SOMEONE HAS TO FAIL

SOMEONE HAS TO FAIL

THE ZERO-SUM GAME OF PUBLIC SCHOOLING

David F. Labaree

HARVARD UNIVERSITY PRESS
Cambridge, Massachusetts & London, England   *2010*

Library of Congress Cataloging-in-Publication Data

Labaree, David F., 1947–
    Someone has to fail : the zero-sum game of public schooling / David F. Labaree.
        p. cm.
    Includes bibliographical references and index.
    ISBN 978-0-674-05068-6 (alk. paper)
    1. Educational change—United States. 2. Public schools—United States.
3. Students with social disabilities—United States. I. Title.
    LA212.L33 2010
    370.973—dc22   2010012646

To David Tyack and Larry Cuban

CONTENTS

INTRODUCTION

We Americans have long pinned our hopes on education. It's the main way we try to express our ideals and solve our problems. We want schools to provide us with good citizens and productive workers; to give us opportunity and reduce inequality; to improve our health, reduce crime, and protect the environment. So we assign these social missions to schools, and educators gamely agree to carry them out. When the school system inevitably fails to produce the desired results, we ask reformers to fix it. The result, as one pair of scholars has put it, is that school reform in the United States is "steady work." The system never seems to work the way we want it to, but we never give up hope that one day it will succeed if we just keep tinkering.[1]

This book is an attempt to explain how this system came about, how it works (and doesn't work), and why we keep investing so heavily in it even though it continues to disappoint us. At heart, this is a story grounded in paradox. The education enterprise is arguably the greatest institutional success in American history. It grew from a modest and marginal position in the eighteenth century to the very center of American life in the twenty-first, where it consumes a stunning share of the time and treasure of both governments and citizens. Key to its institutional success has been its ability to embrace and embody the social goals that we have imposed on it. Yet in spite of recurring waves of school reform, schooling in the United States has been unable to realize these goals.

When people continually repeat behaviors that turn out badly for them, we consider it a sign of mental illness. In this sense, then, the American tendency to resort to schooling is less a strategy than a syndrome. We have set up our school system for failure by asking it to fix all of our most pressing social problems, which we are unwilling to address more directly through political action rather than educational gesture. When it fails, we fiddle with the system and try again. Both as a society and as individuals, we continue to vest our greatest hopes in an institution that is clearly unsuited to realizing them.

The system's failure is, in part, the result of a tension between our shifting social aims for education and the system's own organizational inertia. We created the system to solve critical social problems in the early days of the American republic, and its success in dealing with these problems fooled us into thinking that as time passed we could redirect the system toward new problems. But the school system has picked up substantial momentum over the years, which makes it hard for us to turn it in a new direction.

The system's failure, however, is largely the result of another tension, between our social goals and our personal hopes. School reformers have acted as the agents for society, seeking to use schools to create capable citizens and productive workers and to cure our social ills. Since their initial success early in the nineteenth century, however, these reformers have been mostly unable to achieve these goals through schools. In contrast to reformers, individual consumers of education have seen schools less as a way to pursue grand social designs than as a way to pursue intensely personal dreams of a good job and a good life. As we will see, compared with school reformers, consumers have had a much stronger impact in shaping both school and society; but in the process they have pushed the system in contradictory directions because they want sharply different benefits from it.

Throughout the history of American education, some consumers have demanded greater access to school in order to climb the social ladder, while others have demanded greater advantage from school in order to protect themselves from these same social climbers. Obligingly, the school system has let us have it both ways, providing access *and* advantage, promoting equality *and* inequality.

A key to understanding the American school syndrome is to recognize that our schools have never really been about learning. The impact of school on society over the years has come more from the form of the school system than from the substance of the school curriculum. Schools have been able to create community by bringing together a diverse array of citizens under one roof and exposing them to a shared social and cultural experience, but for these purposes the content of the curriculum hasn't mattered as much as its commonality. In the country's early days, schools helped create citizens for the republic, and more recently they have helped assimilate immigrants. But in many ways the school system's greatest social impact has come from its power to allocate social access and social advantage. And this was more the result of which students entered school and which graduated from it than of what they learned in between.

A LITTLE HISTORICAL BACKGROUND: WAVES
OF SCHOOL REFORM IN THE UNITED STATES

The best way to understand the school syndrome is first to explore where the American school system came from and then examine how it works. So let me give a brief outline of the major social movements that tried to establish and reform the system. This will serve as a map to help the reader follow the historical discussion of schooling in the first three chapters and as background for the analysis of the present-day school system that I develop in the rest of the book.

The first educational reform effort in the United States was the common school movement in the early and mid-nineteenth century. This was a strikingly successful effort by Whig reformers to resolve a crisis that nearly overwhelmed the United States during its early years. The problem was that the republic was new and fragile, fighting to overcome a two-thousand-year history whose clear moral was that republics don't last. In the 1820s and 1830s, American society faced a rapidly growing market economy, which brought great wealth and opportunity but also threatened two elements that were critical to keeping the republic intact—a rough equality of conditions among citizens and a strong culture of civic commitment. By creating a publicly funded and controlled system of public schools that drew together everyone in the community, the common school movement played a critical role in the larger process of institution-building during this period, helping to preserve the republic without putting a damper on economic growth. The invention of the public school system was part of a grand compromise between democratic politics and capitalist markets that has proven essential for the durability of the United States as a liberal democracy. In the process of accomplishing this grand compromise, the common school movement established the basic organizational structure and political rationale for the public school system, both of which have endured to the present day.

The second major reform movement in the history of American education was the progressive movement, which spanned the first half of the twentieth century. The progressive movement in education was something of a catchall, which encompassed a wide variety of individual elements. But the movement had a few core orientations that justified the common label. In loose conjunction with the larger progressive political movement, all of the factions of educational progressivism were reacting to the social and political crisis of the early twentieth century. This crisis was less fundamental and threatening to American society than the one that faced the Whig reformers in the common school movement. The government was secure and the old liberal democratic bargain still held. But the problem was to find a way for government and society to manage the new environment, which included a new corporate economy, growing inequality, angry labor relations, rapid growth of cities, and a huge wave of immigrants from southern and eastern Europe.

Educational progressives came up with two related responses. What they had in common was a hostility toward the traditional academic curriculum, a focus on adapting education to the developmental needs and individual abilities of students, a concern for accommodating the influx of immigrants to the United States, and a need to reconfigure secondary education in order to deal with the flood of new students entering the country's rapidly expanding high schools. One strand of this movement was the child-centered progressives, led by John Dewey and his followers. The other was the administrative progressives, led by a large group of professional educators. As I will show, the administrative progressives were by far the most effective group in changing the structure of secondary education in the United States, but despite their best efforts over fifty years, even they were not able to overturn the core patterns of teaching and learning in American classrooms.

In the last fifty years, we have seen a series of efforts to reform American education. First was the desegregation movement in the 1950s and 1960s, which gradually grew into a broad movement for making American schools inclusive. It ended legal segregation by race, and it also worked to reduce the barriers between girls and boys and between the able and the disabled in American schools. Second was the school standards movement, which began in the 1980s and then took on new life in 2002 with passage of the No Child Left Behind Law. It sought to use curriculum guidelines and high-stakes testing to raise the level of academic achievement in schools and to reduce the differences in achievement between advantaged and disadvantaged students. Third was the school choice movement, which began as a political force early in the 1990s. It aimed to break the public monopoly on education by empowering individual consumers, and by the early

2000s, it extended its scope by arguing that inner-city residents should have the same school options that wealthy suburbanites had always enjoyed.

WHAT SCHOOLS CAN'T DO AND WHAT THIS BOOK WON'T DO

The history of American school reform helps us see what has made reform so ineffective. Reformers have continually tried to impose social missions on schools and then failed to accomplish them, because consumers—the families who send children to school—have had something entirely different in mind. Consumers have wanted schools to allow them to accomplish goals that are less noble socially but more resonant personally: to get ahead and stay ahead. The school system, I argue, emerged as the unintended consequence of these consumer preferences, expressed through the cumulative choices made by families trying to fortify the future of their children through the medium of schooling. In short, the vision of education as a private good (formed by the self-interested actions of individual consumers) has consistently won out over education as a public good (formed by the social aims of reform movements).

My argument is that schooling in America has emerged from this history as a bad way to fix social problems but a good way to express (if not realize) personal dreams. The problem is that these dreams are deeply conflicted and thus the school system is conflicted as well. We want it to meet the ambitions of our children and also to protect them from the ambitions of other people's children. So schooling lets us have it both ways. The costs, however, are high. We find ourselves in harness to the system we created, which continually spurs us on to greater academic effort without ever letting us reach the finish line. After all, the only way schooling can both let my child get ahead of yours and yours stay ahead of mine is by constantly expanding the system upward, which allows every increase in educational access to be followed by an increase of educational advantage. Both parties in this competition find their educational costs rising without being able to change their relative position in the race. In this way, the system really lets us have it, both ways.

That is what this book is about, but I also want to make clear what it is not about. This book is not a guidebook for reformers and policymakers. I'm not trying to reform schools or set educational policy; my approach is analytical rather than prescriptive. I have no intention of providing answers for the reader about how to fix schools or how to fix society. Instead of reforming schools, my aim is to explore how the school system developed and how it works, in its own peculiar way.

I am not touting the system or trashing it; I'm simply trying to understand it. And in the process of developing an understanding of this convoluted, dynamic, contradictory, and expensive system, I hope to convey a certain degree of wonder and respect for it. I have to admire how it does what we want it to do, even as it shrugs off what we ask it to do. In its own way the system is extraordinarily successful, not just because it is so huge and continues to grow so rapidly but because it stands at the heart of the peculiarly American approach to promoting the public welfare. As we will see, this approach emerged early in our history. Unlike Europeans, who in the nineteenth century chose to promote social *equality* by constructing an elaborate *welfare* system, Americans chose to provide social *opportunity* by constructing an elaborate *school* system. We're still living with the consequences of that choice.

PLAN OF THE BOOK

Chapter 1 examines the evolving social missions for education promoted by American school reformers, from the common school movement in the early nineteenth century to the standards and choice movements in the early twenty-first century. In it I show a shift from political to economic purposes, and a parallel shift ⸺ from schooling citizens to schooling consumers. Chapter 2 explains the founding of American schooling, looking at the colonial approach to education, the emergence of the social crisis of the early nineteenth century, and the invention of the common school system in response to this crisis. Chapter 3 looks at the reshaping of the school system in the progressive era, triggered by the social crisis at the start of the twentieth century, when both reformers and consumers saw schools, especially high schools, as the answer. I conclude that the common school movement imposed an indelible stamp on the form, function, and rationale of the American school system, but by the progressive era consumers were calling the shots. By the 1920s all of the central elements of the American system of schooling were locked in place. These were best exemplified by the central educational invention of the period, the tracked comprehensive high school, which opened its doors to all but also carefully monitored the exits.

At this point in the book I turn from a historical account of school reform to a structural analysis of why progressivism and subsequent reforms were so ineffective in reforming schools, especially in changing the core of teaching and learning in classrooms. Chapter 4 focuses on one factor that has made reform difficult: the organization of the school system. It turns out that the loose coupling of the various segments of the school system and the weak control over instruction by school administrators have buffered the classroom from reform efforts. Chapter 5 focuses on another factor, the structure of teaching as a professional practice, which has meant that teachers need to develop a personal style of instruction that can motivate the learning of unwilling students in the self-contained classroom. This in turn has made teachers understandably reluctant to alter their practice in response to demands from reformers.

In the last part of the book I link the historical argument from the first three chapters (the various efforts of school reformers to solve social problems) with the structural argument in chapters 4 and 5 (the organizational arrangements and teaching practices that have impeded these efforts). In Chapter 6, I explore the reasons for the feeble ability of school reform to have a major impact on the key social problems that reformers have stressed: to promote citizenship, social equality, social mobility, and economic productivity. This discussion continues in Chapter 7, where I examine in detail the most prominent American rationale for schooling and school reform in the twentieth and twenty-first centuries: to increase the productive skills of the workforce and promote economic growth. In the end, I argue, schools have turned out to be a weak and inefficient economic investment, and the most useful learning that students acquire in schools comes from doing school rather than learning the curriculum. In Chapter 8 I pull these pieces together, looking at why the school syndrome has persisted in the United States, why the American school system has been so resistant to reformers, and why consumers have trounced reformers in the effort to shape school and society. In the end, the system does what we want as consumers, even if it doesn't do what we ask as reformers, and that is a mixed blessing. As a result, we find ourselves trapped on an educational treadmill of our own making, running hard just to stay in place.

FROM CITIZENS

TO CONSUMERS

1

For better and for worse, the American system of education is truly a marvel. Compared with other countries, public education in the United States has been extraordinarily accessible. It emerged early, expanded quickly, and then rapidly extended access to high school and college. In the process, the United States claimed the distinction of having the first educational system in the world to attain something approaching universal elementary schooling, universal high school attendance, and mass higher education.

But the picture of American education is not all rosy. For one thing, to call it a system at all is something of a contradiction in terms, because it also has the distinction of being radically decentralized, with some 14,000 school districts responsible for setting policy and running schools. And that's before we take into account the large and complex array of public and private colleges in the United States. Even though the educational role of the federal government has been growing in the last several decades, it is still hard to find any structure of education in the world that is more independent of national control. In addition, to applaud the American system of schooling for its great accessibility is to recognize only half the story, since the system balances radical equality of access with radical inequality of outcomes. Students have an easy time gaining entry to education in the United States, but—depending on what school they attend, what program they take, and what degree they earn—they have strikingly different educational experiences and gain strikingly different social benefits from their schooling. One other characteristic of the American educational system further dims its luster, and that is the chronically mediocre academic performance of its students. In world comparisons over the last few decades, American elementary and secondary students have consistently scored at a level that is below average.

In short, the American system of education is highly accessible, radically unequal, organizationally fragmented, and instructionally mediocre. In combination, these characteristics have provided a strong and continuing incentive for school reformers to try to change the system, by launching reform movements that would seek to broaden access, reduce inequality, transform governance, and improve learning. But at the same time that these traits have spurred reform efforts, they have also kept reformers from accomplishing their aims.

For example, every effort to expand access for new students at a given level of the system has tended to provoke counter-efforts to preserve the educational advantage of the old students. When high school enrollment began to expand sharply at the start of the twentieth century, the response was to establish curriculum tracking in the high school (with the new students ending up in the lower tracks and the old students in the upper tracks) and to spur the old students to extend their education to the college level. But such efforts by some to preserve educational advantage by extending it to the next-higher level have in turn provoked countermeasures by others to expand access at that level. So by the midtwentieth century, growing demand for college access brought a flood of new students to higher education. But this just continued the cycle of action and reaction, since the new students largely enrolled in new institutions that were set up to handle the influx—regional state universities and community colleges—while the old students enrolled at the established higher status institutions and then started attending graduate school in large numbers.

Another impediment to reform is the local autonomy of districts, schools, and classrooms in the American educational system, which has made it hard for reform initiatives to reach the heart of the system where teaching and learning take place, and particularly hard to implement reforms that improve classroom learning. Aggravating this tendency has been one additional characteristic of the system, which is that most educational consumers have shown preference for a school system that provides an edge in the competition for jobs more than for one that enriches academic achievement. We have continually demonstrated interest more in getting a diploma than getting an education.

Undaunted by all these impediments, educational reformers have continually tried to change the school system in order to bring it in line with emerging social goals. In this chapter, I look at the goals that reform movements have projected onto the American school system over the years. Here I'm focusing not on the impact of reform but on its rhetoric. As found in major reform documents, the shifting language of reform shows how the mission of the school system evolved over time, as reformers repeatedly tried to push the system to embrace new goals and refine old ones in an effort to deal with an expanding array of social challenges. After defining the trajectory of reformer wishes for the schools in this chapter, I then look at the depth of reform outcomes for the schools. In chapters 2 and 3 I show how the common school movement created the American school system in the nineteenth century and how the progressive movement sought to transform it at the start of the twentieth century. Then, in succeeding chapters, I examine why the impact of reform movements has only rarely extended beyond the level of rhetoric. But for now my focus is on the way ideas about schools developed across an array of major reform movements in the history of American education.

SHIFTING THE FOCUS OF SCHOOLING FROM CITIZENS TO CONSUMERS

This is a story about the evolving language of educational reform in the United States. It starts in the early nineteenth century with a republican vision of education for civic virtue and ends in the early twenty-first century with a consumerist vision of education for equal opportunity. The story is about how we got from there to here, drawing on major reform texts that span this period. It is also a story about how we developed the ideas about education that laid the groundwork for the American school syndrome.

This rhetorical change consisted of two main shifts, each of which occurred at two levels. First, the overall balance in the purposes of schooling shifted from a political rationale (shoring up the new republic) to a market rationale (promoting social efficiency and social mobility). And the political rationale itself evolved from a substantive vision of education for civic virtue to a procedural vision of education for equal opportunity. Second, in a closely related change, the reform rhetoric shifted from viewing education as a public good to viewing it as a private good. And the understanding of education as a public good itself evolved from a politically grounded definition (education for republican community) to a market-grounded definition (education for human capital).

I explore these changes through an examination of a series of reform documents that represent the major reform movements in the history of American education. These include: Horace Mann's *Fifth* and *Twelfth Annual Reports* as Secretary of the Massachusetts Board of Public Education (1841 and 1848), reflecting the common school movement; the *Report of the Committee of Ten on Secondary School Studies,* appointed by the National Education Association (1893), a document that served as a foil for the progressive movement; *The Cardinal Principles of Secondary Education,* a report of the National Education Association's (NEA)

Commission on the Reorganization of Secondary Education (1918), which laid out the agenda for the dominant strand of the progressive movement; *Brown v. Board of Education of Topeka,* decision of the U.S. Supreme Court (1954), the core text of the desegregation movement; *A Nation at Risk,* report of the National Commission on Excellence in Education (1983), which kicked off the standards movement; the No Child Left Behind Act (2002), which made the movement federal law; and two major books from the school choice movement.[1]

The evolution of educational rhetoric in the United States fits within a larger, cross-national pattern in the evolving republican conversation about schooling. Republican ideas played a foundational role in the formation of public education in a number of countries during the long nineteenth century, and stretching from the American Revolution to the Great Depression. Although this role varied from one context to another, the republican vision in general called for a system of education that would shape the kind of self-regulating and civic-minded citizen that was needed to sustain a viable republican community. That system was the modern public school. At the heart of its mission was the delicate and critical task of balancing two elements at the core of republican thinking—the autonomous individual and the common good. The primary contribution of the school was its ability to instill a vision of the republic within future citizens in a way that promoted individual choice while inducing them to pursue the public interest of their own free will. This effort posed twin dangers: too much emphasis on individual interests could turn republican community into a pluralist society defined by the competition of private interests; but too much emphasis on community could turn the republic into an authoritarian society that sacrificed individual freedom to collective interests. A liberal republican society requires an educational system that can instill a commitment to both individual liberty and civic virtue.

As I show below, over time the rhetoric of education in the United States shifted from a political vision of a civic-minded citizen to a market vision of a self-interested consumer. But the idea of republican community did not disappear from the educational mission. Instead the political goal of education shifted from producing civic virtue in the service of the republic to producing human capital and individual opportunity. The end result, however, was to redirect the republican vision of education sharply in the direction of private interests and individual opportunities.

COMPETING SOCIAL GOALS FOR SCHOOLING

A major factor in the transformation of reform rhetoric was the market. While a number of reform efforts—the common school movement, the progressive movement, the civil rights movement, the standards movement, and the school choice movement—occupied center stage in the drama of school reform, the market initially exerted its impact from a position off stage. Over time, however, the market gradually muscled its way into the educational spotlight, shaping both the structure of the school system (by emphasizing inequality and discounting learning) and, more recently, the rhetoric of school reform (by emphasizing job skills and individual opportunity). In the current period, when the market vision has come to drive the educational agenda, the political vision of education's social role remains prominent as an actor in the reform drama, frequently called upon by reformers of all stripes. (I examine here the way the standards and choice movements both belatedly adopted political rhetoric after originally trying to do without it.) But the definition of this political vision has become more abstract, its deployment more adaptable, and its impact more diffuse than in the early nineteenth century, when a well-defined set of republican ideals drove the creation of the American system of common schools.

The American language of educational goals arises from the core tensions within a liberal democracy.[2] One of those tensions is between the demands of democratic politics and the demands of capitalist markets. A related issue is the requirement that society be able to meet its collective needs while simultaneously guaranteeing the liberty of individuals to pursue their own interests. In the American setting, these tensions have played out through the politics of education in the form of a struggle among three major social goals for the educational system. One goal is *democratic equality*, which sees education as a mechanism for producing capable citizens. Another is *social efficiency*, which sees education as a mechanism for developing productive workers. A third is *social mobility*, which sees education as a way for individuals to reinforce or improve their social position.

Democratic equality represents the political side of our liberal democratic values, focusing on the role of education in building a nation, forming a republican community, and providing citizens with the wide range of capabilities they need to make decisions in a democracy. The other two goals represent the market side of liberal democracy. Social efficiency captures the perspective of employers and taxpayers, who are concerned about the role of education in producing the job skills required by the modern economy (human capital) and seen as essential for economic growth and general prosperity. From this angle the issue is for education to provide for the full range of productive skills and forms of knowledge required in the complex job structure of modern capitalism. Social mobility captures the perspective of educational consumers and prospective employees, who are concerned about the role of educational credentials in signaling to the market which individuals have the productive skills that qualify them for the jobs with the most power, money, and prestige.

The collectivist side of liberal democracy is expressed by a combination of democratic equality and social efficiency. Both aim to have education provide broad social benefits, and both see education as a public good. Investing in the political capital of citizens and the human capital of workers benefits everyone in society, including those families that do not have children in school. In contrast, the social mobility goal represents the individualist side of liberal democracy. From this perspective, education is a private good that benefits only the student who receives educational services and owns the resulting diplomas, and its primary function is to provide educational consumers with an edge in the competition for good jobs.

With this mix of goals imposed on it, education in a liberal democracy has come to be an institution at odds with itself. After all, it is being asked simultaneously to serve politics and markets, promote equality and inequality, construct itself and, as a public and private good, serve collective interests and individual interests. Politically, its structure should be flat, its curriculum common, and enrollment universal; economically, its structure should be hierarchical, its curriculum tracked, and enrollment marked by high rates of attrition. From the perspective of democratic equality and social efficiency, its aim is socialization, to provide knowledge that is useful for citizens and workers; from the perspective of social mobility, its aim is selection, to provide credentials that allow access to good jobs, independent of any learning that might have occurred along the way.

These educational goals represent the contradictions embedded in any liberal democracy, contradictions that cannot be resolved without removing either the society's liberalism or its democracy. Therefore, when we project our liberal democratic goals onto schools, we want schools to take each of these goals seriously but not to push any one of them too far, since to do so would put other, equally valued goals in jeopardy. We ask it to promote social equality, but we want it to do so in a way that doesn't threaten individual liberty or private interests. We ask it to promote individual opportunity, but we want it to do so in a way that doesn't threaten the integrity of the nation or the efficiency of the economy. As a result, the educational system is an abject failure in achieving any one of its primary social goals. It is also a failure in solving the social problems assigned to it, since these problems cannot be solved in a way that simultaneously satisfies all three goals. The apparently dysfunctional outcomes of the school system, therefore, are not necessarily the result of bad planning, bad administration, or bad teaching; they are an expression of the contradictions in the liberal democratic mind.

THE COMMON SCHOOL MOVEMENT: SCHOOLS FOR THE REPUBLIC

As secretary of the Massachusetts Board of Public Education in the 1840s, Horace Mann became the most effective champion of the American common school movement, which established the American public school system in the years before the Civil War. As we will see in the following chapter, its primary accomplishment was not in increasing literacy, which was already widespread in the United States, but in drawing public support for a publicly funded and publicly controlled system of schooling that served all the members of the community.

Mann's *Twelfth Annual Report,* published in 1848, provides the most comprehensive summary of the argument for the common schools. In it he made clear that the primary rationale for this institution was political: to create citizens with the knowledge, skills, and public spirit required to maintain a republic and to protect it from the sources of faction, class, and self-interest that pose the primary threat to its existence. After exploring the dangers that the rapidly expanding market economy posed to the fabric of republican community by introducing class conflict, he proclaimed:

> Education, then, beyond all other devices of human origin, is the great equalizer of the conditions of men—the balance-wheel of the social machinery. . . . The spread of education, by enlarging the cultivated class or caste, will open a wider area over which the social feelings will expand; and, if this education should be universal and complete, it would do more than all things else to obliterate factitious distinctions in society.[3]

A few pages later, he summed up his argument with the famous statement, "It may be an easy thing to make a Republic; but it is

a very laborious thing to make Republicans; and woe to the republic that rests upon no better foundations than ignorance, self-
ishness, and passion."[4] In his view, then, schools were given the
centrally important political task of making citizens for a republic. All other functions were subordinate to this one.

In the political rhetoric of the common school movement, we
can also see some other themes with a more economic flavor that
will become the centerpiece of later reform movements. One is
the importance of education in reducing social differences by
enhancing social opportunities for all, as shown in the passage
above. Another is the value of education as an investment in human capital. Mann devoted part of his *Fifth Annual Report* (issued in 1841) to the latter issue, where he drew on his survey of
manufacturers to demonstrate that, "If it can be proved that the
aggregate wealth of a town will be increased just in proportion to
the increase of its appropriations for schools, the opponents of
such a measure will be silenced. The tax for this purpose, which
they now look upon as a burden, they will then regard as a profit-
able investment."[5]

Yet his defense of the human capital rationale for schooling
is backhanded at best. He was a little embarrassed to be talking
about the crass economic returns on education, as he explained
in his introduction to this discussion: "This view, so far from being the highest which can be taken of the beneficent influences
of education, may, perhaps, be justly regarded as the lowest. But
it is a palpable view."[6] Thus economic arguments are useful in
drawing needed support to the common schools, but they play
merely a supporting role in the "higher and nobler" mission of
supporting republican community. Only in the twentieth century
would such economic arguments take center stage.

EMERGING CONSUMERISM: SCHOOLS
FOR SOCIAL MOBILITY

If Horace Mann and the other leaders of the common school movement were reluctant to portray education as a way to promote

worldly gain, the students and parents who pursued education were less so. Compelled by the need to survive and the ambition to thrive in a market economy, citizens quickly began to think of education as something more than a politically desirable way to preserve the republic; they also saw it as a way to get ahead in society. As we will see in the next chapter, reading, writing, and the manipulation of numbers were essential for anyone who wanted to function effectively in the commercial life of the colonial and early national periods of American history. Individuals did not need republican theory or compulsory schooling laws to make them pick up these skills, which is one reason why literacy was a precursor rather than an outcome of the common school movement in the United States.

But this compelling rationale for education—schooling for social mobility—was not something that appeared prominently in the rhetoric of school reform until well into the twentieth century. One reason for this silence was that the idea of education as a way to get ahead was a matter of common sense in a society that was founded in market relations. It was not the subject of reform rhetoric because this idea was already widely accepted. Another reason was that people felt a bit embarrassed about voicing such a self-interested motive for education in the face of the selfless religious and political rationales for education that dominated public discussion in the American colonies and the early United States. But the absence of such talk did not belie the reality that commercial motives for schooling were strong.

This relative silence about an important factor shaping education resonates with an important paradox in the history of school reform identified by David Tyack and Larry Cuban, in their book *Tinkering toward Utopia*.[7] Reform rhetoric swirls around the surface of schools, making a lot of noise but not necessarily penetrating below the surface; while evolutionary forces of structural change may be proceeding powerfully but slowly outside of view, making substantial changes over time without ever necessarily being verbalized or becoming part of a reform agenda.

The story I am telling in this chapter is about the interaction between these two levels—the changing rhetoric of educational reform in the United States over the past two hundred years and its relationship with the quiet but increasingly potent impact of market forces on American schools. I suggest that the rhetorical shifts in subsequent school reform movements were attempts to reach an accommodation between economy and society through the institution of education, which turned increasingly critical as education itself became more economically useful to both employers and employees in the late nineteenth and twentieth centuries.

In *The Making of an American High School*,[8] I explored the way in which educational consumerism emerged as an unintended consequence of the invention of the public high school in the nineteenth century. Central High School was founded in Philadelphia in 1838 for the most whiggish of reasons. Its founders liked to call it "the school of the republic," and they saw it as an effective way to encourage middle-class families to send their children to the new common schools, thus making these schools a true embodiment of republican community. But in order to make the high school sufficiently attractive to draw (male) students from the best private schools, they inadvertently created a highly marketable commodity—with a marble facade, the latest scientific equipment, and a faculty of distinguished professors— which became the object of intense competition among educational consumers.

The new high school introduced a form of educational distinction that was highly visible (Central was the only school of its kind in a large city), culturally legitimate (it was open to anyone who could meet its academic standards), and scarce (it offered a degree to only one in a hundred of the students entering the school system). These characteristics made a Central diploma quite valuable as a way for students to distinguish themselves from peers, even though at the time the job market was not exerting demand for the skills acquired in a secondary education. But by the 1890s, when growing clerical and managerial jobs created a market for high school graduates, the enormous political demand for access forced the school system to expand from two high schools (Central and its female counterpart) to a whole system of community high schools throughout the city. The newcomers ended up in the lower tracks of the newly expanded high school while the students from the high school's older, middle-class constituency ended up in the upper tracks, which helped accommodate both access and advantage in the same school. The resulting institution—the tracked comprehensive high school—served as the model for secondary education for the next one hundred years.

COMMITTEE OF TEN: COMMONALITY WITHOUT CITIZENSHIP

In 1893, at the same time that consumer pressure was starting to transform secondary education in Philadelphia and elsewhere, a committee proposed to the National Educational Association (NEA) a new structure for the high school curriculum. The Committee of Ten on Secondary School Studies was made up of six professors, three high school principals, and the U.S. Commissioner of Education; Charles W. Eliot, the president of Harvard, served as chair. The committee's report is interesting less for its impact, which was minimal, than for its iconic status in later educational debates. It occupied a transitional position, as the final attenuated expression of the common school movement, poised to be swept away by the emerging progressive movement. The progressives dismissed the report with scorn, calling it the last gasp of a discredited vision of traditional academic schooling pushed on the schools by a group of self-interested college professors. Contemporary critics of progressivism—like Diane Ravitch, David Angus, and Jeffrey Mirel[9]—see the report as the road not taken, which would have saved us from the ravages of progressive reform and which in some ways was resurrected and reaffirmed by the standards movement in the late twentieth century.

For our purposes, I will focus on what is usually seen as the main issue in a very long report, the committee's insistence that the high school curriculum should be quite similar in length and content for all students, whether or not they were heading to college. There is much about this argument that is resonant with the common school reformers, but the rhetorical representation of the argument is markedly different. The report stated that "every subject which is taught at all in a secondary school should be taught in the same way and to the same extent to every pupil so long as he pursues it, no matter what the probable destination of the pupil may be, or at what point his education is to cease."[10]

This proposal would have resonated with Horace Mann and the other members of the common school movement, since it would preserve the republican practice of education as an experience shared by the whole community. Schooling should supply citizens with a common set of abilities they need to engage in political life, and it should offset the differentiating tendencies in the market economy with an emphasis on building republican community. Both argue for a common curriculum. But as we have seen, in Philadelphia and elsewhere, the market was driving the high school curriculum in the other direction, differentiating curriculum choices and school experiences according to a student's class background and future prospects. In many ways this report can be read—as Ravitch, Angus, and Mirel do—as a cry for preserving a common education at just the point that the institution was moving sharply toward class-based tracking.

But what a muted cry it was. Gone is the grandiloquent language of Horace Mann, the appeals to the high-level political values, the passionate vision of education as the savior of society. In a report of nearly 19,000 words, there is not a single use of terms like "citizen," "republic," or "democracy." Replacing republican rhetoric is the cautious, circumscribed, bureaucratic language of a committee of professional educators. In the fifty years since Horace Mann wrote, the common school system he promoted had succeeded beyond his wildest dreams. It had become the standard model for American education, defining what future generations would come to see as the "grammar of schooling."[11] It had expanded from elementary to grammar to high school. And it had generated a professional corps of teachers and administrators and college professors who saw their work as a professional practice rather than a political vocation.

And so the committee used a coolly professional rhetoric, narrowly confined to the issues at hand, sticking strictly to the business of schooling. This made the report appropriate to its audience of educators in the NEA, but it left the committee's proposals without a solid political grounding in the surrounding society. If it is not for the benefit of building republican community, then why should high schools have a core curriculum? The report does not really answer this question, except for a feeble wave in the direction of efficiency: "The principle laid down by the Conferences will, if logically carried out, make a great simplification in secondary school programmes."[12] In the absence of solid grounding, the committee allowed the progressives to attribute its recommendations to a conservative desire to preserve traditional school subjects and to impose the requirements of an antiquated college curriculum on the modern high school.

ADMINISTRATIVE PROGRESSIVISM: SCHOOLS FOR SOCIAL EFFICIENCY

The progressive education movement burst on the scene in the United States at the start of the twentieth century. It was a complex movement with a wide range of actors and tendencies embedded within it, but two main strands in particular stand out. Child-centered progressives (such as John Dewey and William Kilpatrick) focused on teaching and learning in classrooms, advocating child-centered pedagogy, discovery learning, and student engagement. Administrative progressives (such as Edward Thorndike, Ellwood Cubberley, and David Snedden) focused on the structure of school governance and curriculum, advocating a mission of social efficiency for schools, which meant preparing students for their future social roles. I focus on administrative progressivism here for the simple reason that they won and the pedagogues lost in the competition over exerting an impact on American schools.[13]

In 1918, the Commission on the Reorganization of Secondary Education (chaired by Clarence Kingsley) issued a report to the NEA titled *Cardinal Principles of Secondary Education,* which spelled out the administrative progressive position on education more clearly and consequentially than any other single document. The report announces at the very beginning that secondary schools need to change in response to changes in society, which "call for a degree of intelligence and efficiency on the part of every citizen that can not be secured through elementary education alone, or even through secondary education unless the scope of that education is broadened."[14] According to the authors, schools exist to help individuals adapt to the needs of society; as society becomes more complex, schools must transform themselves accordingly; and in this way they will help citizens develop the socially needed qualities of "intelligence and efficiency."

This focus on social efficiency, however, didn't deter the authors from drawing on political rhetoric to support their position. In fact, perhaps reacting to the Committee of Ten, or learning from its failure to have a lasting impact on schooling, the authors framed this report in explicitly political terms. In a 12,000-word report, they used the terms "democracy" or "democratic" no fewer than 40 times, an average of 1.5 usages per page; the terms "citizen" or "citizenship" appear 16 times. (The words "republic" and "republican" are nowhere to be found.)

What do they mean by democratic education? At one point, in bold-faced type, they state that "education in a democracy, both within and without the school, should develop in each individual the knowledge, interests, ideals, habits, and powers whereby he will find his place and use that place to shape both himself and society toward ever nobler ends."[15] So democracy is about organizing individuals for the benefit of society, and education is about readying individuals to assume their proper place in that society. This is as crisp a definition as you can find for socially efficient education.

The commission follows up on this statement of principles to spell out the implications for the high school curriculum: "This commission, therefore, regards the following as the main objectives of education: 1. Health. 2. Command of fundamental processes. 3. Worthy home membership. 4. Vocation. 5. Citizenship. 6. Worthy use of leisure. 7. Ethical character."[16] What a striking array of goals for education this is. In comparison with Horace Mann's grand vision of schooling for the republic, we have a list of useful functions that schools can serve for society, only one of which focuses on citizenship. Furthermore, this list confines the rich array of liberal arts subjects, which constituted the entire curriculum proposed by the Committee of Ten, to a single category; the authors give it the dumbed-down and dismissive title, "command of fundamental processes"; and they assign it a parallel position with such mundane educational objectives as "worthy home membership" and "worthy use of leisure."

Later in the report, the commission spelled out an important implication of their vision of secondary education. Not only must the curriculum be expanded radically beyond the academic confines of the Committee of Ten's vision, but it must also be sharply differentiated if it is going to meet the needs of a differentiated job structure:

> The work of the senior high school should be organized into differentiated curriculums. . . . The basis of differentiation should be, in the broad sense of the term, vocational, thus justifying the names commonly given, such as agricultural, business, clerical, industrial, fine-arts, and household-arts curriculums. Provision should be made also for those having distinctively academic interests and needs.[17]

The commissioners are explaining that their call for a socially efficient education in practice means vocationalism, with the vocational skills required by the job market driving the curriculum and slicing it into segments based on the specific jobs toward which students are heading. Any leftover space in the curriculum could then be used for "those having distinctively academic interests and needs."

This report, the keystone of the administrative progressive movement, represents two major transformations in the rhetoric of the common school movement. First, whereas Mann's reports used economic arguments to support a primarily political purpose for schooling (preparing citizens with civic virtue), the Commission's report turned this upside down, using political arguments about the requirements of democracy to support a vision of schooling that was primarily economic (preparing efficient workers). The politics of the *Cardinal Principles* thus provides a thin democratic veneer on a structure of socially efficient education, dressing up what would otherwise be a starkly utilitarian vision.

Second, in *Cardinal Principles* the administrative progressives preserved the common school movement's understanding of education as a public good. There is no talk in the report about education as a kind of personal property, which offers selective benefits to the credential holder; instead, the emphasis is relentlessly on the collective benefits of education to society. What is new, however, is this: Whereas the common school men defined education as a public good in political terms, the progressives defined it a public good in economic terms. Yes, education serves the interests of society as a whole, said these progressives; but it does so not by producing civic virtue but by producing human capital.

THE CIVIL RIGHTS MOVEMENT: SCHOOLS FOR EQUAL OPPORTUNITY

If the administrative progressive movement marginalized the political argument for education, using it as window-dressing for a vision of education as a way to create productive workers, the civil rights movement brought politics back to the center of the debate about schools. In the 1954 decision of the U.S. Supreme Court, *Brown v. Board of Education of Topeka*,[18] Chief Justice Earl Warren, speaking for a unanimous Court, made a forceful political argument for the need to desegregate American schools. The question he was addressing was whether to overturn the Court's doctrine of "separate but equal," established in *Plessy v. Ferguson* in 1894, as a violation of the clause in the Fourteenth Amendment to the Constitution (passed at the end of the Civil War) that guaranteed all citizens the "equal protection of the laws." In past cases, the Court was able to duck the question by ordering school systems to equalize the funding of black and white schools. But in this case, "the Negro and white schools involved have been equalized, or are being equalized, with respect to buildings, curricula, qualifications and salaries of teachers, and other 'tangible' factors," which forced the Court to address the central issue: "We come then to the question presented: Does segregation of children in public schools solely on the basis of race, even though the physical facilities and other 'tangible' factors may be equal, deprive children of the minority group of equal educational opportunities? We believe that it does."

The Court's reasoning moved through two main steps in reaching this conclusion. First, Warren argued that the social meaning of education had changed dramatically in the ninety years since the passage of the Fourteenth Amendment. In the years after the Civil War, "The curriculum was usually rudimentary; ungraded schools were common in rural areas; the school term was but three months a year in many states, and compulsory school attendance was virtually unknown." As a result, education was not seen as an essential right of any citizen; but that had now changed.

> Today, education is perhaps the most important function of state and local governments. Compulsory school attendance laws and

the great expenditures for education both demonstrate our recognition of the importance of education to our democratic society. It is required in the performance of our most basic public responsibilities, even service in the armed forces. It is the very foundation of good citizenship. Today it is a principal instrument in awakening the child to cultural values, in preparing him for later professional training, and in helping him to adjust normally to his environment. In these days, it is doubtful that any child may reasonably be expected to succeed in life if he is denied the opportunity of an education. Such an opportunity, where the state has undertaken to provide it, is a right which must be made available to all on equal terms.

This led to the second part of the argument. If education "is a right which must be made available to all on equal terms," then the question was whether segregated education could be seen as providing truly equal educational opportunity for black and white students. Here Warren drew on social science research to argue that "To separate [black students] from others of similar age and qualifications solely because of their race generates a feeling of inferiority as to their status in the community that may affect their hearts and minds in a way unlikely ever to be undone." He continued by quoting from a finding by a lower court in the case: "Segregation with the sanction of law, therefore, has a tendency to [retard] the educational and mental development of negro children and to deprive them of some of the benefits they would receive in a racial[ly] integrated school system."

In combination, these two arguments—education is an essential right and segregated education is inherently harmful—led Warren to his conclusion: "We conclude that, in the field of public education, the doctrine of 'separate but equal' has no place. Separate educational facilities are inherently unequal. Therefore, we hold that the plaintiffs . . . are, by reason of the segregation complained of, deprived of the equal protection of the laws guaranteed by the Fourteenth Amendment."

The argument in this decision was at heart political, asserting that education is a constitutional right of every citizen that must be granted to everyone on equal terms. In this sense, it was a striking change from the *Cardinal Principles* report, which used the words "democracy" and "citizenship" to support an argument that was at heart economic. But note that the political vision in *Brown* is quite different from the political vision put forward by Mann. For the common school movement, schools were critically important in the effort to build a republic; their purpose was political. But for the desegregation movement, schools were critically important as a mechanism of social opportunity. Their purpose was to promote social mobility. Politics was just the means by which one could demand access to this attractive educational commodity. In this sense, then, *Brown* depicted education as a private good, whose benefits go to the degree holder and not to society as a whole. The Court's argument was not that granting access to equal education for blacks would enhance society, both black and white; instead, it argued that blacks were suffering from segregation and would benefit from desegregation. Quality education was an important form of property that they had been denied, and the remedy was to give them access to it.

Note the language of the decision: "In these days, it is doubtful that any child may reasonably be expected to succeed in life if he is denied the opportunity of an education." Schools enable individuals to succeed in life, and politically we cannot deny them this opportunity. This is an argument that shows how much schools had come of age more than one hundred years after Horace Mann. Once created to support the republic, in a time when schools were marginal to the practical business of making a living, they had become central to every citizen's ability to get a good job and get ahead socially. In the process, however, the political vision of education has changed from a substantive focus on producing the citizens needed to sustain the republic to a procedural focus on providing social opportunities. The idea of education as opportunity was already visible in Mann, but it was subordinated to the political project; here educational opportunity has become the project, and politics has become the way to assert your right to it.

THE STANDARDS MOVEMENT 1.0: SOCIAL EFFICIENCY AND COMMONALITY

In 1983, the National Commission for Excellence in Education produced a report titled *A Nation at Risk*, which helped turn the emerging standards effort into a national reform movement. It is useful to think of this movement in relation to its predecessors, both in the way it drew from them and the way it reacted against them. From the Committee of Ten the standards movement drew the idea of a core academic curriculum for all students, which in turn stood as a harsh rebuke to the diffuse, differentiated, and nonacademic curriculum posed by *Cardinal Principles;* yet *A Nation at Risk* also shows a clear affinity with *Cardinal Principles* by defining the primary purpose of education as social efficiency. At the same time, the standards movement's emphasis on academic content and learning outcomes served as a counter to the civil rights movement, which focused primarily on access to educational opportunity rather than on the substance of learning; and its stress on education as a public good contrasted with *Brown*'s emphasis on education as a form of individual benefit.

The report got off to a fast start, issuing a dire warning about how bad things were and how important it was to reform the educational system.

> Our Nation is at risk. Our once unchallenged preeminence in commerce, industry, science, and technological innovation is being overtaken by competitors throughout the world. . . . We report to the American people that while we can take justifiable pride in what our schools and colleges have historically accomplished and contributed to the United States and the well-being of its people, the educational foundations of our society are presently being eroded by a rising tide

of mediocrity that threatens our very future as a Nation and a people.[19]

This passage set the tone for the rest of the report. It asserted a vision of education as an intensely public good: All Americans benefit from its successes, and all are threatened by its failures. The nation is at risk. This was in striking contrast with the vision of education in the *Brown* decision, which depicted education as a private good, one that was critically important to the possibility of social success for every individual. In that view, it was black educational consumers who were at risk from segregation, not the nation.

But the report represented education as a particular type of public good, which benefited American society by giving it the human capital it needed in order to be economically competitive with other nations.

> We live among determined, well-educated, and strongly motivated competitors. We compete with them for international standing and markets, not only with products but also with the ideas of our laboratories and neighborhood workshops. America's position in the world may once have been reasonably secure with only a few exceptionally well-trained men and women. It is no longer.[20]

The risk to the nation posed here was primarily economic, and the main role that education could play in alleviating this risk was to develop a more efficient mechanism for turning students into productive workers. In parallel with the argument in *Cardinal Principles, A Nation at Risk* asserted that the issue of wealth production—which Horace Mann saw as one of the "inferior motives" for supporting public education—was the most important motive in seeking higher educational standards.

The report's first three recommendations spelled out the core substance of the changes at the top of the priority list for the standards movement. Under the heading "Content," the commission recommended "that State and local high school graduation

requirements be strengthened and that, at a minimum, all students seeking a diploma be required to lay the foundations in the
Five New Basics," which included three to four years of English,
math, science, and social studies, plus some work in computer
science.[21] Under the heading "Standards and Expectations," the
commission recommended "more rigorous and measurable standards, and higher expectations, for academic performance and
student content." In particular, this meant that "Standardized tests
of achievement (not to be confused with aptitude tests) should be
administered at major transition points from one level of schooling
to another and particularly from high school to college or work."[22]
Under the heading "Time," the commission recommended "that
significantly more time be devoted to learning the New Basics.
This will require more effective use of the existing school day, a
longer school day, or a lengthened school year."[23]

In stressing the need to refocus attention on a core academic
curriculum for all students, *A Nation at Risk* stood as a rebuke
to the differentiated and vocationalized curriculum of the *Cardinal Principles* and a bow in the direction of the Committee of
Ten, but it embraced the *Principles'* vision of education for social efficiency. It used a modest form of political rhetoric to support the standards effort (using some version of "citizen" eighteen times and "democracy" two times in a nearly 18,000-word
report, and including one quote from Jefferson), but the emphasis here was on education as a way to produce the human capital
rather than *Brown*'s emphasis on education as a way to promote
individual opportunity. And by focusing on student learning rather
than student access, it also represented a turn away from the equal
opportunity concerns of the *Brown* decision.

SCHOOL CHOICE MOVEMENT 1.0: CONSUMERISM
AND SOCIAL EFFICIENCY

The school choice movement had its roots in Milton Friedman,
who devoted a chapter to the subject in his 1962 book, *Capitalism*

and Freedom. But the movement really took off as a significant
reform effort in the 1990s, and a major text that shaped the policy
discourse of these movement was a book by John Chubb and Terry
Moe—*Politics, Markets, and America's Schools*—which was published by the Brookings Institution in 1990. The argument they
raised in favor of school choice consisted of two key elements.
First, they used the scholarly literature on school effectiveness to
argue that schools are most effective at promoting student learning if they have the greatest degree of autonomy in administration,
teaching, and curriculum. Second, they argued that democratic
governance of school systems necessarily leads to bureaucratic
control of schools, which radically limits autonomy; whereas
market-based governance, based on empowering educational consumers instead of empowering the state, leads to more school autonomy. As a result, they concluded, we need to shift from democratic to market control of schooling in order to make schools
more educationally effective.

Like the standards movement, the choice movement inverted
the rhetorical priorities of the common school movement, putting markets before politics. But the approach was more radically pro-market than the one proposed in *A Nation at Risk,*
because Chubb and Moe argued that democratic politics was in
fact the reason that schools performed badly, and the remedy was
to remove schools from democratic control and hand them over
to educational consumers: "Our guiding principle in the design
of a choice system is this: public authority must be put to use in
creating a system that is almost entirely beyond the reach of public authority."[24] Markets, they argued, are simply more efficient
at promoting the school autonomy needed for effective teaching
and learning: "In a market setting, then, there are strong forces at
work—arising from the technical, administrative, and consumer-
satisfaction requirements of organizational success—that promote school autonomy." By contrast, "In the public sector, the
institutional forces work in the opposite direction. The raison

d'être of democratic control is to impose higher order values on schools, and thus limit their autonomy."[25]

The authors welcomed the fact that, by shifting control from a democratic polity to the educational consumer, the proposed school choice system would change education from a public good to a private good.

> Under a system of democratic control, the public schools are governed by an enormous, far-flung constituency in which the interests of parents and students carry no special status or weight. When markets prevail, parents and students are thrust onto center stage, along with the owners and staff of schools; most of the rest of society plays a distinctly secondary role, limited for the most part to setting the framework within which educational choices get made.[26]

In this way, then, the rhetoric of the school choice movement at the close of the twentieth century represented the opposite end of the scale from the rhetoric of the common school movement that set in motion the American public school system in the middle of the nineteenth century. In educational reform rhetoric, we have moved all the way from a political rationale for education to a market rationale, and from seeing education as a public good to seeing it as a private good. Instead of extolling the benefits of having a common school system promote a single, virtuous republican community, reformers were extolling the benefits of having an atomized school system serve the differential needs of a vast array of disparate consumer subcultures.

STANDARDS 2.0: BROADENING THE BASE WITH A POLITICAL APPEAL TO EQUAL OPPORTUNITY

The start of the twenty-first century saw an interesting shift in the rhetoric of the standards movement and the choice movement, as both incorporated the language of equal opportunity from the civil rights movement. Whether these changes represented a change of heart or merely change of strategy is beyond the scope of my discussion here. My focus in this chapter is on the changing rhetoric of reform, and in both cases the change helped broaden the appeal of the reform effort by expanding the reasons for joining the movement. In their original form, both movements ran into significant limitations in their ability to draw support, and both turned to a very effective political argument from the civil rights movement to add passion and breadth to their mode of appeal.

A *Nation at Risk* made a strong case for supporting educational standards and accountability on the grounds of social efficiency. Although this approach was necessary and effective in encouraging governors and legislators to pass enabling legislation at the state level (by asserting that schooling is a sound public investment), it was not sufficient to gain the support of Congress and the general public for a national standards initiative. Talking about education as an investment in human capital made the reform sound sensible and prudent as a matter of social policy, but it was difficult to get people excited about this effort. Not for nothing is economics known as the dismal science, and the economic rationale for education was not very inspiring at the grassroots level.

In addition, by assigning schools the task of increasing the stock of human capital, the standards movement was treating schooling as a public good, and like any other public good, this left education with what economists call a free-rider problem. Since we all gain benefits from a public good (like public safety or clean air) whether or not we directly contribute to it, it is difficult to maintain such goods on a voluntary basis. Individuals may choose to invest in a variety of other projects that bring them a direct personal return as long as they can get a free ride on the collective benefits of schooling.

One way to gain support for a public good is through a universal mandate such as taxation; another is to appeal for support on idealistic grounds. For educational reformers a political appeal can help turn free riders into active supporters, but A *Nation at Risk* made a political appeal in a manner that was limited and not terribly effective. Its main approach was to depict the consequences of educational failure as a threat to the viability of the United States as a nation in global competition; thus the apocalyptic language in the report's opening passages. However, the threats posed by "the rising tide of mediocrity that threatens our very future as a Nation and a people" would have felt rather remote to the average citizen and congressperson. Both the first President Bush and President Clinton used this strategy in trying to launch a national standards policy, and both failed. However, in January 2002, the second President Bush signed into law a wide-reaching piece of standards legislation passed with broad bipartisan support.

The title of this law explains the rhetorical shift involved in gaining approval for it: The No Child Left Behind Act.[27] Listen to the language in the opening section of this act, which constitutes the most powerful accomplishment of the school standards movement: "The purpose of this title is to ensure that all children have a fair, equal, and significant opportunity to obtain a high-quality education and reach, at a minimum, proficiency on challenging State academic achievement standards and state academic assessments." This end would be accomplished by aligning education "with challenging State academic standards," "meeting the educational needs of low-achieving children in our Nation's highest-poverty schools," "closing the achievement gap between high- and low-performing children," "holding schools accountable for improving the academic achievement of all students," "targeting . . . schools where needs are greatest," and "using State assessment systems designed to ensure that students are meeting challenging State academic achievement and content standards."

What we find here is a marriage of the standards movement and the civil rights movement. From the former comes the focus on rigorous academic subjects, core curriculum for all students, and testing and accountability; from the latter comes the urgent call to reduce social inequality by increasing educational opportunity. The opening sentence captures both elements succinctly.

CHOICE 2.0: A PARALLEL APPEAL
TO EQUAL OPPORTUNITY

The school choice movement had a rhetorical problem that was similar in some ways and different in other ways from the one facing the standards movement, but the message of equal opportunity worked just as well for choice reformers as it did for standards reformers. What was similar about the choice problem was the difficulty in selling choice as an exercise in efficiency. Chubb and Moe stressed that market-based schools are more effective than politics-based schools, but effectiveness alone is not the kind of issue that mobilizes citizens to support a major change in the way schools are structured. That is particularly the case for the choice movement, since the proposed transformation was such a radical departure from the time-honored pattern of school governance established in the common school era. Standards reformers were tinkering with curriculum and tests; choice reformers were attacking the democratic control of schools. It is hard to win a political fight in the United States if you cede the pro-democracy position to your opponents. Compounding the problem was the possibility that market-based schooling would intensify social inequality by allowing schools to segregate themselves along lines of class and race in response to consumer preferences. If the possible benefits were defined only as greater school effectiveness and the possible costs were defined as a retreat from democracy and equality, then the battle for school choice looked hopeless. A series of ballot failures in proposals for school vouchers seemed to confirm this judgment.

In the late 1990s, however, the politics of school choice became more complex with the introduction of a new approach to the choice movement's rhetorical repertoire. There is no canonical source to draw from in exploring this change; instead, it was a rhetorical shift that spread widely throughout the movement. As one possible example among many, I use a book by Julian Betts and Tom Loveless, *Getting Choice Right,* published in 2005 by Brookings, which also published the book by Chubb and Moe. The essence of the shift in emphasis from the earlier book was captured in the new book's subtitle: "Ensuring Equity and Efficiency in Educational Policy." Adding equity changed the valence of the choice argument. Instead of being seen as a threat to social equality, choice now could be presented as a way to spread social opportunity to the disadvantaged.

At the start of their book, Betts and Loveless agree with the judgment that "school choice in the United States is here to stay and likely to grow."[28] The only issue is how to implement it effectively.

> Indeed, the question of school choice is not an "if" or a "when." We have always had school choice in the United States, through the right of parents to send their child to a private school and through the ability of parents to pick a public school for their child by choosing where to live. Clearly, affluent parents have typically been the main beneficiaries of these forms of school choice.
>
> In recent decades new forms of school choice have arisen that have fundamentally changed the education landscape. In many cases these new mechanisms have provided less affluent families with their first taste of school choice.[29]

This shift toward a rhetoric of equal opportunity dramatically changed the way the choice argument was received, and also it transformed the political complexion of the effort. Once favored primarily by libertarians, economists, and free-market Republicans, it was now able to pick up support from a variety of sectors. One major supporter was Howard Fuller, a black community leader and former Milwaukee school superintendent, who headed the pro-choice organization Black Alliance for Educational Options (BAEO). He argued that

We must give low-income and working-class parents the power to choose schools—public or private, nonsectarian or religious—where their children will succeed. And we must give all schools the incentives to work to meet children's needs. Consider the power of choice in the hands of families who have little or no power because they control no resources. Consider how the absence of choice will continue to consign their children to schools that the affluent parents who oppose choice would never tolerate for their own children.[30]

With the new political turn, even Marxist economists Samuel Bowles and Herbert Gintis came to argue that school choice could enhance social equity.[31] Adding equal opportunity to the argument helped broaden the appeal of both the standards and choice movements.

CONCLUSION

This has been a story about the changing rhetoric of American school reform. We have seen a transition from a political vision to a market vision of schooling; from a focus on schooling as a way to create citizens for an emerging republic to a focus on schooling as a way to allow citizens to get ahead in a market society. During this century and a half, however, we have not seen the political argument for schooling disappear. Instead, we have seen it become transformed from the argument that schooling promotes civic virtue among citizens to the argument that schooling promotes social mobility among consumers. In the latter form, the political vision of schooling has retained a strong rhetorical presence in the language of school reform.

Yet the persistence of a political argument for schooling has come at a cost. Gone is the notion that schools exist to promote civic virtue for the preservation of republican community; in its place is the notion that schools exist to give all consumers access to a valuable form of educational property. This is a political vision of a very different sort, which transforms education from a public good to a private good, and from a source of political community to a source of individual opportunity. As we will see in later chapters, by undermining education as a public good and empowering educational consumers, this evolved vision of the American school system provides the rationale for the current school syndrome.

FOUNDING THE AMERICAN
SCHOOL SYSTEM

2

As we have seen, American reformers over the years have asked schools to pursue an expanding array of goals, first to create citizens and then later to create workers and consumers as well. Understanding this helps to give us a sense of what social purposes people wanted schools to serve, but it doesn't tell us much about the nature of the school system. Rhetoric and reality are never very closely aligned in social life, and this is especially true in American education, where reformers have had little luck in realizing their goals.

In this chapter, I explore the foundation of the American school system in the first part of the nineteenth century. This creation story provides important insight into the peculiarities of the system. For one thing, it is the only case in the history of American education where a reform movement really succeeded. The common school movement invented the American school system as the response to a social and political crisis that threatened the survival of the American republic in its early years. Remarkably, this system not only reflected these goals in its form and function; it went a long way toward resolving the social problem it was asked to address. There has never been anything like it since. In addition, this creation story is important because 150 years later the system that the common school men created is still very much with us. It remains a publicly funded, publicly controlled, and radically decentralized system, which focuses more on being accessible than on teaching the curriculum. In Chapter 3 we will see how the system underwent a restructuring during the progressive era, but that change was more a modification than a transformation.

To understand the common school system, therefore, is to understand many of the peculiarities of American schooling today. Both the success of the common school movement and the persistence of its handiwork in the ongoing organization of schooling help to explain two central components of the American school syndrome: our enduring faith in school reform (it worked for them, so it should work for us) and our continuing inability to make the system they created work to realize our own purposes.

EDUCATION IN COLONIAL AMERICA

Colonial America had no system of education. Instead it offered a loose collection of informal ways to provide basic literacy and numeracy skills to most of the population and to supply advanced learning to a few. Parents taught their own children in the home, or if they could afford it they hired a tutor. Churches provided religious education for the young, which required them to offer literacy training as part of the process. Parents contracted with master craftsmen to take on their sons as apprentices, which meant not only teaching them a trade but also teaching them to read, write, and figure. In a variant of this practice, parents frequently boarded out their children with another family, which in turn agreed to educate them as part of the arrangement. Often a woman in the neighborhood would take in students for a fee and teach them the basics in her own home. For education beyond the most basic level, independent schoolmasters in one-room schools taught students who paid a modest tuition; and on a more formal basis, grammar school education took place in academies, some of which had government charters. At the highest level, there were a few colleges (most of which ended up as today's Ivy League institutions), with formal charters, a faculty, and a mandate to prepare clergy and other professionals. Most students received some form of education during this period, and most of these did not attend anything resembling a school.

Only in New England was there a systematic effort by colonial governments to establish schools for all (white) members of a community. Boston established a public Latin school in 1635, only fifteen years after the Mayflower, and Harvard College was chartered in 1636. In 1647, the Massachusetts Bay Colony passed a law requiring that towns of a certain size should establish a primary school and that larger towns should also establish a grammar school. Other colonies in New England gradually followed suit by requiring the public provision of schooling in local communities. Although the middle-Atlantic colonies did not adopt the same laws, they did support a variety of less formal ways of supporting education; in the South, support for schooling was slower in building.

A study by Kenneth Lockridge shows that these efforts to provide education in the American colonies had a significant impact on the literacy of the population, especially in New England. He found that male literacy in New England reached 60 percent in 1660, 70 percent in 1710, 85 percent in 1760, and 90 percent in 1790.[1] In contrast, male literacy among non-slaves in the other colonies remained constant at around 67 percent throughout the 1700s. This was slightly higher than estimates for male literacy in England during the same period, which hovered around 60 percent, but markedly lower than New England, which may have been the first region in the world to achieve something approaching universal literacy in its white male population.[2]

How did the New England colonists do it? Lockridge notes that colonial literacy tended to be higher in general for males and the wealthy, and also for those who lived in an area that had

more population density, more commerce, and that drew immigrants who were literate on arrival. Most of these factors favored New England to a small degree, but they were not enough
to explain the region's advantage over the other colonies, much
less over the mother country. Instead, the major factor that promoted schooling in New England during this period was the
intensity of the community's commitment to Protestant religion,
especially the Puritan version that characterized the original English immigrants to the region. Elsewhere in the colonies alternative forms of Christianity were dominant, such as Catholicism in
Maryland, Anglicanism in Virginia and Delaware, and a mix of
Protestant denominations in New York, New Jersey, and Pennsylvania. But in New England, the strict brand of reform Protes-
tantism predominated.

At the core of the Protestant faith—especially in the Calvinist
version—was the belief that worshippers had a direct connection to God, which, in contrast with Catholic belief, was not
mediated by the church and its priesthood. As a result, the faith-
ful could not afford to be left illiterate, which would make them
dependent on a literate clergy to interpret and transmit the gospel. Instead they needed direct access to the word of God in order
to maintain their faith, and this required learning how to read.
Therefore, at the heart of the push for schooling in colonial America was a profoundly conservative vision of education's mission:
to preserve piety and maintain the faith. The extraordinary language of the 1647 Massachusetts law that mandated schooling
vividly makes this argument for education:

> It being one chief project of that old deluder, Satan, to keep men from
> the knowledge of the Scriptures, as in former times by keeping them
> in an unknown tongue, so in these latter times by persuading from
> the use of tongues, that so at least the true sense and meaning of the
> original might be clouded by false glosses of saint seeming deceivers,
> that learning may not be buried in the grave of our fathers in the
> church and commonwealth, the Lord assisting our endeavors.

It is therefore ordered, that every township in this jurisdiction, after the Lord hath increased them to the number of fifty householders,
shall then forthwith appoint one within their town to teach all such
children as shall resort to him to write and read . . . ; and it is further
ordered, that where any town shall increase to the number of one
hundred families or householders, they shall set up a grammar school,
the master thereof being able to instruct youth so far as they may be
fitted for the university.[3]

Thus only through education could congregants acquire "the true
sense and meaning" of the Bible and thereby save themselves from
the "false glosses of saint seeming deceivers." Such a mission was
too important to be left to chance or to the option of individual
parents. Instead it required action by public authority to make
schooling happen.

Although the primary rationale for communities to provide
education in colonial America was the pursuit of a religious ideal,
another, more pragmatic reason quietly emerged that pushed individuals to seek education on their own. In order to engage in
commerce, people needed to be reasonably good at reading,
writing, and arithmetic. Without these skills, storekeepers and
merchants and tradesmen and clerks would be unable to make
contracts, correspond with customers, or keep accounts. From
this angle, schooling was a practical necessity for anyone who
hoped to make a living in commercial activity. It was possible
for subsistence farmers to do without these skills, although it
would have certainly limited their prospects for advancing beyond this condition; and tradesmen could hire literate clerks to
handle correspondence and recordkeeping, but this would have
been inefficient and risky. From the beginning, trade was a central fact of American life. A key reason for Britain to establish
colonies in America in the first place, and to keep supporting
them for two hundred years, was to increase trade within the
empire. Therefore, colonists had a strong incentive to acquire
the skills they needed in order to take part in these commercial
activities.

So although religion was the reason for establishing schools, once schooling became available commerce emerged as a reason for consumers to pursue education on their own. And this second impulse is the best way to understand the growth of literacy in the 1700s. During this period, the colonies were becoming more secular in the way they governed (even in New England) and the colonists were becoming more diverse in the way they worshipped; but at the same time the colonial population was growing in size and density, and commercial life was expanding rapidly. Under these conditions, consumers increasingly saw the advantage, even the necessity, of gaining a basic education, whatever their religious beliefs, and growing residential density meant that they were more likely to find some form of schooling in their own community to meet their needs.

An Emerging Pattern

So before there was an American system of education—before there was even an American nation—schooling in America was an important and growing component of ordinary life, and it educated a larger share of the populace than did schooling in the rest of the world. The two factors that propelled this growth of schooling, however, were quite different in character. From the view of religion, schooling was the pursuit of a high ideal, a way to keep the faith and promote piety. Religion gave schooling a public rationale that was explicit, openly expounded by preachers, political leaders, journalists, and parents. From the view of commerce, schooling was the pursuit of a mundane interest, a way to make a living in an increasingly trade-oriented economy. This rationale for schooling was well understood but only rarely made explicit. The prevailing religious rhetoric about education, backed by the full authority of scripture, made it difficult for anyone to argue the case in public for schooling as a way to get ahead financially, since to do so would seem at best unworthy and at worst irreligious. And the two factors differed not only in the goal they set for schooling but also in the agents who would carry out this goal. Whereas the religious view stimulated top-down efforts by government and the church to promote and provide education for the populace, the commercial view stimulated bottom-up efforts by individual consumers to pursue education for their own ends.

From the colonial period to the present, the economic rationale for schooling in the United States has gradually grown in intensity, and in the twentieth century it became increasingly explicit as a primary goal for education. Meanwhile, the religious rationale for schooling has gradually faded into the background, giving way to more secular educational goals. During this entire time, however, the pressures that have sought to shape educational change in the United States have continually taken the form of these two early impulses to provide and pursue schooling.

The history of American education is in many ways an expression of this ongoing tension between schooling as the pursuit of gradually evolving cultural ideals and schooling as the pursuit of increasingly compelling economic practicalities. The first of these rationales is what has propelled most educational reform movements, which have demanded that schools adapt themselves to new ideals and help society realize these ideals—whether this ideal be religious faith, civic virtue, economic efficiency, racial equality, or individual liberty. These ideals have formed the core of the rhetoric of the major school reform movements.

The second rationale is what has propelled individuals to demand educational opportunity and avail themselves of it when it is made available. Until the last fifty years, this second form of pressure for educational change had flown under the radar, and was largely missing from the language of reform documents and educational politics. While the first approach has set waves of reform episodically rolling across the surface of education, the second has been the source of a steady current of incremental change flowing beneath the surface. As David Tyack and Larry Cuban point out, in their seminal essay on American schooling, the history of school reform in the United States has been an odd mix of turbulent reform rhetoric, which has only modestly affected the underlying structure of schooling, and a slow and silent evolutionary process, which has exerted substantial change in this structure over a sufficiently long period of time that this change is barely visible.[4] As many educators have noted over the years, schools are perpetually in the throes of one reform after another, but at the same time they seem to keep plowing ahead with business as usual. The more things change, the more they remain the same. We see this paradoxical pattern repeated frequently throughout the story of American school reform.

SCHOOLING AFTER THE REVOLUTION

By the 1790s, most white Americans were receiving some form of education, at least enough to provide basic skills, and increasingly this education was taking place in some form of school, especially if they lived in cities or major towns. Literacy had become the norm for men, and in New England it was nearly universal. The schools themselves were a mixture of public, private, and religious institutions, funded by a combination of private fees and public subsidies. The biggest change in this period, however, came not from the amount of schooling, which had been climbing steadily for decades, but from a new political rationale for schooling.

The Revolution and the formation of the United States as a nation led to an intense conversation among political leaders about the need to provide a secure basis for the new republic by promoting the education of all citizens. The founding fathers knew their history. From ancient Rome to Renaissance Florence, the record of republics had not been promising. In one case after another, republican government fell prey to a well-understood array of threats to its existence—torn apart by a combination of unrestrained self-interest, the raw pursuit of political power, and class divisions in the republican community. One way they saw that would shore up the prospects for the new American republic was with education.

The emerging republican argument for education had three central components. First was the need to instill civic virtue in future citizens, which would make them committed to the preservation of the republic and willing to devote themselves to the public good. Benjamin Rush focused in particular on civic virtue in his widely disseminated essay on republican education, which was first published in 1786:

> The business of education has acquired a new complexion by the independence of our country. The form of government we have assumed has created a new class of duties to every American. It becomes us, therefore, to examine our former habits upon this subject, and in laying the foundations for nurseries of wise and good men, to adapt our modes of teaching to the peculiar form of our government.[5]

What this meant in practice was that schools needed to instill in students a willingness to abandon self-interest in support of the republic. "Let our pupil be taught that he does not belong to himself, but that he is public property. Let him be taught to love his family, but let him be taught at the same time that he must forsake and even forget them when the welfare of his country requires it."[6]

A second component of the republican rationale for education was to give individuals the knowledge and skill they needed in order to carry out their role as citizens at the high level of effectiveness required in the life of a republic. Thomas Jefferson emphasized this aim in the opening section of the preamble to his proposed Bill for the General Diffusion of Knowledge, written in 1778. After expressing concern about the historical tendency for republican governments in which "those entrusted with power have, in time, and by slow operations, perverted it into tyranny," he continues, "it is believed that the most effectual means of preventing this would be, to illuminate, as far as practicable, the minds of the people at large, and more especially to give them knowledge of those facts, which history exhibiteth, that . . . they may be enabled to know ambition under all its shapes, and prompt to exert their natural powers to defeat its purposes."[7]

A third goal of republican education followed naturally from the first two: that a viable republic required a system of schooling that could instill both civic virtue and civic skill in all citizens regardless of wealth and social position. Only in this way would it be possible to construct a true republican community, in which capabilities and commitments were widely shared and social inequalities would not interfere with carrying out civic functions. Jefferson's preamble concluded with this point:

> it becomes expedient for promoting the public happiness that those persons, whom nature hath endowed with genius and virtue, should be rendered by liberal education worthy to receive, and able to guard the sacred deposit of the rights and liberties of their fellow citizens, and that they should be called to that charge without regard to wealth, birth or other accidental condition or circumstance.

To make this possible, those who could not afford to pay for schooling should be "educated at the common expense of all."[8]

This republican mission for education substantially raised the stakes by making the effort to ensure that all citizens had access to effective schooling into an essential function of government. The haphazard patchwork of mechanisms that emerged during the colonial period to provide some form of schooling for most individuals now seemed wholly inadequate. For this reason, leaders argued that schooling was too important to be left to chance or to be distributed according to social position. So in the first decades of the nineteenth century, New York and Philadelphia developed large systems of public schools, which were supported by public funds and governed by publicly appointed boards, and other cities followed suit.

The catch, however, was that these were designed as charity schools. In order to enroll their children in these schools, parents needed to go to city hall and declare themselves paupers, while families that had sufficient resources were expected to provide education for their children at their own expense. This development gave the poor expanded access to formal schooling, and it set a precedent for establishing a public system of education, but it did not realize Rush's vision of "producing one general and uniform system of education" that would "render the mass of the people more homogeneous." Instead it tended to reinforce class differences by establishing a distinction between schools for us and schools for them. This distinction became particularly troubling when in the 1820s and 1830s the young republic had to confront a social crisis that threatened to destroy it.

A SOCIAL CRISIS FOR THE NEW REPUBLIC

The United States went through some tough times in its early years, and the second decade of the nineteenth century was particularly trying. First came the War of 1812 with Great Britain. The fighting lasted for three years and ended in a draw, but not before the country had gone through substantial destruction and citizens had watched in humiliation as the president fled the capital to escape from invading troops, who then sat down to eat his dinner before burning down the White House. Coming on the heels of war was the Panic of 1819, which wiped out all of the growth in personal income from the previous twenty years. What followed, however, was one of the strongest periods of economic growth in American history, lasting all the way to the Civil War. There are a number of compelling explanations for the rapid economic growth in the latter part of this period, including the rise of factory production, railroads, and widespread immigration from Germany and Ireland. But none of these factors was in place in the 1820s, when the boom began.

What was going on in the late teens and twenties, however, was an extraordinary growth in the country's economic infrastructure—in particular a huge government investment in building turnpikes and canals. These internal improvements in the U.S. transportation system sharply reduced the cost of transporting goods, which meant that for the first time farmers and craftsmen in rural areas could sell their produce in major cities on the East Coast. By connecting previously isolated segments of the economy, the new trade routes helped create regional markets for goods and even the beginnings of a national market. The result was a boom in trade and also a sharp increase in competition among all of the producers along these routes. Instead of operating within a geographically constricted setting, with a small group of producers catering to a small group of local consumers, producers such as wheat farmers and shoemakers found themselves having to adapt to an economic situation where the numbers of buyers and sellers were effectively unlimited. This in turn led to a dramatic transformation in the mode of production for goods, in the relations between owners and workers, and in the structure of communities.

This transformation was a kind of revolution, a market revolution.[9] As I noted earlier, America had a market economy from the earliest colonial days, but large-scale trade had been confined to a few port towns. For everyone else markets were local, narrowly restricted by poor transportation and communication. But when goods and information were suddenly able to cross great distances at low cost, this brought a severe challenge to America's economic, social, political, and religious life. The result was the destruction of one social order without a clear indication of what new social order would arise to take its place, leaving a vacuum of authority that threatened the foundations of the fragile new republic. And the significance of these events for the history of American school reform is that reformers came to the conclusion that the primary institutional way to resolve this crisis was to develop a broadly inclusive system of public schools.

A useful way to understand both the nature of this social turbulence in the 1820s and the rationale for seeing education as the solution to the problem is to examine a particular case of social change and social reform close-up. Rochester, New York, presents an ideal case to consider in this regard, since it served as the site for a natural experiment in radical social change. Starting out as a tiny agricultural village, which had only fifteen inhabitants in 1812, it became the fastest-growing city in the United States in the 1820s. The reason for this rapid growth is easy to identify: the Erie Canal. And we can even establish the exact starting date for the change process. Construction on the canal began in 1817, and on October 1, 1823, the waterway reached Rochester, connecting the city to Albany 225 miles east and, by way of the Hudson River, all the way to New York City. On that day, the national market came to Rochester, riding on the first canal boat. With this arrival, everything in Rochester changed.

The National Market Comes to Town: The Case of Rochester, New York

Because of its relation with the Erie Canal, Rochester presents a useful way to understand the social crisis of the 1820s and the impetus for social reform during this period, and what allows us to interpret this case is Paul Johnson's stunning study of the city in the throes of social transformation, *A Shopkeeper's Millennium: Society and Revivals in Rochester, New York, 1815–1837*.[10] In this book he details the social transformation that took place in the city after the arrival of the canal and shows how citizens experienced this transformation as a crisis of the spirit. His analysis allows us to understand both the threats and the opportunities inherent in this transformation, which was happening at the same time across the United States. This upheaval prompted reformers to invent a series of social institutions that came to shape American society for the next two hundred years, and the model for these institutions was the common school.

In 1818, when construction work on the canal began in earnest, Rochester had about 1,000 residents, and from this point on its population grew at a rate of about 25 percent a year into

the early 1830s. In the first few years of this expansion, the social structure of the town retained a distinctly traditional character, following long-standing patterns of precapitalist economic
and social relations. Surrounding farmers sold their produce in
town, and craftsmen made goods to order for customers in the
area, with local custom setting the prices for their wares. Farm
work was organized by family, with little need for outside labor.
Craft work was organized around the family of the master craftsman, who took in apprentices to learn the trade and journeymen
to carry out production, all of them living in the master's house
and eating at his table; the goods were sold in the master's shop.
Children on the farm expected either to take over the family
farm or to buy their own land and become independent farmers.
Apprentices expected to become journeymen and eventually
hoped to set up their own shops as master artisans.

Social authority rested with the head of household, who was
also the owner of the farm or the shop. Because of property
qualifications for the electorate, these owners were also the prime
political actors. Demand for goods was modest and steady, restricted by a geography that also limited the options and thus
the leverage of consumers. As a result, there was little pressure
for farmers or shopkeepers to increase productivity. Workers in
the craft shop earned room, board, and a small amount of pay,
which they received regularly even though orders came in more
episodically; the shopkeeper-craftsman had to maintain a stable
workforce to meet average demand and could not easily add or
drop employees in response to fluctuations in this demand. When
there were no orders to fill, the workers would quit early.[11]

All this suddenly changed with the arrival of the national market. Cheap transportation by canal boat opened up enormous
economic opportunity for farmers and craftsmen alike. Instead of
having sales restricted to customers within walking distance,
they could sell their wares to anyone living along the 365-mile
length of the canal, plus anyone living along the rivers that connected with the canal. Beyond this was the world, since at the

western end the canal connected with the Great Lakes and the entire upper Midwest; at the eastern end it linked up with the Hudson; and at the mouth of the Hudson was New York City, where ships could take their goods up and down the coast and across the ocean. A wide-open market meant wide-open opportunity for farmers and craftsmen to get rich by expanding production to meet the new demand.

But at the same time that the canal provided great opportunity, it also opened up great economic risk. Every wheat farmer was suddenly competing with every other wheat farmer across New York State and beyond, and every shoemaker was competing with every other shoemaker in Buffalo, Albany, New York City, and all points in between. Because of the huge increase in the potential market, producers in Rochester could sell vastly more goods than they had before, but because of the huge increase in competition, they could do so only if they lowered their prices to a competitive level. Otherwise they would easily be driven out of business. The only options were to increase the volume and intensity of production in your business or fold up shop and go to work for someone else who was more successful in negotiating the new market situation. In order to survive, much less thrive, in this environment, producers had to raise productivity by sharply reducing the cost of producing every bushel of wheat and every pair of shoes. This meant increasing the amount of goods produced for every hour of labor and every acre of land, increasing the volume of output, and reducing the cost of labor, all in order to compensate for the drop in prices.

Johnson carefully traces the social consequences of these market pressures in Rochester with the arrival of the Erie Canal, and in doing so he provides insight into the same series of changes that were going on more gradually across the country during the period from about 1815 to 1860. As in Rochester, the growth of cheap transportation and the connection with wider markets in the United States was steadily lowering prices and wages and changing the way people worked and lived. Under these new conditions, master craftsmen could no longer afford the economic inefficiencies that came with the old model of work relations. Since they were now producing goods for consumers far away, they could no longer work to order but had to turn toward volume production of standardized goods. They could only pay workers when there was work to do and had to supervise them closely to get the most productivity during working hours. In order to maintain flexibility in matching work hours to product demand, they could no longer support apprentices and journeymen in their homes, since they had to be able to drop and add workers as needed. So, workers increasingly lived in their own housing in a separate section of the city, which freed them from the social authority of the master but at the same time left them wholly dependent on their own declining and irregular wages as the sole support for themselves and their families.

In Rochester and across the country during this period, the shift toward a market economy led to a series of major problems—social, political, religious, and economic—which merged into a single overarching crisis in American society.[12] The social problem was in part a question of authority. In the face of wage labor, the old, unquestioned authority of the farm and business owner was disappearing and there was nothing to take its place, a change that liberated workers but also raised fears of anarchy and rebellion. In addition, since the key to survival was now the ability to command wages in the market, this left families poorly equipped to handle the dependents in their midst—the old, the young, and the ill—who were not able to care for themselves much less earn a living wage. The political problem was the potential destruction of republican community in the new economy, with its emphasis on personal autonomy, the pursuit of individual interest, and the growing separation between social classes. Under these conditions, how could the republic instill civic virtue in its citizens without restricting their newly won liberties, and how could it reduce social differences sufficiently to allow citizens to continue thinking of themselves as political equals?

The religious and moral problem was how people could take part in a competitive market economy, with its emphasis on individual self-reliance instead of social dependence, and still remain good Christians with a high standard of morality. And the economic problem was how to resolve all of these other problems without constricting individual initiative and the market economy, which were so effective at increasing wealth and improving the standard of living. Going back to a more traditional society did not seem possible or even attractive, either for the workers who had submitted to it or the farmers and masters who had dominated it; but the social, political, and spiritual consequences of the new market economy were truly frightening.

Reform to the Rescue

If necessity is the mother of invention, then crisis is the mother of reform. Crisis conditions in a society create a powerful demand for possible solutions, which in turn encourages social entrepreneurs to develop innovative reform measures and test them out in practice. Local innovations that demonstrate the greatest apparent success spread quickly to other locations, winning the reformer public acclaim, social influence, and political power. In the 1820s and 1830s, the rise of a national market economy in the United States created a strong demand for social reform to deal with the market's disruptive side effects, and the result was an amazing flowering of reform ideas, which in turn led to the most productive period of institution creation in American history.[13]

The reformers who stepped forward to meet this challenge can be loosely labeled as Whigs. This group, however, was not limited to members of the Whig Party, which was formally established in 1833 in response to Andrew Jackson's new Democratic Party. The Whig Party was a prime mover at the national and state levels in efforts to promote development of the market economy (by supporting construction of canals and turnpikes to spur trade and by supporting the tariff to protect industry) while simultaneously supporting development of new institutions to soften the impact of the market on society. But the urge to establish these new institutions extended well beyond the confines of this party and long preceded its formation, when, during the late teens and twenties, whiggism was lodged in the nationalist wing of the old Democratic-Republican Party founded by Jefferson. In states like New York, where the Jacksonian Democrats became the dominant force, the Whig impulse played out through Democratic politicians.

Whiggism broadly conceived was a particular stance toward progress that cut across party lines, if not across class lines. At its heart was a desire to reconcile the market economy with the republic, to develop an approach that would accommodate the one without destroying the other. Whigs tended to be masters, merchants, and farmers who prospered or hoped to prosper in the new setting (and people aspired to join their ranks). They wanted to enjoy the benefits of the market while also preserving the republic, and their efforts at institution-building were closely aimed at accomplishing this kind of delicate balance. This Whig effort was part of the larger American compromise, starting in 1789 and continuing to this day, which has continually sought to strike just the right balance between the prime elements in a liberal republic. They sought to preserve economic liberty while also preserving republican politics. The Whigs were the group that arose to reestablish this balance when the market economy posed the most severe threat to a liberal republic that Americans have ever faced.[14]

Most of the institutions created during the years before the Civil War are still with us in some form or other. These include the penitentiary, the hospital, the insane asylum, the poorhouse (now superseded by welfare and social security), and the common school. At one level, all these institutions were designed to provide a social support system to replace the system that was destroyed by the market. They took care of the various dependent populations that used to be supported through a person's affiliation with a family farm or family shop. Each institution dealt with a particular dependent group that was left hanging by the wage labor system, a group that was incapable of supporting itself in the labor market and was also too much of a burden for wage-earning families to manage on their own. These institutions took care of those who were too criminal (the penitentiary), too sick (the hospital), too crazy (the asylum), too old and poor (the poorhouse), and too young (the school) to earn wages and thus care for themselves. With the rise of a market economy, wage earners were not able to deal with these dependents on their own, since to do so would remove them from the wage labor force and leave their families without support. Whigs argued that the government needed to step in to fill the gap, providing a new kind of safety net for the populace while at the same time freeing up more people in their productive years to enter the workforce and make a contribution to the economy.

But Whig reformers in Rochester (and in the United States more generally) saw a bigger mission for reform than the need to provide a social safety net for workers in the new market economy. At a deeper level, they wanted to resolve the core problem at the heart of the liberal republican compromise: how to create a moral and politically stable community that was made up of self-interested individuals; how to accommodate the republic with the market. The grandest of issues was at stake here: Could we maintain social order, the accumulation of wealth, individual liberty, and republican community—all in the same society? Rochester, like the rest of the United States, settled on an answer right around 1830. In Rochester's case, the answer took a singular form. The great evangelical preacher, Charles Grandison Finney, came to town in 1830 and stayed for a year. By the time he was done, he had turned the city upside down and established a stable basis for a new social order.

Prior efforts by civic leaders to establish social stability in Rochester had failed miserably. During the late 1820s, city government, churches, and civic organizations had tried to fill the vacuum left by the decline in the social authority of masters by imposing such authority through law. Leaders sought to close bars, ban drinking, and prohibit activities on the Sabbath, all in the name of restoring social order. But with the disappearance of property qualifications for voting and the introduction of the secret ballot, the city's broader and freer electorate soundly rejected these initiatives. And this was as much a failure of vision as an electoral defeat for the first wave of reformers. The problem was that imposing order from above was not only unfeasible in the new political environment; it was also economically counterproductive, since it threatened to restrain those individual liberties—free labor and free enterprise—that were so critical to the market economy. So reform took a turn away from imposition and toward education.

Finney was the most famous evangelist in the Second Great Awakening, the powerful wave of religious revival that swept across the United States in the period before the Civil War. His preaching in Rochester helped to establish that city as the heart of what came to be known as the Burned-Over District, the central and western part of New York State (along the route of the Erie Canal) that was the site of the most intense series of revivals in the country during this period. He succeeded in establishing a new social and moral order in the region, not through the force of law but through the power of persuasion, employing his superb preaching skills in service of a powerful theological message directed at the troubled citizens along the canal. His message was perfectly suited to the problems they faced in this difficult time of social transition. In Finney the social crisis had found the social reformer with the skills and message that were best adapted to respond to this time of trouble and opportunity.

His theology was based on the principle of salvation by grace. Individuals could only save their souls if they were willing to make the decision to accept the grace of God and then to rededicate themselves to a new life as Christians. And the revival process was enormously effective in encouraging people to make this choice by using social modeling and social pressure. When people arrived at a revival, they found that their social betters—the local masters, merchants, and landowners—had already accepted grace and were welcoming newcomers to join them. And the revival's combination of public exhortation, public prayer, and social outreach made it hard to resist the offer of the good news, along with entry into the community of true believers who were also social leaders. But at the heart of this choice was more than social approval and social mobility; it was a profound decision to replace external control with internal control. Coming forward at the revival to accept the gift of grace meant agreeing to accept the precepts of social authority, internalizing these rules for behavior, and them imposing them on yourself. It meant giving up drink, developing sober work habits, observing the Sabbath, and being a productive member of your religious and social community.

Here was a formula for restoring social, political, and religious authority in a market economy; a formula that showed how individuals could be self-interested economic actors and still be orderly townspeople, civic-minded citizens, and upstanding Christians, all the while avoiding the kinds of traditional social controls that would undermine the freedoms needed for free enterprise. For masters, Finney offered a new social order based on sharing self-regulation with their workers rather than imposing control on them. For workers, he offered an answer that reinforced their freedom from the master by allowing them to impose regulation on themselves; and since this new pattern of behavior was the same for workers and entrepreneurs, it offered the possibility that the one could become the other.

Grounding their efforts in this revivalist Protestant frame for reconstructing the antebellum social order, the Whigs invented a powerful and enduring series of social institutions that were designed to carry it into social practice. Intended to establish a balance between the republic and the new economy, and modeled after the structure of the religious revival, these institutions saw their primary function as education. Reformers established the penitentiary, hospital, asylum, poorhouse, and school, all as educational institutions. Like Finney's revivals, these institutions sought to persuade, inculcate, and educate individuals to regulate themselves; and like the revivals, they used mechanisms of social pressure and routines of habit-building to accomplish their educational goals.

Although many, maybe most, of these institutions have tended over the years to hover closer to warehousing than educating their clients, that was not the primary intent of their Whig founders. As I have noted, taking care of those whom the family could no longer handle was a secondary goal of the institutions, yet the primary goal was not custody but conversion. The penitentiary was supposed to be a place for the inmate to become penitent, develop new work habits, and then return to society as a self-regulating and productive participant. The hospital and asylum were supposed to rehabilitate patients and prepare them to take on responsibilities as citizens, family members, and workers. The poorhouse took care of the elderly who were unable to take care of themselves, but it also sought to retrain the younger and more able inmates in order to reintroduce them into the labor force. Every correctional officer, nurse, and attendant in these institutions was considered a kind of teacher.

Of all these institutions, the common school was the most comprehensive and the most fundamental. Whereas the others focused on discrete subgroups of the population, the school focused on the entire cohort of the young, and as a result its goals were broader and its potential social impact greater. The idea was to provide one place in every community where every child would receive instruction, and the primary focus would be on moral and political education. The notion of education for economic growth was not in the vocabulary of the common school movement. Instead, the explicit aim of the movement was to provide students with an educational experience that would encourage them to become self-regulating moral and political actors in society. Without resort to external supervision, they would be obedient to moral standards and committed to civic virtue. In the verbal shorthand of the movement, the school was focused on making citizens. And in line with the republican vision of education that came from Rush and Jefferson, this meant that a critical quality of the common school was its commonness. Citizens could not come together into a republican community unless the social differences among them were kept sufficiently modest that they would be able to find common ground. Under these circumstances, the mix of private, parochial, and pauper schools that was in place in the 1820s was no longer suitable for the task.

THE COMMON SCHOOL MOVEMENT

In the introduction to this book, I argued that Americans over the years have loaded enormous responsibility onto public education by asking it to take the lead in solving one major social problem after another. And as I have been showing in the current chapter, that process of placing massive responsibilities and high expectations on the schools was present at the birth of the U.S. public school system in the years before the Civil War. The social problems in United States in the 1820s and 1830s were potentially catastrophic—threatening the dissolution of community, morality, and republic—and the key social response that reformers devised to solve these problems was to create the common school. The stakes don't get any higher than this. Of course, school reformers have always claimed that the stakes are high. But what distinguished the common school movement from all of its successors in the history of American school reform was that this reform movement accomplished its goal. More recent educational reformers have aimed for a lot and accomplished a little, but the common schoolmen established a system of education that not only reflected their goals but for the most part realized them. And the system they established, with only modest addition and alteration, is still with us today.

The common school movement spanned the years from 1830 to 1860. Its most prominent national leader was Horace Mann, a Whig politician who in 1837 became the first Secretary of the State Board of Education of Massachusetts and then used this position to promote the cause of the common schools. His speeches and widely republished annual reports reached a broad audience across the country. Massachusetts was a natural base for the movement, since it had the earliest start in developing public education with the "old deluder Satan" act of 1647. But, provoked by a common set of social problems, school reform efforts emerged spontaneously in a number of locations around the country, carried by dozens of local leaders who freely borrowed from each other until their efforts converged into a national movement. And the leaders of the common school movement were also frequently involved in efforts to establish other parallel Whig institutions at the same time. For example, Roberts Vaux led the Philadelphia campaign for a common school system in the 1820s, but he was best known as the founder of Eastern State Penitentiary, the widely copied model for the new prison as reformatory. Along the way he also played a leading role in establishing Philadelphia asylums for the deaf, the blind, and the insane. For Whig reformers like Vaux (a Quaker and a Jacksonian Democrat), all of these institutions were closely related answers to the same problem.

To understand the nature of the common school movement, we need to establish first what it was *not* trying to do. It was not an effort to persuade Americans to see education as important. As we have seen, education was already playing a prominent role in American life. It was not an effort to increase school enrollment, since such enrollments were already quite high. A study by Carl Kaestle and Maris Vinovskis shows that educational enrollments in Massachusetts were at a high level at the start of the nineteenth century and remained flat during the common school period through the middle of the century.[15] It was also not an effort to raise the literacy rate, which was already nearly universal in

New England and elevated in the rest of the country. Instead, its central aim was to channel the existing school enrollments in every community into a single, publicly governed community school.

The problem for the movement was how to bring about this end. Different religious and ethnic groups were accustomed to having their own schools, and the middle and upper classes were comfortable in paying tuition for their children. Added to this was the problem that public schools bore the stigma of charity. If only the poor and the unaffiliated continued to attend the public schools, they would fail to accomplish their grand republican aims. But removing the pauper test and opening the doors of the public school to everyone would succeed only if the whole community would be willing to accept the invitation.

One approach reformers took to selling the common schools was political, to emphasize the need for universal education in order to shore up the republic. As one leader of the movement in Philadelphia put it grandiloquently: "Ignorance in the masses is the aliment of usurpation and the safe-guard of tyranny. Education, confined to the favoured few, makes but a janizary guard for the tyrant. The only pedestal on which Liberty can stand erect, forever firmly poised, is UNIVERSAL EDUCATION."[16] Another approach to selling the reform was religious, to build on the evangelical Protestant vision of sharing the faith, with masters inviting workers to join them in reforming themselves in response to the gift of grace. So reformers portrayed the common school as an ideal institution for instilling the new morality of self-regulation.

A third marketing approach was social, to stir up fears of the social disorder that would run rampant without an effective institution for socializing the public. And if all these rhetorical approaches didn't work, there was also the option of luring the well-to-do with special inducements. For example, the 1836 law that established the common school system in Philadelphia also established a high school. The leaders of the new school system deliberately made the high school more attractive than the best private academies in the city—with a marble edifice, the latest scientific equipment, and a faculty of distinguished professors—and then announced that students could only be admitted to the high school if they had first attended the common elementary schools.

The arguments worked, and in one community after another there emerged a structure of schooling in the new mold. By the outbreak of the Civil War, all of the elements of the new educational system were firmly in place.

THE COMMON SCHOOL SYSTEM, THEN AND NOW

It is worth pausing at this point to analyze the components of the common school system. At one level, the structure of the system poses promise for reformers, showing how a school reform movement can be truly effective by creating a system whose form and function align closely with the movement's guiding ideas. But at another level, it also poses caution for reformers, showing how the organizational machinery of a school system created for one purpose can make it ill suited for other purposes. The school system put in place by the common school movement had the following emergent characteristics: community-wide enrollment, public control, local control, age grading, teacher training, big government, and curriculum marginality. Let's consider the nature of each of these elements and also the implications of each for later school reform efforts.

Community-Wide Enrollment. The most important principle defining the common school was that it drew its students from the entire surrounding community. The Whig-republican mission made this central. By including students from all walks of life and putting them through the same educational experience, schools could help alleviate the growing class divisions in the new market society. Students would emerge from this experience with a lot in common, which would help offset substantial differences in other parts of their lives, and which would help prepare them to interact as members of the same republican community. In addition, the school experience would focus on instilling in all students a degree of self-regulation, which would allow them to function as independent citizens, workers, and community members while still maintaining a common commitment to civic virtue, work ethics, and public morality.

The tradition of the community school has remained important throughout the history of American education. In the nineteenth century, the community was inclusive by social class and gender but not when it came to race, since blacks, Indians, Chinese, and Hispanics were all consigned to separate institutions if they were educated at all. The mid-twentieth century saw efforts to broaden access to racial minority groups through the desegregation movement, which then expanded the community even more widely by seeking to include students with disabilities into the regular classroom and to end tracking by gender. More recently, the school standards movement has drawn on this tradition to argue for imposing a common academic standard on all students in order to make sure that no child is left behind.

But sometimes the community school has been a bone of contention for reformers. Administrative progressives in the early twentieth century sought to track students by ability and future job, which introduced de facto segregation by social class and immigrant status and later by race. And the contemporary school choice movement has argued for breaking up the public school monopoly, which compels everyone in a given geographical area to attend the local public school, in order to allow consumers to select alternative private schools and public charter schools that are tailored to their values and wishes.

Public Funding. The common schools could not enroll everybody in the community without drawing on public funds to overcome differences in ability to pay. The earliest common schools often supplemented public appropriations with fees charged to students, but these were generally waived for students who could not pay and gradually disappeared over the years. This shift toward public subsidy of education from a mixed public-private model meant that education quickly became a dominant issue in state and local politics, since schools devoured such a large portion of the public purse. No longer only a matter for private concern, schooling took center stage, where it was exposed to withering critiques as well as public acclaim and was subjected to a variety of public pressures. After all, the thinking went, since we're already paying for schools, shouldn't they be doing something about the latest looming social problem? So the intensely public character of the common school system made it the target of recurring efforts at social reform.

Local Control. From the very beginning, control of the common schools was radically localized. Decisions about funding, hiring, and curriculum rested in the hands of the elected (or sometimes politically appointed) board of a local school district, and for a long time the districts were quite small. One-school districts were the norm in rural areas and smaller towns. No one knows the actual numbers of districts in the nineteenth century; but when the federal government starting counting districts in 1938, after forty years of aggressive efforts at consolidation, there were still 120,000. Now they number about 14,000.

One consequence of this structure of local control is that it created a legacy of weak school administration. For most of the nineteenth century, school administration was so decentralized and districts were so small that administration was a part-time job. In most districts, with only one school, the principal and superintendent were the same person. In larger districts, the grammar school master or high school principal was superintendent; there was no administrative staff. True professional administration did not start to emerge until the latter part of the century and then only in the larger cities.

For reformers over the years, this decentralized structure has posed both a problem and an opportunity. The problem is this: How can you disseminate reforms and implement them at the local level when governance is so widely dispersed? One answer has been for reformers to push for an increased role by the state and federal governments; another has been to push for mechanisms, like curriculum standards and testing requirements, that restrict district autonomy and bring local practice in line with reform policies. But so far, neither approach has managed to make more than a dent in local resistance to outside reform initiatives.

The opportunity posed by decentralization is that there are many ways to try initiating reforms within the system. You don't have to rely on a process of dispersion from the center to the periphery; instead, you can try something new in a remote district without the support of a national reform movement or state educational policymakers. As a result, the system encourages a process of reform that is diverse, dispersed, and chronic. Every school potentially becomes an independent site of reform experimentation. This makes it easy for us to use school reform repeatedly to address social problems, which is a key element of the American school syndrome.[17]

Age Grading. In rural areas and small towns, one-room schools remained the norm long after the establishment of the common school system. (Fewer than 400 persist today, but as recently as 1919 there were 190,000.)[18] But in most towns and cities, a more complex structure of the school emerged quickly with the arrival of universal education. In response to the growing size of the school, educators started dividing students into manageable groups, and age was a natural basis for this since it correlated with cognitive development. But age grading also arose from ideology. The common school mission called for a form of education that was powerful enough to instill within students a deep sense of citizenship, self-regulation, and moral conscience. By organizing students by developmental stage, educators created the possibility that the whole class could be taught the same subject at the same level and that forces of peer pressure and emulation could help reinforce the learning process. In this sense, the age-graded school drew on insights from the revival movement and its techniques for promoting conversion.

Age grading, however, came to pose particular challenges for future educational reformers. When over time a gap emerged between the age of students and their level of academic achievement, educators faced the dilemma of which criterion to use in promoting students to the next grade. This tension between social promotion (by age) and merit promotion (by achievement) has been a chronic concern for reform movements over the years. Opting for social promotion, progressive reformers chose to group students in each grade by their differing abilities and curriculum levels. Opting for merit promotion, reformers in the standards movement have pushed to establish common achievement and curriculum standards for students in each grade.

Teacher Training. For common school reformers, schooling was too important for political and social life to be left to private option and private funding; and it followed that teaching in the common schools was also too important for leaders to leave the preparation and recruitment of teachers to chance. So common school reformers worked hard to develop public normal schools that could provide teacher preparation. But normal schools remained relatively scarce until the latter part of the nineteenth century, and even by 1900 they were not preparing a majority of teachers. Most elementary teachers came to the classroom with little more than the experience of having completed the course of study that they were now trying to teach. Under these circumstances, the normal schools often played a role that was less practical (preparing teachers) than symbolic (providing a model of what teaching should be). (The term "normal school" came from the French *école normale,* and it carried the meaning of setting the norm for schooling.) Accompanying the move toward normal schools was a parallel effort to establish state certification of teachers, with both intended to ensure that the common schools were able to carry out their mission.

One result of these efforts to develop systematic preparation of teachers was that every subsequent school reform movement needed to launch a parallel movement to reform teacher education if it was going to have teachers who would teach in line with the reform. Another was that if reformers came to feel that teacher education institutions were part of the problem rather than part of the solution, they could always look to establish alternative routes into teaching that would bypass education schools to supply reform-minded instructors to the classroom. The current movements for academic standards and school choice have pursued both of these options.

Big Government. Like the rest of the common school enterprise, the establishment of normal schools bore the imprint of the Whig vision for early America. In an interesting parallel with New Deal reformers a century later, Whig reformers felt that they could save capitalism from its own dangerous side effects only by sharply enhancing the role of government. In the 1930s this meant expanding government to provide social security, increased welfare, bank regulation, public insurance, and public employment. In the antebellum period, this meant expanding government to provide canals, turnpikes, and railroads; penitentiaries, hospitals, asylums, and poorhouses; common schools and normal schools. This amounted to a huge increase in the role of the state, enlisting it in the effort to protect both the market economy and the political and social structure of the country. As we have seen, Whig reformers asked the state to assume two major functions that had not been part of its purview before that point. Reformers asked to take on the care of the dependent members of society, who were unable to earn their way in a wage labor economy and who could no longer be supported by their families. And they also asked the state to take on the education of the populace in order to create a new kind of self-regulating citizen, soul, and conscience. The common school system was the largest institution for pursuing the first goal, and it was the model for all other institutions in carrying out the second.

Ever since the common school movement, school reformers have debated how best to use the powers of government to render schools more effective in solving social problems. As schools kept taking on new roles, they also needed to add new staff, specialists, curriculum units, and administrators, which amounted to a large increase in the size and social intrusiveness of government. The progressive movement was a particularly extensive development of schooling in this direction. But recently we have seen a growing reaction to the school as the extension of big government. In particular, the school choice movement has launched a frontal assault on the legitimacy of government schools, arguing that schooling works best if government cedes control to empowered consumers, who select the schooling for their children in a competitive educational market.

Curriculum Marginality. The aspect of the common school system that had perhaps the greatest long-term impact was its emphasis on commonality over content. Recall that Americans were already highly literate before the invention of the common school, so the massive public investment in constructing the school system in the mid-nineteenth century did little to increase rates of literacy. The system did not even increase the likelihood that a young person would receive an education, since that was already taking place in some form or other for most Americans in the early part of the century. What the system did do was increase the likelihood that young people, in company with a cross section of the local community, would acquire their education in the setting of a formally constituted school, which was publicly controlled, age graded, and run by a trained teacher. The system's primary accomplishment was to provide a shared experience of schooling for the populace. This helped to create a new form of community for a liberal republic; and it also helped to socialize students in new norms of self-control and internalized social values that prepared them to play the role of self-regulating actors in a market economy.

One thing the system never emphasized, however, was learning the school curriculum. Not that these schools lacked formal study in school subjects—far from it. They had students read textbooks, listen to lectures, practice their lessons, do homework, and take tests to determine how much they had learned. After all, that's what schools do. But aside from the basics of literacy and numeracy training, the specific content of this curriculum was less important than the process of learning it in the company of peers and in the setting of a classroom. Community came from being socialized in the values of a liberal republic and from having the shared experience of schooling. What students learned about math, science, literature, and history—the four core school subjects then and now—was beside the point. Horace Mann wrote a lot about the political aims of schooling, and his fellow common school reformer Henry Barnard wrote a book about school architecture, but neither showed much interest in talking about the importance of learning school subjects. In many ways, for them and for the common school movement in general, the common form of the schools *was* its content. Being there was the most important thing.

At the elementary level, which was the primary focus of the common school movement, schooling was all about open access and shared experience. But this started to change at the end of the nineteenth century, when elementary schools were filling up and a sharply increasing number of students began to attend high school. High school at that point was a markedly uncommon experience, shared by fewer than 10 percent of students, and the relative scarcity of a high school education granted its recipients a form of invidious distinction. This is not to say that the subjects learned in high school were any more socially salient than the subjects learned at the lower levels of the system. Social advantage did not arise because the high school content was useful but because access to these subjects was limited. Thus, in the twentieth century the key issue in the politics of education became this new tension between the open access and the special advantage that schooling could provide individual consumers. The central fights that emerged were over who would get access to high school (and later college) and how families with educational advantage could retain their edge in the face of growing enrollments at one level of the system and then another.

So one legacy of the marginality of curriculum in the common school system is that it helped spur the ongoing struggle over access to schooling. Another is that it provided the central issue for a new reform movement that—finally, after 150 years of public schooling in the United States—sought to make learning the curriculum the system's central aim. The standards movement in the late twentieth century was the first major American reform effort that focused on trying to improve the quality of student achievement in school subjects. We have yet to see how successful that effort will be.

A SCHOOL REFORM THAT WORKED

In this book about the social role of schools and the limits of school reform, the common school movement is the one big success story. It was a school reform that worked, and none of the later reform movements came close to realizing their goals the way it did. The common school movement demonstrated its power in two ways. It had a huge impact on the educational system, effectively creating a structure of schooling in its own image; and it played a critical role in resolving the social crisis that provoked reform in the first place. Let's look at each of these in turn.

I think I have already established the first point in the preceding analysis, where I showed how the central organizational characteristics of the common school system expressed the core

vision of the common school movement. The reformers had some
distinct advantages in creating a system that realized their vision,
all deriving from newness. The United States was a brand-new
country, which in revolution had shrugged off much of its British
inheritance and thus was free to invent new traditions instead of
following old ones. It had educational practices that preceded the
development of the common school, but it had no preexisting
school system, whose precedents, habits, and organizational momentum might have acted as a drag on radical reform. In the
1820s, the country was undergoing a social transformation that
was so threatening to its existence that modest incremental change
seemed inadequate to the task and dramatic forms of social innovation seemed prudent and even conservative. In response to this
challenge, school reformers found themselves part of a broad
movement to invent new social institutions, each part of which
reinforced the others. And operating at a time only thirty years
after the founding of the United States, the Whig reformers
could pursue social reinvention free of the kind of social under-
tow that would have restricted the scope of innovation in a more
established society.

Common school reformers successfully built on these advantages to construct a school system whose core organizational characteristics faithfully expressed the Whig agenda. Community-
wide enrollment, public funding, and local control produced an
inclusive and self-regulating community in the school, which in
turn promoted the possibility of creating and reinforcing republican community. Age grading and teacher training promoted the kind of modeling, social pressure, peer competition,
and professional instruction that would push students to learn
and take to heart their new roles as citizens. And the invention
of the common school system exemplified the Whig view that
education in the broadest sense—inducting the populace into
the new social order—was the responsibility of an expansive
state.

Making the case that the common school movement had a powerful impact on the school system is relatively easy, but establishing that this action was effective in solving the social problems that first provoked the reform is potentially more difficult. After all, the movement had extraordinarily ambitious goals: establish a new social order by educating the new citizen. It's hard to measure the outcomes of such an effort and even harder to attribute these outcomes to a particular institutional invention. But I think there is compelling evidence that this is a reform that was able to accomplish much of what it set out for itself.

A new social order did indeed replace the old one in the years before the Civil War, and this new order resolved the crisis of the 1820s by filling the void left by the sudden collapse of the previous organization of social and economic life. This is exactly what the common school reformers were aiming to do. Of course, it could simply have been a coincidence, which had nothing to do with the construction of a common school system. But this new social order was organized precisely along the lines sought by the Whigs who were behind the common school and the other related efforts to establish new institutions in the antebellum years. It effected a grand compromise between the market and the republic, saving republican community while preserving the rapidly expanding market economy.

At the core of this balancing of competing interests was the Whig vision of the need to construct a new citizen for the republic, a new soul for the church, and a new conscience for society. As realized in the new social order, this vision would allow individuals to participate as self-interested entrepreneurs and workers in the market economy by ensuring that they internalized the political, religious, and moral controls that were needed in order to maintain the United States as a Protestant republican nation. The common schools could not take all the credit for this stunning reconstruction of society, since there were many other institutional innovations that moved this agenda forward. But all of these new institutions shared a common form and function, and all of them were constructed around the educational model set by the common schools. Under the circumstances, it's hard to see how the common school movement could be denied major credit for bringing about the resolution of the great social crisis of the early republic.

If this is what the common school movement accomplished, what kind of legacy did that leave to the American educational system and its social role in American life? First, the common school system had a structure that was perfectly attuned to the demands of the early nineteenth century but not necessarily well adapted to the American society that evolved over the next two hundred years. Future reform movements would struggle with the problem of trying to accommodate this old system to new social missions.

Second, the common school movement set a dangerous, even impossible, precedent by presenting the public schools as the most effective way to fix social problems, including the most deep-seated and difficult. As a result, it prompted later reform movements to try to use the schools to repair society and perfect its members, extrapolating from the Whig experience in the antebellum United States to other situations. In the later period, however, the advantages of newness had long since evaporated, and the entrenched organization of the school system resisted redeployment against problems that were markedly different from those it was designed to solve.

Third, the system established schooling as a central focus of the American experience. The school became the central institution in every community, the largest expenditure for every local government, and the primary locus of growing up for every citizen. As such, it became the natural technology for dealing with social problems, large and small, and the natural scapegoat for any failures in these efforts at social improvement.

Fourth, the system placed a priority on the experience of schooling over the experience of learning. Gaining access to school was the key for individual consumers, and educational success came to be measured in time served rather than subjects mastered. In these terms, then, the crucial question for parents in the twentieth century became: How many years of schooling do my children have compared with yours?

THE PROGRESSIVE EFFORT TO
RESHAPE THE SYSTEM

3

When the common school movement created the American system of elementary education in the years before the Civil War, it set in motion an educational enterprise with a distinctive structure and rationale. The new system took on responsibility for educating the kinds of morally centered citizen-entrepreneurs that the liberal American republic needed for its survival. But once the system was established and began to gain organizational momentum, it also became an inviting target for reformers. Why limit its function to keeping the faith and preserving the republic when there were so many other problems it could address? Once the common school system was up and running and apparently a great success, it seemed only natural to ask it to take on new roles and new missions. Engineering the system seemed like the hard part. Now all you needed to do was to come up with new ways to use this educational machinery. As we will see in later chapters, reforming and redirecting the system was a lot harder than it looked. But the urge to fix society by reforming schools proved irresistible, and a series of reform movements worked hard to deploy the system for their own ends. In this chapter, I examine the movement for progressive education in the United States in the first half of the twentieth century, which was the first major effort to reform the school system put in place by the Whigs.

In thinking about the accomplishments and failures of educational progressivism, it's important to keep in mind a point that emerged in the first two chapters: school reform and school change are two different things. Reformers try to change schools in a particular direction that aligns with their vision for school and society, but they often fail. And schools can change in response to factors that are independent of reform efforts. By nature, reform is an organized change effort that states its purposes clearly and creates a structure to help it achieve these goals. But change can happen without benefit of either an explicit agenda or a mobilizing organization.

In this book I refer to non-reform-based forces for educational change as educational markets or educational consumerism. Market-based and consumer-driven social processes are ones where individual motives are independent of collective results, where the invisible hand of the market may take things in a direction that none of the individual actors intended. From this perspective, educational consumerism is ·the sum of the choices about education that individual parents and children make, based on the social and economic benefits that they will gain personally by attaining higher levels of schooling and acquiring the associated credentials. Since the aim of these actors in pursuing education is personal rather than collective gain, they treat education as a private good, whose benefits are owned exclusively by the degree holder and do not extend to society as a whole.

In contrast, as we saw in Chapter 1, for a long time American school reform movements treated education only as a public good, whose benefits flowed to society as a whole. This started changing in the middle of the twentieth century with the arrival of consumerism as an explicit theme of school reform, beginning with the desegregation movement and continuing on in the movements for standards and choice. But before then, consumer pressures on education in the United States acted as the silent partner (or competitor) of school reform movements, exerting a significant impact on the school system but without raising a ruckus in the process.

In the colonial era, reform defined a religious purpose for schooling. But consumers assigned it a more practical purpose, to prepare themselves and their children so they could pursue their own interests effectively in a market economy. In the common school era, reform defined a political purpose for schooling. But consumers gave it a more practical purpose, making it an arena for gaining educational and thus social advantage. This meant picking up more education than their peers, which in this period could be done by completing grammar school and attending high school. Set up for political purposes (to draw support for the public school system), the high school set off a consumer competition for access and advantage in schooling. In this chapter, I carry the story forward into the progressive era.

The spur for the progressive movement was a social, economic, and political crisis that confronted the United States at the end of the nineteenth century. This crisis brought two kinds of pressures to bear on the school system. One came from a large-scale reform movement—administrative progressivism, the dominant wing of the educational progressives—which sought to establish a new social and economic order around the principle of social efficiency, with particular attention to the high school. The other came from educational consumers—families with children near school age—whose response to the social crisis also focused on the high school, where they sought to resolve conflicting demands for democratic equality and social mobility on this, the most exclusive and valuable part of the school system. Working-class families pushed for greater access to this institution, and middle-class families pushed to preserve the social advantage they had long enjoyed by occupying most of the seats in the high school classroom.

These cross pressures from both reformers and consumers led to a restructuring of the school system that represented a grand compromise among the competing visions of education. And the institution that embodied this compromise most fully was the new comprehensive high school, which allowed all students in the community to attend and then channeled them into different program tracks based on their academic ability and future social role. This effort to balance alternative goals in a single structure of schooling established a model for American schools that has lasted into the twenty-first century.

THE ROOTS OF PROGRESSIVISM

The movement for progressive education emerged at the end of the nineteenth century in the United States, became a major force in the first decade of the twentieth century, and lasted for another fifty years. Its major chronicler, Lawrence Cremin, set its end date at 1955, when the Progressive Education Association finally disbanded. The movement was so big and lasted so long that historians have had difficulty defining just what it was all about. Most have concluded that it was less a single movement than a collection of related movements that shared a common language.[1] Under these circumstances, perhaps the best way to come to grips with progressivism is to consider its origins, the same approach we used with the common school movement. For if major social reform is the offspring of social crisis, as I suggested in Chapter 2, then the first step in trying to understand the nature of the progressive education movement is to figure out the nature of the crisis that provoked it. Put another way, what was the problem for which progressive education was seen as the solution?

Just as the common school movement emerged in the early nineteenth century as an extension of a broad program of Whig political and social reform, educational progressivism arose at the very end of the century from a broad movement for progressive political and social reform. The Whig and progressive movements were both political responses to a dramatic transformation of the

American economic and social structure, and both sought to establish a new social order that would balance long-standing political goals and new socioeconomic realities. For the Whigs, the problem was the emergence of a national market economy; for the progressives, the problem was the emergence of a corporate industrial economy. Both of these moments were tipping points in the economic and social development of the United States, when a series of changes converged at the same time and—accelerated by new technologies of transportation, communication, and organization— suddenly shifted the country's social relations and productive capacities in a new direction.

Each transformation posed a significant political challenge. Early in the century the explosion of the market economy compelled reformers to invent a series of new social institutions that could preserve republican virtue from the ravages of acquisitive individualism and could also provide new social systems of support for those who were unable to support themselves in the market. Late in the century the explosion of the corporate industrial economy compelled reformers to develop political and social institutions that would allow democratic government to assert itself in the face of rich and powerful corporate monopolies and also provide some measures that would help accommodate members of society to the new social order.

Rise of the Corporate Industrial Economy

The corporate industrial revolution at the end of the nineteenth century began as a continuation and acceleration of the changes initiated by the market revolution in the 1820s and 1830s. The rapid growth in transportation and communication that started with the canal and turnpike picked up momentum in the 1840s with the arrival of the steamship, the railroad, and the telegraph. Together these inventions represented another quantum leap in foreshortening time and space, which created a true national market for agricultural and manufactured goods. Like the Erie Canal, these advances sharply expanded opportunities for people to grow wealthy through trade and also increased the intensity of competition. Farmers and manufacturers felt ever more pressure to reduce costs and increase productivity, so they could lower prices sufficiently to hold their own in the newly enlarged marketplace. Success meant great wealth; failure meant bankruptcy and going to work for someone else.

Competitive pressure spurred a variety of efforts to restructure work in a way that would cut labor costs. One such method was to develop new sources of power to augment manual labor. First came water power, which drove the weaving machines in the first New England textile mills. Then came the steam engine, which quickly showed itself to be the most adaptable and efficient mechanism to power the economy, driving ships on the rivers, locomotives on the rails, and machinery in production facilities. The need to control labor costs and harness large-scale alternative power sources pushed manufacturers to shift production from the artisan's shop to the full-scale factory, which in turn required large amounts of capital and an ability to manage an increasingly complex production process.

The emerging factory system of production combined capital and management with another factor that provided a huge advantage in controlling manufacturing costs and enhancing competitiveness—a radical increase in the division of labor.[2] In the early system of manufacture, the division of labor meant that craft shops specialized in different products, with cordwainers making shoes for people and blacksmiths making them for horses. Within the shop itself, work was divided according to skill level, ranging from apprentice to journeyman to master, and individuals could move through these roles over the course of a career. The master craftsman could and frequently did create the entire product.

The market revolution early in the century began to drive a wedge between master and journeyman, but in the factory the division of labor became more extreme and the gaps between skill levels became harder for individuals to cross. Even before the advent of large-scale machinery, manufacturers found it advantageous to break down the work of production into a series of small tasks that could be carried out by workers with relatively little skill. They could hire a large number of laborers at a low wage to do this work and then assemble the complex product at the end of the process. The key here was to separate conception from execution, with engineers designing the production process, managers overseeing it, and laborers carrying it out. Since laborers learned only a tiny part of overall task of fabricating the final product, they had little ability to demand higher pay or move up the ladder. The introduction of steam-powered machinery only widened the gap between labor and management, since most of the work of laborers in the factory devolved into the repetition of simple manual tasks where they had no real chance to learn the whole process.

By the middle of the nineteenth century, therefore, improvements in transportation and communication, an increasingly competitive national market, the development of steam power, and the growth of the factory system combined to create a highly productive manufacturing base across the northeastern and midwestern states, which proved its prowess by helping the North defeat the largely agricultural South during the Civil War. After the war, economic development took off from this base, fueled by an extraordinary series of inventions. The introduction of the Bessemer converter in the 1850s made it possible to mass-produce steel, and the steel industry expanded rapidly in the postwar period. In the 1870s came the invention of the telephone, the phonograph, and the electric trolley car; in the 1880s came electric lighting, the gasoline engine, and the automobile.

By the 1890s, the United States was emerging as the world's greatest industrial nation. The scale of production had increased enormously since the middle of the century and the size of factories had increased proportionately. What was new at this stage, however, was not just an increase in the size of the production system but a transformation in the way it was managed. The master craftsman running his own shop at the start of the century gave way to the proprietor running his own factory in the middle of the century, which in turn gave way to the corporation managing a series of factories at the end of the century.

The emergence of corporate domination of industry represented a shift from personal control by the owner to institutionalized control by a team of professional managers, who were answerable to a diffuse and distant array of stockholders. The division of labor had spread now into management, with discrete staff and line positions organized into elaborate hierarchies. In parallel with what happened on the factory floor, white-collar roles like clerk and secretary, which used to offer apprenticeship for future proprietors, turned into deskilled, subordinate positions that offered incumbents little promise of being able to learn the business and climb to the top. The corporation not only organized the work of multiple factories but also organized the productive process. Driven by increasing pressures to control costs and increase income, corporations sought to impose a rationalized structure of control on the entire operation, from acquiring raw materials, through all the stages of production, marketing, and distribution. And by the 1890s, corporations were forming into trusts in an effort to control entire industries and thus protect themselves from competitors.

The emergence of the corporate industrial economy at the end of the nineteenth century brought on a series of major social dislocations in American life. One was a sudden surge in immigration, as the new economy's insatiable demand for unskilled labor drew large numbers of immigrants to work in factories and mines. The first great wave of immigration to the United States occurred in the wake of the market revolution, bringing workers from Germany, Ireland, and England. The second wave, from 1890 to 1924 (when federal law closed the door), was much larger, bringing millions of immigrants from southern and eastern Europe.

Another major change was rapid urbanization, as immigrants from abroad and also from the American countryside poured into the major cities where industrial jobs were located.

When people got to the city, they found that the new American economy was prone to both boom and bust. Two deep depressions wracked the country in the latter part of the century. The Panic of 1873, set off by the collapse of the Jay Cooke bank, led to a decline that lasted for the rest of the decade; and the Panic of 1893, set off by overbuilding of railroads, brought a depression that continued until 1900.

These conditions—with wages and skills declining, opportunities for advancement closing down, and the economy in radical flux—prepared the ground for industrial strife. Labor unions were emerging to assert the rights of workers in the face of the new corporate management, and this led to two of the ugliest industrial confrontations in American history. In 1892 there was the Homestead strike at the Carnegie Steel works near Pittsburgh, which started as a lockout of workers who sought to unionize and then led to battles between strikers and Pinkerton guards hired by the company. After the Pinkertons surrendered the plant to the strikers, the governor deployed the state militia, which crushed the strike and destroyed the union. In 1894 there was the Pullman strike, when the company cut wages by 25 percent in response to the Panic; workers went on strike and were supported by more than 100,000 railroad workers across the country. The government prosecuted the strike leader, Eugene Debs, and sent him to prison.

In many ways, the situation in the 1890s was parallel to the situation in the 1820s, but in others it wasn't. The social crisis of the progressive era was serious and troubling, but it wasn't nearly as threatening to state and society as was the market revolution in the early nineteenth century that provoked the Whigs and the common school reformers. The state wasn't at risk of collapsing, only of becoming irrelevant and peripheral in the face of corporate power. The United States at the time was emerging as a dominant industrial economy in the world, and after victory in the 1898 Spanish-American war it was also emerging as an imperial power. Government and society clearly needed reform, but the situation wasn't as desperate as it had been when the republic and economy were in a new and fragile state. So progressives had a strong platform from which to launch a reform movement, but in the face of a less perilous situation they were not in a position to sweep away the opposition and fully realize their reform goals.

The Rise of Political Progressivism

Progressivism as a political movement arose in response to the social crisis brought on by the corporate industrial revolution at the end of the nineteenth century. It was a loosely organized movement with a broad array of aims, but they all revolved around what Robert Wiebe, the leading historian of progressivism, called "the search for order."[3] In particular, progressives sought to establish a new kind of political and social order, which was appropriate to the time and able to respond effectively to the period's social crisis. Like the Whigs earlier in the century, the progressives wanted to establish a new balance between enduring political and moral values and the new economic realities. They posed questions such as: What did democracy mean in a corporate, industrial, urban, and multicultural society such as the one that had developed in the United States? How could government intervene in the economy to alleviate the social dislocations it had caused without destroying the new economy's enormous capacity to produce wealth and raise the standard of living? And if we needed a much stronger and more interventionist government in order to deal with the emerging power of the large corporations, how could this government remain truly responsive to its citizens?

To create a new order that would provide solutions to these problems called for a multistranded political movement. One strand focused on producing a new kind of democracy. The ideal of republican community seemed better suited to the city states of preimperial Rome and Renaissance Florence than to the political reality of the turn-of-the-century American industrial city. Citizens needed tools to allow them to reassert control over an expanded government, so progressives pushed through legislation authorizing initiative, referendum, and recall, which allowed citizens to sidestep a legislature that often seemed beholden to the trusts and take direct action on important issues.

A second strand focused on social justice. This meant developing institutions for dealing with the social effects of the new economy: establishing settlement houses and deploying social workers to intervene with the poor; developing special courts for juvenile delinquents; passing laws to restrict child labor, limit the work day, and permit unions. A third strand focused on regulation. This meant trying to balance big business with big government, breaking up the largest trusts, and establishing an array of government agencies for intervening in the economy, such as the Interstate Commerce Commission, the Federal Reserve Bank, and state public utility commissions. A fourth strand focused on social efficiency. This meant rooting out government corruption, replacing ward-level urban political machines with elite political bodies, placing public institutions in the hands of professional administrators, and fostering a broad efficiency in the workings of society and economy.

THE EMERGENCE OF EDUCATIONAL PROGRESSIVISM

The movement for progressive education emerged within the context of the broader progressive movement in the United States.[4] As Lawrence Cremin has noted, progressive education was not one movement but several, since "the movement was marked from the very beginning by a pluralistic, frequently contradictory, character," which meant that "throughout its history progressive education meant different things to different people."[5] Historians disagree about how to label the various tendencies within the

movement. Herbert Kliebard identifies three, which he called social efficiency, child development, and social reconstruction.[6] Robert Church and Michael Sedlak see two forms, which they call
conservative and liberal.[7] David Tyack calls these two tendencies
administrative and pedagogical.[8] The latter terms are the most
descriptive, but "pedagogical" doesn't roll off the tongue easily, so
I refer to the two as "administrative" and "child-centered."

These two strands of the progressive education movement
were strikingly different in their effect on the American system of
schooling. Ellen Lagemann argues that "one cannot understand
the history of education in the United States during the twentieth
century unless one realizes that Edward L. Thorndike won and
John Dewey lost." She goes on to note, "If Dewey has been revered
among some educators and his thought has had influence across a
greater range of scholarly domains . . . Thorndike's thought has
been more influential within education. It helped to shape public
school practice as well as scholarship about education."[9]

Although Dewey and the child-centered progressives lost the
fight to reshape the structure of schools, they nonetheless had a
major and continuing impact on the rhetoric of education. In contrast, Thorndike and the administrative progressives managed to
effect enduring changes in both rhetoric and the formal structure
of schooling, but had a limited impact on the core of teaching
and learning.[10] To explore the difference between the two reform efforts and the limitations on both, let's consider the aims
of each of these tendencies in the progressive movement.

These two tendencies had several orientations in common,
which helped justify the common label applied to them and which
often put them on the same side in reform efforts. One is that they
both shared a belief in the importance of child development. Both
sought to establish a system of education that was designed around
the needs and capabilities that students had at different stages of
their intellectual and social development. But the strongest link
between them was their antagonism toward the traditional

academic curriculum. They both detested the practice of basing school subjects in academic disciplines instead of tailoring these subjects to the practical needs of modern life. The two strands of progressivism, however, took these two common orientations in very different directions.

Child-centered progressives saw developmentalism as a rationale for rejecting the traditional curriculum in favor of classroom processes that would harness individual student interests and abilities and would foster engaged, self-directed learning. A broad vein of romanticism runs through this form of progressivism, which saw learning as a natural process that would occur best if artificial mechanisms like schools and curricula would just get out of the way of children's natural urge to learn.[11] Child-centered progressives resented the traditional curriculum because they saw it as a conspiracy to impose adult mind-sets and adult roles on children who needed the freedom to explore childhood and develop their own learning styles. They were more concerned about having students learn to learn than learn the curriculum. In their view, the ideal school would revolve around student initiative and student inquiry; focus on discovering knowledge instead of presenting knowledge; emphasize active and engaged learning over passive recitation of the text; organize study around projects, which drew on student interests and which synthesized knowledge and skill from multiple disciplines; and create a school as a democratic community, modeling values of justice and cooperation for later life. In addition to Dewey, some of the major players in child-centered progressivism were William Heard Kilpatrick, Harold Rugg, and Boyd Bode.

Administrative progressives dropped the romanticism of their child-centered counterparts in favor of a hard-headed utilitarianism. Instead of Dewey's focus on naturalistic teaching and learning, they tended to focus on school governance, professional administration, and scientifically designed formal curriculum. The two main principles of administrative progressive reforms were social efficiency and differentiation. Social efficiency meant training and empowering professional administrators to manage school systems instead of leaving them at the mercy of school boards filled with amateurs. It meant organizing a system of education that would prepare graduates to play future roles as productive workers and capable members of the community. It meant shifting the curriculum away from academic and toward vocational education. It meant sharply differentiating the curriculum and the whole school experience, so that schools would mirror the differentiated patterns of work and life. And it meant aggressively testing student abilities in order to place them in the correct subjects and at the correct ability level in that subject. In addition to Thorndike, some of the major administrative progressives were David Snedden, Ellwood P. Cubberley, Charles H. Judd, and John Franklin Bobbitt.

Another way to understand the difference between the two kinds of educational progressivism is to locate them in relation to the core issues within the larger progressive political movement. The two focused on different components of the progressive agenda. Child-centered progressives tended to emphasize the idealistic side of progressivism, especially *democracy* and *social justice*. They saw themselves constructing democratic communities in the classroom, promoting community values like justice and equity, and liberating students from the yoke of curricular oppression. They showed disdain for the pragmatic concerns of their administrative counterparts. The latter, on the other hand, tended to revel in a pragmatic approach to education, with special emphasis on *social efficiency* and *regulation*. They approached school as administrators rather than as teachers, and they were intent on using regulatory powers to make the school system work more efficiently and on using schools to help make American social and economic life more efficient as well. They showed disdain for the romanticism inherent in the agenda of the pedagogues.

The administrative progressives were more effective than their alter egos in responding to the social crisis of the late nineteenth century.[12] That, after all, is what reformers are supposed to do: fix things. From the educational perspective, this crisis posed two problems for school reforms to resolve. In terms of the classic educational goals that have long driven the politics of American education, one was a problem with social efficiency, while the other was a problem with the balance between democratic equality and social mobility. The first problem affected the producers of education and provoked a response from school reformers; the second affected the consumers of education and provoked a response from these consumers. The consumer response came first.

SCHOOL CONSUMERS RESPOND TO THE CRISIS

For the consumers of schooling—families and students who saw school as a way to get ahead or stay ahead—the problem posed by the late-century crisis was more complicated and less visible than the social efficiency problem that later faced progressive reformers. Recall the pattern from the colonial period, in which some issues gained vivid expression in the language of reform while others remained largely unvoiced. Until the mid-twentieth century, the individual interests of educational consumers in attaining an education (to provide access to a good life and a good living) tended to be an unspoken but nonetheless important factor in shaping educational change. Since the founding of the common school system, schools had served the interests of consumers in two conflicting ways: by providing open access to educational opportunity for everyone in the white population (democratic equality) and also by providing a source of educational advantage to those who pursued education at a higher level than others (social mobility).

This tension between equal access and unequal outcomes was there in the system from the very beginning, and it grew during the nineteenth century. Gradually, the lower level of the system filled up, as students were drawn into the public schools and then over time extended the number of years they remained in school. According to one estimate, the average American student attended school for 210 days in 1800, 450 days in 1850, and 1,050 days in 1900.[13] Translating this into years of schooling is tricky because of variation in the number of days students attended school per year, but census estimates suggest that in 1910 the average American over age 25 had spent about eight years in school.[14] Thus, by the turn of the century, American schools had largely filled up through the eighth grade, which meant that the only place for expanding enrollments to go were into high school. High schools such as Central High in Philadelphia had long been elite institutions that held no more that a tiny percentage of the students in the American school system (in 1880 high school students accounted for only 1.1 percent of public school enrollments in the United States).[15]

But to keep a public institution this exclusive is simply unsustainable in a democratic society, where potential consumers of a high school education are able to make their wishes known at the ballot box. The pressure for access grew strong during the long depression of the 1870s, when families were looking for alternative ways to launch their children into the occupational world, and when teenagers were available to attend high school since they were unable to find work. The educational records from Philadelphia in the 1870s show a large amount of public agitation for access to Central High, which was still the city's only high school for boys. Finally, in the 1880s the political pressure for access led Philadelphia and other urban districts across the country to start opening a series of new secondary institutions to meet the demand. The result was a huge expansion in high school enrollments, which doubled every ten years from 1880 through 1930, rising from 100,000 at the start of this period to nearly 4.5 million at the end.[16]

For working-class families, the expansion of the high school offered the opportunity to obtain what had been an elite level of education, which might qualify their children for positions in the growing white-collar workforce. The expansion gave them access to a scarce high school diploma and a good job, just at the point when factory work was clearly becoming a dead end. But for middle-class families, whose children had long occupied a disproportionate number of seats in the high school classroom, opening the doors to this institution threatened to dilute the social advantage that high school had provided them during much of the nineteenth century. These same families faced a squeeze from the new corporate economy, which had disrupted the way that middle-class families passed on social position to their children. Being middle class used to mean owning a shop, and parents passed the shop along to their children to secure their income and social standing. But in the new economy, small businesses were overwhelmed by competition from corporations, in retail as well as manufacturing (this was also a boom era for department stores), so middle-class families had to find other ways to give their children a good start in life.

During the nineteenth century, the high school provided the answer for middle-class families, since acquiring a high school education clearly distinguished their children from the vast majority of other children, who had only attended grammar school. For families who were in fear of falling down the class scale in the new social order, the high school offered a kind of alchemy. It promised to transform economic and social capital into cultural capital in the form of schooling, allowing people with a modicum of wealth and position to acquire a scarce educational credential for their children—a high school diploma—which would then give them priority access to better jobs. Passing on social advantage to their children by means of a diploma instead of a proprietorship had an added benefit for these middle-class families. Inheriting your father's business just showed that you were well born; acquiring an academic degree showed that you were smart—qualified on your own merits to take on any number of attractive jobs.

PROGRESSIVE REFORMERS RESPOND TO THE CRISIS

All of these changes were going on before the movement for progressive reform in education really got started after 1900. At the turn of the century, administrative progressives like David Snedden, Edward Thorndike, and Ellwood Cubberley were just beginning their work of studying education and agitating for reform, and the movement's main reform document, the *Cardinal Principles* report, wasn't even published until eighteen years later. In response to the corporate industrial revolution of the 1890s, the new reform movement developed a set of educational reforms that focused on two main concerns of the larger progressive movement, regulation and social efficiency, both of which were central in the effort to establish a new social order.

Within this frame, administrative progressives pursued a series of related goals. First, they established professional administration for the school system. In the nineteenth century, the title of school principal was just shorthand for the school's principal teacher, but the new school order mandated a division of labor between administrators and teaching staff, paralleling the division of labor in both factory and corporate management.

Second, they took the atomized and autonomous collections of schools from the previous century, consolidated them into larger school districts, and organized the schools within districts into a staged hierarchy. This ushered students through a series of school grades, which paralleled the graded structure of work, leading from elementary school to junior high school (a progressive invention) to high school and possibly to college. Students gained admission to each level only if they accumulated the required credits at the level below and obtained a diploma that certified this accomplishment. By creating a rationalized sequence for the entire system, from first grade through college, they integrated the system, made its structure more transparent, and eased the movement of students up through the levels. As part of this sequencing process, progressives developed a set of preparatory course requirements that students needed to complete in high school in order to qualify for college, the so-called Carnegie units, which the Carnegie Foundation for the Advancement of Teaching established in 1906.

Third, progressives also tried to shift the emphasis of education toward vocational training. We saw this emphasis strongly enunciated in the language of the *Cardinal Principles,* but the vocational shift was more symbolic than substantive. A recent study shows that at the height of progressive influence, vocational courses never made up more than 20 percent of the courses taken by students, and the core academic subjects never fell below 60 percent.[17] In addition, vocational education in the twentieth century was notoriously ineffective at training people for work, since it tended to restrict training to a single role (when careers call for the ability to move across jobs) and since it typically trained students for yesterday's jobs. But by elevating social efficiency and workforce preparation as the prime goals of schooling, administrative progressives did change people's thinking about school, shifting the rhetorical emphasis from the republic in the common school era to the economy in the progressive era.

Finally, the progressives introduced tracking. They took what had been a common high school curriculum and split it up into a series of different programs, each with its own array of subjects. Administrators then sorted students into the appropriate program based on their tested ability, their motivation, and their likely future occupation. The best predictor for the latter, then as now, was their current social position. This new curriculum structure promised to provide students with the particular skills they needed to carry out their future work role effectively. To make this process reassuringly scientific, progressives introduced standardized ability testing and developed principles of curriculum construction.

CONSTRUCTING A GRAND COMPROMISE:
THE COMPREHENSIVE HIGH SCHOOL

The most significant change in American education during the progressive era arose from the interaction between the social efficiency reforms of the progressive movement and the social mobility demands of educational consumers. By the first decade of the twentieth century, high school enrollments were already expanding rapidly and a major debate arose about how to handle this influx of students. On one side were ardent vocationalists like Snedden, who wanted separate high schools for each occupational trajectory, and this decade saw a proliferation of high school types that reflected this view: industrial high schools, mechanical high schools, commercial high schools, academic high schools. On the other side were liberal progressives like John Dewey and leaders of labor unions, who argued that this differentiated form of education would reinforce class differences and restrict opportunity; they pushed for a comprehensive high school that would stand as a natural extension of the common school and would integrate the entire community.

By 1910, a resolution to this debate emerged. It took the form of a grand compromise between the two positions. And, more important for the story I'm telling here, it also represented a grand compromise between the aims of administrative progressive reformers and the demands of educational consumers. The former wanted social efficiency; the latter wanted both equal access (democratic equality) and social advantage (social mobility). The institutional innovation that embodied all three of these aims within its conflicted heart was the tracked comprehensive high school—the prize creation of the progressive era.

The solution had two critically interconnected parts. First, the new institution confirmed that the high school would open its doors to a broad stream of new students, thus potentially diluting the value of the high school degree for its traditional middle-class recipients. But it channeled those new students into the

lower tracks in the high school curriculum, particularly the industrial arts, mechanical, and commercial courses, while most
middle-class students ended up in the top track, labeled academic. The academic track functioned much like the old exclusive high school, with the same kinds of students enrolling in it
as had done so in the days before the high school embraced a
broader constituency. At the same time, however, a large number
of students were gaining access to a high school education who
had been denied it in the past.

In this way, the tracked comprehensive high school accomplished a kind of balance among the goals of social efficiency,
democratic equality, and social mobility. It allowed everyone
access to high school, but different groups had different educational experiences within this high school, which in turn led to
different social outcomes. This institution offered a portion of
equality and advantage and efficiency all at the same time and in
the same institution, thus establishing an example of blended
goals for the entire American educational system. In the United
States we like institutions that can meet all our needs, no matter
how contradictory they are and no matter how difficult it is to
meet all of these goals in one setting. Our school system continues to demonstrate this genius for absorbing new social goals and
blending them together.

The second part of the solution that emerged in the interaction between educational progressives and consumers at the start
of the twentieth century was closely connected to the first. Students could gain an edge by landing in the top track in the new
comprehensive high school, but the key benefit of this position
was that it gave them privileged access to education at the next
level up, the university. This followed an earlier pattern. Recall
that when the common school opened up elementary education
to everyone, middle-class families started flocking to the high
school in order to gain a step on the competition; and then when
the progressives opened up high school to everyone at the end of
the century, middle-class families started channeling their chil-

dren into college. This is a model that the American educational system has been following throughout its history. Democratic politics demands that we open up education to everyone, which then drives the more advantaged educational consumer to pursue education at the next higher level. This eventually spurs democratic demands for open access to that new level, which then drives families seeking an edge to send their children to an even higher level. In 1840, the two levels were elementary school and high school; in 1900 they were high school and college; and in the 1970s (when higher education was filling up) they were college and graduate school.

IMPLICATIONS OF SCHOOL CHANGE IN THE PROGRESSIVE ERA

The primary contribution of the common school movement was to establish a system of publicly controlled and community-based elementary schools with a strong political vision. The primary contributions of the progressive movement were to restructure the system in line with a social efficiency vision and to create the comprehensive high school. Let's consider the implications of each of these changes for the American school system and American society.

Sharply Expanding the Goals of Schooling

By reconstructing schools around the ideal of social efficiency, progressives at one level were changing the rationale for schooling from the republican mission of the common school era to the economic mission of the progressive era. This meant reorienting schools away from building republican community and toward building a productive and efficiently organized economy. But the change had broader implications than this for the story of school reform in the United States. The turn toward social efficiency was not just a change in focus but also a radical expansion of the social mission of schooling. As we saw in Chapter 1, social efficiency was an umbrella concept that incorporated a wide range of goals for public education that were nowhere evident in the original conception of the common school system. Recall that the *Cardinal Principles* report spelled out no fewer than seven such goals: "1. Health. 2. Command of fundamental processes. 3. Worthy home membership. 4. Vocation. 5. Citizenship. 6. Worthy use of leisure. 7. Ethical character."[18] All seven goals were laid out within the broader context of social efficiency, which saw the overarching aim of schooling in the task of making children useful members of society. And only goals two, five, and seven (fundamental processes, citizenship, and character), were in line with the aims of the system's founders in the early nineteenth century. The others were brand new, each representing a new social problem for which the commission was proposing school as the solution.

Poor public health was a problem that posed a threat to the social utility of adult members of society, since it would impede their ability to be economically productive and might turn them into a public burden. The answer included teaching classes in health education, hiring school nurses, and imposing vaccination requirements for school attendance. The effort to foster worthy home membership translated into programs in home economics, which sought to ensure that girls would pick up the skills in cooking, sewing, and housekeeping that they would need in order to become good wives and mothers. The absence of these domestic skills would lead to dysfunctional families, which would be unable to turn out a citizens and workers who were well nourished, well socialized, and productive. As with poor health, the threat posed by poor homes was a particular concern for the families of immigrants and the lower classes.

Schooling for vocation meant developing programs of vocational education, which included everything from wood shop, mechanical drawing, typing, and shorthand to car repair, bookkeeping, and cosmetology. Worthy use of leisure meant programs to train students to use their nonworking time in constructive ways that would support the larger social roles. A key goal along these lines was to maintain physical fitness, which led schools at all levels to develop classes in physical education. The common school movement had laid out an enormously ambitious agenda for the American school system, asking it to do no less than construct a new social order—by developing citizens, creating self-regulating moral actors, and establishing a republican community. The progressive movement also had an ambitious agenda for the schools, asking it to construct a new social order for the corporate industrial age. But it tacked on a number of social goals for schools that extended well beyond the political and moral aims of the common schoolmen. In so doing, it established a precedent for future reformers to call on schools to take on an ever-enlarging array of social problems to solve with new school programs. The American pattern of assigning the most demanding current problems to schools for a solution was now firmly in place.

Reformers and Consumers, Access and Advantage, Form and Content

The progressive creation of the comprehensive high school—with its mix of openness and tracking, equality and inequality, access and advantage, social utility and personal utility—established a model for education in the twentieth century, one that is still very much with us in the American system of education. Balancing opposites is something that American schools have always been good at. It leads to an institution that is anything but efficient, since it can't go very far toward achieving any of these goals without undercutting the others. As an embodiment of the contradictions of liberal democracy, however, this model of schooling has no equal. These changes took place during the progressive era, and the movement for progressive education played a part in bringing them about, but reform—a deliberate political effort to realize particular social goals—was only part of the story. Another force in shaping these changes came from educational consumers, who were not trying to reform schools but instead were trying to get ahead and stay ahead in the emergent social order at the end of the nineteenth century. They expressed their preferences through politics, by exerting pressure on political leaders to expand access to the high school, and through markets, by charging through the doors of the newly opened high schools and sorting themselves into its newly developed curriculum tracks.

So in combination with consumer pressures, the progressive education movement had an impact. It played a significant role in the process of developing a new social order in the early years of the twentieth century, helping to shape a social compromise based on a new balance among principles of political access, economic efficiency, and individual advantage. The comprehensive high school was both the symbol of this balance and an important medium for enacting this balance in social practice. But while the educational progressives exerted a significant impact on society, they were limited to having a more marginal impact on education. In Chapter 4, as part of a larger examination of the organizational factors that limit the impact of school reform, I will revisit the progressive case to show how and why this reform movement was never able to have a significant impact on schools beyond the level of school structure. In particular, it never succeeded in altering how teachers taught and how students learned. Since these elements are at the heart of education, that is a severe limitation indeed for any social effort that styles itself as a movement for school reform.

I am suggesting, however, that school reform can have significant social effects without necessarily having significant educational effects; that reform may be better at changing the form of education than its content. Changing the content of learning may not be necessary for either reformers or consumers to accomplish their social ends through schooling if they can accomplish these ends by altering the form of schooling. This means that, as an intervention in social life and as a response to social problems, school reform may be better off tinkering with the school system than trying to transform classroom learning. I will develop this idea further in Chapter 7, but for now let me conclude with this preliminary paradox: maybe academic learning is a side effect of the school system and schooling is the main effect.

What motivates school reformers is the desire to achieve compelling social goals such as democratic equality, social efficiency, and social mobility. They want to fix social problems through the medium of schooling. As an institution designed to mold the next generation, the school system seems ideally suited to take on these tasks; and as a publicly controlled and publicly funded enterprise, it is responsive to political demands. So over the years schools have eagerly taken on new social missions. It's just that they haven't been good at carrying out these missions.

In general, the primary impact of educational reform efforts on elementary and secondary schooling has been at the periphery rather than the core of the school system. Reformers have been able to have a major impact on the rhetoric of education, and the most effective reform efforts have even been able to shape the formal structure of schooling; but they typically have had little impact on the core functions of the school system—how teachers teach and what students learn. As I suggested at the end of the previous chapter, maybe reform can exert a social impact by shaping the structural form of the school system even if it doesn't reshape the system's educational function. We'll explore this idea further later in the book. But it's safe to say that reformers themselves don't buy this argument. They see themselves changing society by changing what students learn in schools. If learning is the object of reform, however, then why has reform had so much difficulty changing the learning process? That is the question I explore in this chapter and the next.

In this chapter, I present an organizational model of the American school system, which allows us to better understand the relative inability of school reform to reach the core of teaching and learning in classrooms. Then I examine the movement for progressive education in the United States in the first half of the twentieth century as a case for understanding the organizational limits of reform. Looking separately at the two main branches of this reform movement, I show that child-centered progressives shaped the rhetoric of education but never penetrated much further, while administrative progressives succeeded in changing rhetoric and in reshaping the formal structure of schooling but failed to shape the practice of teaching and learning in classrooms. In the final section of the chapter, I explore the organizational reasons that U.S. reform movements in general have had more success in changing the form of schooling than its instructional content. In the next chapter, I turn from organizational to educational reasons for the limits of reform, focusing on particular facets of the practice of teaching and the problems of learning that make reforms at the classroom level difficult, not only in the United States but anywhere in the world.

Reforming schools is hard in part because any large-scale effort to transform social programs is hard. Peter Rossi, who has evaluated a number of such programs, formalized these difficulties in a series of "laws," starting with "*The Iron Law of Evaluation:* The expected value of any net impact assessment of any social program is zero." That is: when you evaluate a social program, don't expect to find that it had any significant impact. And this is not because the methodology of the evaluation is defective. Just the opposite, as he notes in a corollary: "The better designed the impact assessment of a social program, the more likely is the resulting estimate of net impact to be zero." Another corollary is that "The more social programs are designed to change individuals, the more likely the net impact of the program will be zero."[1] He argues that this track record of failure and minimal impact arises from the complexity of social programs and the resulting difficulty in figuring out how they work, formulating valid plans for intervention, and successfully implementing these plans.

What is true for social reforms in general is particularly true for education, where social complexity is high, where measuring improvement is a challenge, and where changing people is the central task. School is hard, because it tries to get students to adopt a complex array of values, skills, and knowledge that society wants them to have. And school reform is even harder, because it seeks to get millions of administrators, teachers, and students to adopt the educational attitudes and behaviors that reformers want them to have.

Michael Fullan is both an educational reformer and an educational researcher who surveys the problem of school reform in a book titled *The New Meaning of Educational Change*. He summarizes the issue this way: "Educational change is technically simple and socially complex. . . . A large part of the problem of educational change may be less a question of dogmatic resistance and bad intentions (although there is certainly some of both) and more a question of the difficulties related to planning and coordinating a multilevel social process involving thousands of people."[2] He devotes separate chapters of this analysis to the major actors who populate and complicate the system of schooling: students, teachers, principals, district administrators, consultants, parents, communities, and governments. Trying to mobilize all these actors to move in the same direction is enormously difficult, and Fullan devotes the latter part of his book to a discussion of how to accomplish this, both by building capacity for the actors to pursue change and by developing forms of accountability that will maintain pressure toward particular reform goals.

Another student of reform, Larry Cuban, zeroes in on a key component of the problem of school reform, arguing that the

prospects for educational change vary according to the degree
that reform efforts aim to transform the central functions of schooling. At the core of schooling, he says, are the academic programs
for educating the ordinary child; at the periphery are the programs for students who don't fit into the core curriculum and instead find themselves in areas such as vocational education, special education, and gifted education. He notes that over the years
reformers have been much more likely to effect substantial change
at the periphery of schooling than at the core.[3]

Richard Elmore and Milbrey McLaughlin, two others who
have researched the issue, see the problem of school reform in organizational terms, arguing that the key variable in shaping the
success or failure of reforms is the ability of intended change to
move across the levels of the school hierarchy. In particular, they
point to three levels in the educational system: policymakers,
school administrators, and practitioners. Each of these sets of actors occupies a critical part in the reform process. In theory, the
first frames and initiates the reform effort, the second organizes
and facilitates it, the third adopts and implements it; but each
group of actors lives in its own distinct social and cultural world,
and communication across boundaries is inherently problematic.
These differences make it difficult for change efforts to move
from one level to the next, which means that most reforms get
stalled at the door of the school administrator or the classroom
teacher.[4]

FOUR LEVELS OF THE SCHOOL SYSTEM

In combination, these authors depict a reform process that has difficulty dealing with education's organizational complexity, over-
coming resistance to change in its core functions, and moving
reforms down the hierarchy and into the classroom. Building on
these insights, I have found it useful to model the complexity of
schooling, like Elmore and McLaughlin, as a matter of organizational hierarchy, but extended to four levels, with Cuban's core
functions of schooling occupying the lowest levels.[5] Each level

has its own peculiar set of actors; and each set of actors occupies a distinctive ecological niche, with its own language, media of expression, tools, organizational incentives, and problems of practice. From this angle, the challenge for reformers is to try to move reform down to the core levels of the system without letting it get blocked, deflected, or diluted. Cuban provides a succinct description of the way this system frustrates reform: "Organizations, I have discovered, have plans for reformers."[6]

At the top level of the system is its *rhetoric,* which provides the rationale for the whole enterprise. This is where most reform efforts begin (and frequently end), expending a lot of energy in generating statements of principle, educational visions, rationales for change, frameworks for representing that change, and norms for reconstructed educational practice. The actors at this level are a mixture of policymakers, lawmakers, education professors, judges, and educational leaders; and their primary media are reform reports, speeches, policy papers, journal articles, laws, and court rulings. The rhetorical level is the most open to reform efforts, since the actors are part of the same discourse community and thus are comfortable swimming in its rhetorical currents.

Next is the level of the system's *formal structure.* This is where reform rhetoric needs to be translated into key components of the organizational structure of schooling at the district level, such as educational policies, organizational units, curriculum frameworks, classroom textbooks, and professional development workshops. The actors are school administrators, school board members, curriculum developers, textbook publishers, and workshop leaders. The level of formal structure is harder for reformers to influence, since such an effort means translating national reform principles into forms that will work within the 14,000 local school districts currently in existence in the United States, each with its own organizational structure, school politics, and ways of doing things.

Third is the level of *teaching practice.* This is where reform ideas, if they succeed in passing through the machinery of the school district largely unscathed, need to pass through the door of the self-contained classroom. The actors here are teachers, and the key issue for school reform is the extent to which these practitioners adapt the content and process of their instruction, both to the principles of reform rhetoric and to the local structure of reform implementation. At this level we arrive at the instructional core of the educational enterprise, and reform success depends entirely on the capability and willingness of 3 million American public school teachers in 95,000 schools (using the current U.S. numbers) to take on the reform agenda and put it into practice in their classrooms. I will explore the problem of reform at the classroom level in more detail later in the chapter; but on the face of it, the sheer number, diversity, and geographical dispersion of these teachers and classrooms suggests how hard it is to effect reform at this level of the system.

Last of all is the level of *student learning*. Even if a particular reform effort improbably manages to shape the rhetoric of schooling, alter the structure of some school districts, and penetrate the practice of teachers in some classrooms, it still needs to transform the learning that students take away from their classroom experience if it is going to be declared an educational success. The key actors here are the students, and they present a final barrier to reform that may be the most formidable, especially under the peculiar conditions of teaching and learning that characterize schools in the United States.

The problem of school reform, then, is whether it can move through all four levels of the system, from the rhetorical periphery to the core of teaching and learning in classrooms. Is the reform able to persuade educational opinion leaders at the rhetorical level, reshape the formal structure of schooling at the district level, remold the practice of teachers in individual classrooms, and reconstruct the learning of students in these classrooms? Even though teaching and learning in classrooms would seem to be the only levels that really matter in educational reform, research on the history of U.S. education suggests strongly that reform movements in general have not been successful in reaching down the levels of the system to reconstruct the instructional core. The more successful movements managed to reshape the formal structure of schooling, even if they didn't extend much beyond this point; the less successful movements never moved past the level of rhetoric.

Let's return to the progressive movement as a useful case for trying to figure out why reform at the classroom level has proven so difficult over the years.

ASSESSING THE IMPACT OF THE ADMINISTRATIVE PROGRESSIVES

In the first half of the twentieth century, administrative progressives had a substantial impact at the rhetorical level. In particular, they gave public credibility to the idea that the primary goals of education are to produce human capital and promote social efficiency. The movement's most prominent rhetorical expression, *The Cardinal Principles of Secondary Education* (1918), made these points forcefully on the opening page of the report:

> Within the past few decades changes have taken place in American life profoundly affecting the activities of the individual. As a citizen, he must to a greater extent and in a more direct way cope with problems of community life, State and National Governments, and international relationships. As a worker, he must adjust himself to a more complex economic order. As a relatively independent personality, he has more leisure. The problems arising from these three dominant phases of life are closely interrelated and call for a degree of intelligence and efficiency on the part of every citizen that can not be secured through elementary education alone, or even through secondary education unless the scope of that education is broadened.[7]

The vision of social efficiency carried the day during the progressive era and continued into the latter part of the century as a central theme in the politics of American education. It stood in sharp contrast to the rhetoric of the common school movement, which established the American public school system in the second quarter of the nineteenth century and set the rhetorical tone for American education until the progressives arrived on the scene. The common school leaders provided a purely political rationale for public schooling, portraying it as a mechanism for promoting republican community and creating capable citizens. As we saw in Chapter 1, its most forceful leader, Horace Mann, could barely conceal his contempt for the proposition that these schools might also provide vocationally useful skills and promote economic prosperity. But in the early twentieth century the administrative progressives managed to shift the rhetoric about the purposes of American education from an emphasis on democratic equality to an emphasis on social efficiency. Diane Ravitch, in her study of administrative progressivism *(Left Back)*, argues that the movement's ideas reshaped educational discourse in a way that diminished the intellectual aims of education in favor of a focus on "job training, social planning, political reform, social sorting, personality adjustment, and social efficiency."[8]

Today, the language of education and educational reform is permeated with the practical vision of schooling that was originally promoted by the administrative progressives. Front and center in virtually every reform manifesto, every policy document, and every political speech on educational issues we see a bow toward education's critical role in the nation's economy. In the title of their historical study of the subject, Norton Grubb and Marvin Lazerson label this faith in the economic power of schooling *The Education Gospel.* Economists started taking up the cause in the 1950s. Drawing on Adam Smith's designation of the productive skills of the population as "human capital," they developed the argument that, by expanding schooling, societies are making prudent investments in human capital that will pay great dividends in future economic growth. This view has become the bedrock of educational policy, and reformers, policymakers, and politicians of all stripes now deploy the language of human capital in their visions of public education. At the level of the language of education, the administrative progressives were a huge success.

But administrative progressive reform also reached past the rhetorical level and exerted a substantial impact at the structural level of the school system, with particular emphasis on the organization of school systems and the structure of the formal curriculum. Especially in urban school systems, they succeeded in professionalizing school administration and consolidating governance in the hands of small, elite school boards. In rural areas they launched a remarkable process of consolidation, which during the 1930s alone reduced the number of school systems by 10,000.[9]

Their impact on curriculum was also significant if less dramatic. They tried to broaden traditional school subjects in order to shift them from narrow preparation in academic disciplines to broad preparation for work and life. Their greatest success along these lines was in substituting social studies for history, but they also introduced courses in general math and general science. In addition, they added a set of explicitly vocational courses aimed at preparing students for clerical, technical, and industrial work; and they added courses like home economics and physical education that were aimed at "life adjustment." But in their most significant innovation, they created a differentiated curriculum that organized courses in curriculum tracks, which were distinguished from each other by the students' level of tested academic ability and by their projected future job role. When Lawrence Cremin summarizes the impact of progressivism on schools in his comprehensive history of the movement, he enumerates changes that represented primarily the aims of the administrative progressives and that affected primarily the formal structure of schooling. He lists such changes as introducing the junior high school, expanding the curriculum into nonacademic areas, expanding the extracurricular activities, differentiating courses by vocational trajectory, grouping students by ability, and professionalizing school administration.[10]

A systematic study of the twentieth-century high school curriculum in the United States, by David Angus and Jeffrey Mirel, shows both the extent and the limits of the impact of administrative progressives. They identify a sharp increase in the differentiation of the curriculum by ability level, future job, gender, and social class. They also find a substantial rise in vocational and life adjustment classes and a declining share of academic courses. But the latter changes were less dramatic than the increase in differentiation. As noted earlier, vocational classes never rose above 20 percent of the curriculum and academic subjects hardly ever fell below 60 percent. The largest growth area in nonacademic courses was not vocational classes but physical education, and the largest drop in academic studies was in foreign languages rather than the core academic subjects. By the 1950s, the curriculum was much more differentiated than it had been at the start of the century, but the bulk of schooling still focused on English, math, science, and social studies, and most of the latter was still devoted to history. High school teachers still identified themselves by their disciplinary specialty rather than by the new progressive labels of vocationalism and life adjustment.[11]

The evidence is strong that the administrative progressives had a major impact on American schooling at the rhetorical and structural levels, but the evidence suggests a much weaker impact at the levels of teaching and learning in classrooms. That they were successful in shaping the formal structure of schooling, however, did have some consequences for how teachers taught and what students learned. By defining the outlines of the curriculum and shaping the focus and content of textbooks, they were able to put constraints on what was likely to happen in the classroom. They designed the reformed administrative structure of the school system to help implement the new curriculum. The new regime assigned teachers to classes that were defined by the curriculum, and the content in the available textbooks and other curriculum materials influenced what teachers were likely to teach. As a result, students were more likely to be exposed to some kinds of content over others; and this differential access to knowledge increased the likelihood of some kinds of learning over others.

But these constraints were not as restrictive and as consequential for practice as they might seem in formal terms. Over the years American school administrators have had a strong hold on the administrative apparatus of the school but have been lacking in the necessary tools required to influence the way teachers taught behind the doors of their classrooms. And American teachers, in turn, have been in a weak position to motivate students to learn the content they have been trying to teach. Reshaping curriculum and administration is not as strong an intervention in the core instructional work of schools as it might initially appear. I defer until later in this chapter and the next a more detailed discussion of these limitations on the social efficiency reform of classroom teaching and learning. But one aspect of the approach to reform taken by the administrative progressives served to reinforce their generic weakness in shaping teaching and learning in classrooms: their primary focus was elsewhere.

This was a movement aimed at the formal structure of schooling and not at the instructional core. Many of its leaders were school superintendents and its primary reform target was other superintendents. Its focus was on changing the way school systems were administered and the way curriculum was structured, and they succeeded in both goals, in part because they limited their aspirations and they targeted the elements of schooling that administrators had most directly under their control. A close reading of *The Cardinal Principles* report and other major documents in the administrative progressive canon reveals almost no mention of teachers. There was an assumption that teachers will do what the administration and the curriculum require, but there was no real effort to address the problem of how to bring teaching in line with administrative expectations.

Student learning was also something that administrative progressives assumed instead of trying to facilitate it as a central part of the reform process. This strand of the progressive movement was grounded in Thorndike's theory of learning, which argued that learning is largely not transferable. This means that the curriculum should not focus on training core faculties through exercises in arbitrary subjects like Greek and Latin. The latter approach followed naturally from the once-dominant learning theory known as faculty psychology, which saw the study of classical languages as a way to train the mind for future learning in any area. In contrast to the faculty psychology approach, Thorndike argued that students' learning depends heavily on the particular content they encounter. This meant that schools needed a scientifically differentiated curriculum, which corresponded with all the domains of practical knowledge that students would need as workers and citizens and parents. The beauty of this theory was that it put curriculum in the driver's seat. Once you had set up a carefully designed curriculum to cover all the knowledge students needed, learning naturally followed. Teachers were just there to deliver the curriculum; it was the curriculum that taught the students.

The key was to match up the student with the right curriculum track, and this was where testing came in. The administrative progressives were intensely interested in testing and were aggressive in introducing standardized tests into schools in a massive way. But the testing they emphasized was intelligence testing, which allowed them to place students in the correct track according to each person's ability level. They did not, however, focus on measuring how well students actually learned the curriculum to which they were exposed. Tests to measure learning outcomes were an invention of a reform effort that became prominent in the United States at the end of the twentieth century, the standards movement, whose leaders have learned from the failure of the administrative progressives and deliberately use testing to ensure that curriculum mandates actually lead to the desired student learning.

ASSESSING THE IMPACT OF THE CHILD-CENTERED PROGRESSIVES

In the first half of the twentieth century, child-centered progressives had almost no success in shaping schooling at the level of formal structure. The best evidence for this is the relative success of the administrative progressives at the same level. For the primary accomplishments of the latter were anathema to their child-centered counterparts; the success of the one marked the failure of the other. The focus on curriculum by administrative progressive reforms in this era was itself a major problem, since it ran against the grain of the effort by child-centered progressives to tailor instruction to the interests and initiative of the child. The social efficiency curriculum was designed as a deliberate imposition on children, channeling them in the direction the reformers thought they should go, for the social and economic good; whereas the child-centered form of instruction was supposed to subordinate curriculum to the student. And the form assumed by the reformed curriculum was particularly abhorrent to them. The emphasis on creating an elaborate structure of curriculum tracks, and then assigning students to experience schooling solely within the confines of these tracks, introduced a rigidity to schooling that made it impossible to achieve the kind of naturalistic, student-directed pursuit of learning they envisioned.

The theory of learning behind the social efficiency curriculum also ran in the opposite direction from that of the pedagogues. The administrative progressives saw learning as confined to the specific domain being studied, but the Deweyan progressives were proponents of the transferability of learning. For the former, the curriculum was everything, the object of learning; for the latter, curriculum was a medium through which learning took place, a means to an end, and a variety of means would do. In fact, for the child-centered progressives it was dysfunctional for learning to be trapped in the kind of specialized curricular dead end that

administrative progressive reform mandated for the scientifically tracked student. This was exactly the kind of curriculum that
Dewey warned against in *The Child and the Curriculum:* "exter-
nally presented material, conceived and generated in standpoints
and attitudes remote from the child, and developed in motives
alien to him."[12]

The child-centered progressives also had little luck in introducing their reforms at the levels of classroom practice and student learning. But unlike the administrators, this was not for lack
of effort. The administrative progressives focused on administrative structure and formal curriculum, and they assumed that appropriate teaching and learning would naturally follow; the
child-centered progressives, however, ignored the structural level
and focused entirely on the processes of teaching and learning
within individual classrooms. The success of the administrators
at the structural level is due in part to the fact that this is where
they concentrated their energies and where they engaged their
primary constituency of other administrators. The failure of the
child-centered progressives at the structural level is due in part to
the fact that they discounted the importance of this level and focused on the levels below it. Yet, although they concentrated their
energies on teaching and learning, this didn't keep them from failing there as well. This is what gives their failure at these core levels
the tenor of tragedy. Proponents of the Deweyan credo have been
railing against their fate ever since the second quarter of the twentieth century, when the dimension of their failure started to become
apparent.

Arthur Zilversmit and Larry Cuban are two historians who
have examined the impact of child-centered progressives on the
practice of teaching, and both have concluded that this impact
was modest and transitory.[13] Cuban looked at a variety of sources
(such as photographs, district studies, accounts by visitors, classroom layouts) to determine how much child-centered instruction
was actually taking place in classrooms in New York; Washington,

DC; and Denver during the second quarter of the twentieth century. He classified classrooms as child-centered if they demonstrated progressive characteristics in at least some of five domains: class arrangements (classes organized in student clusters rather than rows), grouping (students working in small groups), talk (students talking a lot and initiating talk in the class), activities (projects, small groups, independent study), and movement (students free to leave their desks). Even in using these generous proxies for child-centered instruction (any one which could be adopted without really carrying out the spirit of Deweyan progressive teaching), he found that the evidence for it was slight. In New York City, from 1920 to 1940, for example, he found that "No more than an estimated one of four elementary teachers, and an even smaller fraction of high school teachers, adopted progressive teaching practices, broadly defined, and used them to varying degrees in the classroom."[14] The most likely elements of the canon to appear in the classroom were activity and movement.

Zilversmit examined the evidence of child-centered teaching in classrooms in the Chicago area in the 1930s and 1940s. His conclusion about this period was:

> Despite the impassioned discussions of progressive education in the 1920s and 1930s, despite the marked progressivism of a few school districts and the increasing importance of progressive ideas in state education departments and teachers' colleges, it is clear that by 1940 progressive education had not significantly altered the broad pattern of American education. The call for a child-centered school had, for the most part, been ignored.[15]

His explanation for this outcome is this: "The ultimate failure was that so much of progressivism's apparent success was rhetorical. While some schools and individual teachers had heeded Dewey's call for a more child-centered school, most had given only lip service to these ideas while continuing older practices."[16] The pattern that these and other historians have noted is that child-centered progressivism was largely confined to a few independent schools, whereas social efficiency progressivism dominated in the public school systems.[17]

If the child-centered progressives largely failed in their primary aim, to reshape teaching and learning in public school classrooms around the principles of child-centered instruction, they did succeed in effecting reform at one level of the educational system. As Zilversmit points out, that was at the level of rhetoric. This was not a minor accomplishment. As Cremin points out in his summary of the state of the progressive project at the middle of the twentieth century, American educators had by then all come to talk about education in the language of child-centered progressivism:

> There is a "conventional wisdom," to borrow from John Kenneth Galbraith, in education as well as economics, and by the end of World War II progressivism had come to be that conventional wisdom. Discussions of educational policy were liberally spiced with phrases like "recognizing individual differences," "personality development," "the whole child," "social and emotional growth," "creative self-expression," "the needs of learners," "intrinsic motivation," "persistent life situations," "bridging the gap between home and school," "teaching children, not subjects," "adjusting the school to the child," "real life experiences," "teacher-pupil relationships," and "staff planning." Such phrases were a cant, to be sure, the peculiar jargon of the pedagogues. But they were more than that, for they signified that Dewey's forecast of a day when *progressive* education would eventually be accepted as *good* education had now finally come to pass.[18]

In the last sentence, Cremin tries to stretch this rhetorical accomplishment into something more substantive. But the weight of this paragraph—in conjunction with the weight of the historical evidence about the impact of child-centered progressivism on teaching and learning—suggests strongly that the impact was primarily limited to the way American educators talked about schooling rather than the way they practiced it.[19] As a result, we had come to use the child-centered language of discovery, engagement, and inquiry to talk about a structure of schooling, a practice of teaching, and a process of learning that were deeply grounded in the social efficiency principles of differentiation and human capital production.

How can we best understand the failure of the child-centered progressives to extend reform beyond the rhetorical level at the same time that the administrative progressives managed to reach the structural level? As I have pointed out earlier, one reason was that administrative progressives focused their attention at a level that they, as administrators, could realistically affect; while the child-centered progressives tried to transform the levels of teaching and learning at the heart of the educational system, where change is particularly difficult and where they had no special leverage, especially with the formal structure and the curriculum in the hands of their opponents. Another, more basic reason is that a romantic appeal for educational reform is in general likely to be less effective than a utilitarian appeal. Education is an enormous enterprise, which requires massive public investment in order to bring about social outcomes of great consequence. Under these circumstances, the investment is easier to justify in support of practical goals like promoting economic growth and providing needed job skills than in support of romantic goals like promoting pleasurable schooling and engaged learning.

SCHOOL ORGANIZATION MAKES IT HARD FOR REFORM TO REACH THE CLASSROOM

The case of progressive reform in the first half of the twentieth century shows that educational reforms have had trouble bringing about fundamental change in the system of schooling. Making change at the rhetorical level has been relatively easy for school reformers. Making change at the structural level has been more difficult, but in limited form it too was possible for well-positioned reformers. However, changing how teachers teach in their individual classrooms has been much more challenging; and changing how and what students learn in those classrooms has proven to be the most daunting of all reform aims.

In the last section of this chapter, I explore some of the structural factors that make reform so difficult at the core levels of the school system where teaching and learning take place. I argue that there are two organizational characteristics of the American school system in particular that make it hard for reformers to change schooling at the deepest level: loose coupling and weak administrative control.

Loose Coupling

The organization of American schooling is loosely coupled.[20] In a tightly coupled system, like a nuclear power plant or a petroleum processing facility, changes or actions in one part of the system quickly travel to other parts. But this is not the way things work in American schools, where the parts of the system operate as semiautonomous segments rather than integrated components of a single entity.[21] Historically, in the United States, state systems of schooling have operated quite independently of each other, and they are only tangentially connected with the federal government. Likewise, school districts have had their own governance structure, funding sources, political constituencies, hiring authority, and organizational cultures, largely buffered from intrusions by state authorities and quite separate from other districts. Within districts, individual schools have a similar degree of independence from each other, as parallel but not closely interrelated, self-contained segments of schooling; and they are also protected from much intrusion from the district administration by their physical isolation from the district office and by their ability to deliver schooling to a particular community more or less on their own.

Within schools, individual classrooms act as separate instructional modules, which are independent of each other and which are cut off from the school principal by their distinctive function (instruction, in contrast with the principal's focus on administration) and their physical isolation (behind the walls of the self-contained classroom). And within classrooms, individual students act as separate units of teaching and learning, each bringing distinctive abilities and motivation to the learning process and thus offering distinctive challenges to the teacher independent of the other students in the class. The relative independence of states from the federal government, districts from the state government, schools from the district, classrooms from the principal's office, and students from the teacher provides functional semiautonomy for both teachers and students in relation to all of the layers above them in the organizational structure of schooling.

Each of the six layers of the organization of American schooling has a similar structure, with a series of parallel and often interchangeable organizational segments (students, classrooms, schools, school districts, and states) operating quasi-independently to deliver an educational service and nested loosely within a higher-level unit (classrooms, schools, districts, states, and federal government) that has the same segmented structure. Individual students are the basic building blocks of this nested structure, which accumulate in stages into classrooms, schools, districts, state systems, and finally a national system. Thus when we talk about the American system of schooling, we're really referring to a series of nested segments that ultimately rest on the teaching and learning of 50 million students that goes on in approximately 3 million public school classrooms, which in turn are nested in 95,000 schools, 14,000 districts, and 50 states.[22] (In 1938, the first year the United States starting collecting data on school districts, the numbers were 25 million students, 900,000 classrooms, 250,000 schools, 120,000 school districts, and 48 states.)[23] Under these conditions, it should not be surprising to find that school reform efforts are hard-pressed to penetrate vertically all the way down through these layers in the system, and to spread horizontally across all the segments in each layer, to reach—at long last—the classroom and the student. Having significant impact on the district level, as the administrative progressives did, was in this view quite an accomplishment.

The standards movement, which arose at the end of the twentieth century in the United States, has been, in part, a major effort to learn from the limitations that this system imposed on reformers by deliberately seeking to create a more tightly coupled system of schooling. This started with federal rhetorical calls for a common set of curriculum standards (in the 1983 report, A Nation at Risk, and updated in the 2002 law, No Child Left Behind), which led to the setting of state curriculum standards reinforced by high-stakes tests; which brought local consequences for districts, schools, teachers, and students who failed to meet performance benchmarks; which in turn helped coerce school districts, schools, and classrooms to align both the formal curriculum at the district level and the curriculum-in-use by teachers at the classroom level with state and federal guidelines. Another element that has helped reinforce this move toward tighter coupling during the standards movement was the trend during the same period to shift the funding for schooling away from dependence on local property taxes (which tend to reinforce district autonomy) and toward the state and federal budgets (which tend to intrude on that autonomy).

Weak Administrative Control over Teaching

Another organizationally distinctive trait of American schooling is the relatively weak control that school administrators exert over teaching.[24] In part, of course, this administrative weakness is a function of loose coupling, which makes it difficult for administrators to reach across the boundaries separating school districts from the state, schools from the district office, teachers from the principal's office, and students from the teacher; and which makes it difficult for changes brought about in one school district to spread to other districts, from one school to others in the same district, from one classroom to others in the same school, or from one student to others in the same classroom. But there is an additional component that weakens the impact of administrators over teaching. The structure of teaching-as-work in the United States is such that school administrators have traditionally been lacking the basic levers of power that enable employers in most occupational settings to motivate employee compliance with their boss's wishes. In most jobs, the employer can manipulate some combination of two core mechanisms to make sure that employees do as they are told. One is fear, the other greed.

Fear works at an elemental level: Do as I say or I'll fire you. In its more sophisticated forms, it presents the employee with a variety of possible punishments short of termination for failing to comply with the employer's expectations, such as demotion, reprimand, transfer to a less desirable posting, relegation to the margins of the work group, reduced perks, and blocked promotion.

Principals in American schools, however, traditionally have held a weak hand in using the fear factor against teachers. Consider the current pattern in the United States, which emerged early in the twentieth century and then was reinforced when teacher unions became strong after World War II. The contract with the teacher union makes it extraordinarily difficult to fire a teacher after she has completed an initial probationary period of three years or so. American teachers enjoy a form of tenure guarantee that, though weaker than the tenure rights of American college professors, is much stronger than in nearly any other occupational setting. To fire a teacher after being tenured is so onerous in its requirements for documentation, due process, and battles with the union that most principals don't even try. So this leaves only lesser forms of punishment that are not as effective in getting the teacher's attention. The principal can provide a negative evaluation, deny special requests, block access to resources, push a teacher to transfer to another school, or assign a teacher to less desirable classes. (The New York City school system maintains a "rubber room" in the administration building for teachers who have been removed from the classroom for cause but can't be fired; they sit around doing crossword puzzles while receiving full pay.)[25] But in the absence of the big gun of termination, these forms of punishment are a weak weapon in the ongoing effort to get teachers to teach the required curriculum in the desired way.

If fear provides the stick for the employer, greed provides the carrot. It is equally simple in its operation: Do as I say and I'll reward you. Jobs in most complex organizations offer a finely tuned array of possible rewards for the employees who perform well in the eyes of their employers, but the two primary modes are pay and promotion. Managers dole out or deny pay increases and promotions based on the degree to which the employee's work meets the manager's expectations. Pay, bonuses, and other forms of financial incentives offer an infinitely flexible mechanism for rewarding employee behavior. And promotions supply a similarly rich series of gradations for offering possible benefits for the compliant employee: a higher grade, a better title, a bigger office, a window, more generous benefits, or a company car.

In American public schools, however, administrators since World War II have had virtually no discretion in allocating either pay or promotion. Pay levels are set by union contracts, and traditionally they are based on only two criteria: the number of years the teacher has served and the number of graduate credits and degrees the teacher has accumulated. Reformers have repeatedly proposed a shift toward merit pay for teachers, and a few districts and their unions have experimented with such plans. But with these few exceptions, school administrators in general have no ability to hand out pay increases to teachers based on their performance in meeting particular educational goals. Administrators also can't offer promotion. Teaching is a horizontal profession, lacking the vertical career path of lawyers in a law firm or professors in a university. Except for high schools, which have the position of department chair, there is no higher-level teaching position to attract the aspirations of teachers. Newcomers to the profession take on the role of teacher in their first year on the job and hold that same role until they retire. Promotion normally comes only by leaving teaching for administration. Again, there have been proposals to create higher tiers of teaching (lead teacher, career professional, board certified teacher), but these have not yet become incorporated into the structure of the profession.[26]

That is the current pattern of teacher tenure, pay, and promotion in the United States. But what were conditions like during the first half of the twentieth century, when the progressive education movement was in full swing? Teacher unions started exerting a major influence in the largest American cities during the first two decades of the twentieth century, affiliating with the American Federation of Teachers (founded in 1912). These efforts lost steam in the 1920s and then redoubled in the 1930s and 1940s.[27] Formal teacher contracts have been the norm in public schools since the second half of the nineteenth century. Initially, these contracts largely consisted of a list of reasons that would warrant termination, although these related primarily to sexual behavior (consorting with a man without a chaperone, marrying) rather than instructional behavior. A teacher shortage in the early 1920s, however, compelled school districts around the country to offer teachers job tenure in order to attract and retain the teachers they needed.[28] In addition to tenure, teacher contracts in the 1920s also began to change the terms of teacher pay. The older contracts had set up a pay scale that offered higher salaries for men; they also offered higher pay for teachers in the upper grades, which created a de facto promotion system for teachers based on seniority, encouraging teachers over time to move up the scale of school grade levels and teacher pay. But in the 1920s teacher shortages and union pressure forced districts to raise pay and also to yield to demands for a single-standard pay scale, which equalized pay between men and women and across grade levels. As a result, the old promotion ladder quickly disappeared while the pattern of rewarding seniority remained. This left a structure of teacher tenure, pay by seniority, and nonpromotion, which approximated the current American pattern.

During most of the twentieth century, therefore, school administrators in the United States largely lacked the ability to fire or promote teachers or to set teacher pay, which left them with few of the resources that administrators in most other workplaces could use to keep employees working in line with the aims of management. This helps explain why it has been particularly difficult for reformers to reach past the second level of the American school system. Even when reformers have partially succeeded in reshaping the formal structure of the school system, as the administrative progressives did, they have still found themselves blocked at the classroom door. And it is this third level of the system, classroom teaching, that constitutes the instructional core of the entire system.

WHY RESISTING REFORM CAN BE A GOOD THING

One way to decide whether a particular educational reform was a success or a failure is to examine how deeply that reform managed to reach down through the levels of the educational system to its instructional core. Reformers have had the most success in shaping the system at the rhetorical level, by changing the way we talk about school. And with the right people and the right proposals, they have even been able to remake elements of the system at the level of formal structure, by changing curriculum and administration, adding a new layer (like the junior high school), and introducing testing. But reformers have had a much more difficult time bringing about significant change at the levels of classroom teaching and student learning.

The movement for progressive education in the early twentieth-century United States has provided an instructive case in point. One strand of the movement succeeding in changing the rhetoric and reforming the structure of school districts, while the other strand had an impact that was limited to the rhetorical level. But both were largely unable to change classroom teaching and student learning. Progressivism was the dominant reform movement in American education during this period, and it drew support from an extraordinary array of educational administrators, professors, theorists, and policymakers; yet its impact on the core of schooling was marginal. I have shown that, in part, this relative failure arose from characteristics that have been specific to the American system of schooling: a loosely coupled structure of organization, which buffered schools and classrooms from changes coming down from above; and a structure of teaching that denied school administrators control over teacher tenure, pay, and promotion, thus protecting teachers from administrative efforts to change the way they taught.

Keep in mind, however, that the failure of a reform movement to accomplish its goals may not be a bad thing for schools or society and that the success of a reform movement may make things worse. I would argue, for example, that American schools would have been better off if Snedden, Kingsley, and the other administrative progressives had failed to impose their social efficiency agenda on the structure of the American school system. They didn't succeed in transforming teaching and learning in classrooms, but they did enough damage as it was—by developing curriculum tracks that effectively sorted students by social class and by giving a vocational spin to schooling that undercut its broader social and political mission. From this perspective, then, blocking a harmful reform is as positive an accomplishment as implementing a beneficial reform. Of course, the judgment about what's harmful or beneficial about a reform is open to debate, since it depends on which educational goal a person values most. Snedden thought vocationalism was great; Dewey thought it was terrible. So Snedden's success was Dewey's failure.

Thinking of the problem of reform this way suggests that we should be cautious about viewing the organization of schooling as a problem that needs to be fixed, just because it makes the reform of teaching and learning difficult. The standards movement that emerged in the 1980s and continues into the early twenty-first century certainly sees the system's organization as a problem. Seeking to avoid the failures of the educational progressives, leaders of this movement have worked hard to introduce mechanisms that would tighten the coupling of the system and make teachers more accountable to administrators. They have set up systems of high-stakes testing, tied them to state-mandated curriculum guidelines, and then developed report cards that display how well each school is doing in raising scores and meeting objectives. They are pushing to have teacher performance, retention, and pay depend on how well that teacher does in raising student scores.

We can measure the effectiveness of the standards movement by the degree to which they succeed in imposing tighter coupling and greater accountability on the school system. If you agree with the goals of the standards movement 2.0—that school reform should focus on making the United States more productive economically and more equitable socially—and if you think that raising academic standards will help accomplish these goals, then success for this reform would be a good thing. But if you feel that the equity claims of the standards movement are just a cover for an educational agenda that privileges economic goals for education over more important social and political goals, then you will be rooting for the educational system to resist these changes. From the latter angle, loose coupling and teacher autonomy are safeguards that prevent reformers from hijacking the school system for unworthy purposes.

Sociologist Charles Perrow wrote a book called *Normal Accidents,* about the ways in which loose coupling can be an advantage for an organization. What prompted this analysis was his evaluation of the 1979 partial meltdown of the nuclear reactor at Three Mile Island near Harrisburg, Pennsylvania.[29] He concluded that some accidents like this one are "normal," in the sense that they are the likely outcome of a particular organizational structure. A nuclear power plant is a tightly coupled system, since it involves a continuous process that connects all parts of the system closely. This means that a problem in one place quickly has ramifications for other parts of the system. And since the interactions are so complex, no safety systems can take into account all contingencies; in fact, safety systems can make things worse by introducing a new cascade of interactions.

So in a tightly coupled system, isolated failures over time inevitably will interact to cause a catastrophic failure of the whole system. (Recall how easily a quirk in a particular application can make a computer crash.) In contrast, loosely coupled systems, like schools, are buffered from this kind of catastrophic failure. Bad teaching in one classroom doesn't necessarily affect the other classrooms in a school; one poor performing school doesn't necessarily have an impact on those around it. Harmful reforms are unlikely to infect the system as a whole, since adoption of these reforms will be spotty rather than systemic. Bad ideas have as much trouble as good ideas moving from state to district to school to classroom, since buffers at each step along the way limit and localize their effects. As a loosely coupled system, the American school system is a terrible medium for transmitting reform, but at the same time, it's a bulwark against the spread of harmful approaches to teaching and learning.

Whether you think this is a positive or a negative trait depends on whether you are an optimist or a pessimist about the possibilities of social improvement through school reform. School reformers by nature are optimists. They are convinced that schools can address important social problems if schools will just change their ways of doing things. As a result, reformers detest the structure of the school system, since it deflects their best efforts to bring teaching and learning in line with reform goals. But if you're a pessimist like me, skeptical about the ability of schools to resolve social problems, then you may well take comfort in the capacity of the school system to resist reform. For reformers, the need for schools to take on the latest social problem is so great, and schools' failure to do so in their current form is so costly for society, that drastic reform of the school system is imperative. Under these dire conditions, they are not terribly worried about promoting catastrophic failure—the educational equivalent of a nuclear meltdown—since in their view it would be hard to make things worse in the school system than they already are.

Almost any change is better than none. Their motto is: Don't just stand there, do something.

But for skeptics like me, making things worse is a likely possibility. The history of school reform is a depressing tale of unintended consequences and serial failures. One of the things that makes school reform "steady work" is that every reform effort creates problems, which then spurs a new reform movement to develop a remedy.[30] The standards movement is trying to fix the problems caused by administrative progressive reforms, which led to curriculum fragmentation and social sorting. Its answer is to focus on developing a higher floor for achievement in a common core of academic subjects. We don't know what will happen next, but we can be assured that another reform movement will emerge at some point to fix the problems caused by the standards effort.

The motto for skeptics comes from Hippocrates: First do no harm. History suggests that doing something in educational reform may well do more harm than good. So it pays to be cautious, consider the implications, and try things out on a pilot basis instead of launching a systemwide reform effort from day one. In this view, it's useful to have a school system that contains problems and resists the infectious spread of educational enthusiasms.[31]

CLASSROOM RESISTANCE

TO REFORM

5

One reason that school reformers struggle to have an impact on student learning is that the organization of the school system makes it hard for reforms to get past the classroom door. But another reason is that, even inside the classroom itself, teachers themselves struggle to get their students to learn. Even if teachers were to buy into the reform agenda fully and try to implement it, they're unlikely to be very successful, since the connection between teaching and learning is indirect at best.[1]

For student learning to take place, teachers must first establish a special kind of personal relationship with the individual students in the class. Without this kind of relationship, students will not learn what schools want them to learn. And teachers can only establish such pedagogically effective relationships if they are allowed the discretionary space to do so. They need this latitude to figure out a way of doing things that works best for the individual students in the class and for the special situations of time and place.

Thus, a central dilemma of school reform: if reformers are going to have an impact on the instructional core of schooling, instead of limiting themselves to the rhetorical or structural levels of the system, they need to change how teachers teach in classrooms; but intruding on teachers in this way threatens to undermine the degree of teacher discretion that is necessary to foster effective learning.[2] Teachers fit the occupational category that Michael Lipsky calls "street-level bureaucrats."[3] These are public service workers whose clients are nonvoluntary, who function under conditions of crushing demand and inadequate resources, where goals are ambiguous or conflicted and where performance in relation to goals is hard to measure. In cases like these (police officers, social workers, teachers), the bureaucracy has no choice but to allow the front-line agent substantial discretion to decide how to apply general policies to the myriad peculiarities of the cases at hand. From this perspective, then, school reform at the classroom level may not only be difficult; it may be counterproductive. And a key reason that teachers often resist reform efforts may be that they are trying to preserve a form of teaching and learning that seems to work and to fend off an alternative approach that might not.[4]

THE NATURE OF TEACHING AND THE PROBLEM OF REFORM

Let me explain some of the key elements in the educational relationship between teachers and students that create barriers to reform at the classroom level.

The Need for Client Cooperation

At the core of the difficulties facing teachers is that, as David Cohen has put it, in a lovely essay on the nature of teaching, "Teaching is a practice of human improvement. It promises students intellectual growth, social learning, better jobs, and civilized sensibilities."[5] This puts it in the same category as psychotherapy, consulting, and social work. One big problem that arises in such a practice is that "practitioners depend on their clients to achieve any results. . . . No matter how hard practitioners try, or how artfully they work, they can produce no results alone. They can succeed only if their clients succeed."[6]

A surgeon can fix the ailment of a patient who sleeps through the operation, and a lawyer can successfully defend a client who remains mute during the trial; but success for a teacher depends heavily on the active cooperation of the student.[7] The student must be willing to learn what the teacher is teaching. Unless this intended learning takes place, the teacher has failed. It was this reciprocal notion of the teacher–student relationship that Dewey had in mind when he noted, "There is the same exact equation between teaching and learning that there is between selling and buying."[8] That is, you can't be a good salesperson unless someone is buying, and you can't be a good teacher unless someone is learning.

Consider how difficult this makes things for teachers and others trying to work as practitioners of human improvement. They most devote enormous amounts of skill and effort to the task of motivating the client to cooperate, and still the outcome is far from certain. The client may choose to spurn the practitioner's offer of improvement—out of apathy, habit, principle, spite, inattention, or whim. In such a field, success rates are likely to be low, and the connection between a practitioner's action and a client's outcome is likely to be, at best, indirect. Therefore, the effectiveness of the practitioner becomes difficult to establish.

Within the field of medicine, we can see some of the consequences of this reciprocity problem. Physicians can treat many bodily ailments (an inflamed appendix, a bacterial infection) with a high degree of success by means of a direct physical or pharmaceutical intervention on the body of the patient. But they are less effective at treating disorders such as obesity or neurosis, in which the treatment requires patients to change behaviors that are damaging to their health. As a result, medicine tends to push such low-yield therapies into the hands of human improvement practitioners, such as counselors, while retaining control over the treatments that are most successful. Teachers don't have this luxury; changing people is their whole job.

The Problem of a Compulsory Clientele

The difficulty of gaining the compliance of the student is made even worse for the teacher because the student is only present in the classroom under duress. A central fact of school life is that, given the choice, students would be doing something other than studying algebra or geography or literature or biology. Part of the compulsion is legal. Most states in the United States require students to attend school until the age of 16, whether they want to or not.

The heavy hand of the law, however, is not the primary factor pushing students to attend school. They are likely to feel the pressure for attendance more directly from their parents (who want school to take care of children during the day, to help them get ahead, even to educate them), from the market (which makes school credentials mandatory for access to a good job), and from their own social desires (school is where their friends are). But the looming presence of a legal sanction is not a minor issue for either student or teacher, and it certainly helps distinguish the classroom from other venues of professional practice, both human-improving and not. After all, how often does a truant officer come knocking when a patient misses an appointment with a counselor or dentist? In addition, most of the incentives to go to school, legal and otherwise, have to do with encouraging students to attend rather than to learn. Students may have to be in school and they may even want to be there, but they are not necessarily there to learn, at least not to learn the official curriculum. If they learn school subjects while attending school, it is because a teacher has actively worked to make that happen.

If successful teaching, as I have noted, requires the willingness of the student to learn, then success is even harder to obtain because the student is there involuntarily. Motivating volunteers to engage in human improvement is very difficult, as any psychotherapist can confirm, but motivating conscripts is quite another thing altogether. And it is conscripts that teachers face every day in the classroom.

No one writes about the consequences of involuntary learning on both teacher and student in more depth or with greater bile than Willard Waller does, in his classic book, *The Sociology of Teaching*. The teacher–pupil relationship is a form of institutionalized domination and subordination. Teacher and pupil confront each other in the school with an original conflict of desires, and however much that conflict may be reduced in amount, or however much it may be hidden, it still remains. The teacher represents the adult group, ever the enemy of the spontaneous life of groups of children. The teacher represents the formal curriculum, and his interest is in imposing that curriculum upon the children in the form of tasks; pupils are much more interested in life in their own world than in the desiccated bits of adult life that teachers have to offer.[9]

Control is therefore the central problem facing the teacher, according to Waller, and every novice approaching the classroom for the first time would certainly agree with him. Just ask students in teacher-preparation programs, and they will tell you that they have learned too much about theories of curriculum and pedagogy and not nearly enough about classroom management, the thing that most worries them about being able to teach. In fact, as Philip Cusick argues, in *The Educational System,* this problem does not go away with time and experience: "control is the major issue and always at the center of teacher–student relations. Orderly behavior can never be expected; it is always problematic and always requires attention."[10]

Of course, teachers have a huge advantage in this struggle for control. They have institutional authority, superior knowledge, and parental sanction, and they are usually bigger, too. But students are not without weapons of their own. Waller again: "Whatever the rules that the teacher lays down, the tendency of the pupils is to empty them of meaning. By mechanization of conformity, by 'laughing off' the teacher or hating him out of all existence as a person, by taking refuge in self-initiated activities that are always just beyond the teacher's reach, students attempt to neutralize teacher control."[11]

The key here is the ability of students to empty teacher rules of their meaning. If the purpose of control for teachers is to facilitate learning, then the best way for students to exact revenge for compulsory education is to comply with the formal reality of teacher control without giving in to its substance by actually learning anything. The result is a compromise in which students acknowledge the teacher's control and the teacher uses this control lightly, making only modest demands on the students as learners. Some authors call this form of accommodation in the classroom "bargaining";[12] others call it constructing "treaties";[13] and in a previous book, I called it a game of "how to succeed in school without really learning."[14]

Waller goes out of his way to focus on, even caricature, the traditional teacher, who relies on direct control to manage the classroom (in characteristically epigrammatic form, he asserts, "Every teacher is a taskmaster and every taskmaster is a hard man."[15]). But teachers in the child-centered progressive tradition also necessarily exert control in the classroom. The difference is that they do so in a manner that is less direct, less visible, and therefore more manipulative than Waller's taskmaster: by engaging student interest and finding ways of attaching it to the required curriculum; by indirectly promoting and modeling correct behavior rather than imposing it by fiat; and by creating an emotional bond with students and using this to motivate compliance with the social order and learning process in the classroom. Students may experience this softer approach to classroom management as more benign and friendly than the heavy-handed use of authority in the traditional approach. It may even be more effective in general as a way to motivate students to learn what the teacher is teaching. But it is no less a mechanism for controlling student behavior.

In countries other than the United States, the structure of education sometimes strengthens the teacher's hand in managing student learning—for example, by organizing the educational system around high-stakes testing of students at critical transition points in their careers in school. Outside the United States, students often have to pass an intensive and comprehensive examination of what they have learned in school in order to get into the most desirable high school or university. An interesting side effect of this is that it shifts responsibility for compelling students to learn the curriculum away from teachers and onto an examination over which the teacher has no control. In the American classroom, where the teacher is responsible for both delivering the curriculum and evaluating the success of students in learning it, the teacher is in the disadvantageous position of having to say to students, "Learn this because I said so" (which provokes student opposition) or "Learn this because you're going to need to know it some day" (which provokes student skepticism because that day seems so far away).

In a system driven by outside examinations, however, teachers can portray themselves as the allies rather than taskmasters of the students in their classes. Under these conditions, the teacher can say to students, "You need to learn this for the exam, which is coming up shortly and will have a big impact on your lives; I can help you pass it." This approach helps teachers undercut some of the student resistance and apathy toward learning, but it doesn't eliminate the problem that compulsion poses for teachers. In fact, high-stakes exams may well exacerbate students' sense of learning under duress—and of learning itself as the acquisition of what Waller called "desiccated bits of adult life"—even as it transfers some of the blame for this away from the teacher.[16] To the extent that the standards movement is now driving the United States in this direction, it too may encounter the pedagogical costs and benefits of high-stakes testing.

The Need to Manage Emotion

Another characteristic of teaching that makes it difficult is the way it requires teachers to establish and actively manage an emotional relationship with students. This is in striking contrast to the norms that govern most professions, including those that focus on human improvement. So consider for a moment some of the characteristics of the prototypical professional relationship, and then consider the implications for teaching that arise from the sharp differences between this and the teacher–student relationship.

First, professional practitioners in general are permitted, even required, to maintain a distinct emotional distance between themselves and the client. They construct the role relationship around a norm of emotional neutrality, according to the rationale that the services of the professional will be most effective in meeting the needs of the client if the professional is able to approach matters from a stance of objectivity. From this perspective, emotional involvement with the client is counterproductive, because it distracts the professional from deploying the analytical and technical skills that will be most valuable in serving the client's interests.

Another characteristic of the professional–client relationship that reinforces the norm of emotional distance is the distinctive narrowness of this relationship. That is, the professional focuses on the particular problem that brings the client to seek professional help in the first place rather than construing this interaction as a diffuse relationship between two people. The doctor focuses on the client's fever, the accountant on the client's tax liability, and the therapist on the client's compulsive behavior. To get involved with the client in the more intense and wide-ranging manner of a close friend may be counterproductive in handling the problem that brought the client to the professional in the first place, and therefore may well be defined as unprofessional conduct.

A third characteristic that defines the professional–client relationship is its achievement orientation. It exists in order to get the job done, and the client will judge its success by how well the professional performs in resolving the problem that originally propelled the client to seek professional help. A fourth characteristic of this relationship is the self-interestedness of the actors. They approach each other as independent agents pursuing their own ends, not as members of a group with shared ends. A fifth characteristic of professional relationships is that they are supposed to be governed by universalistic rather than particularistic rules. This means following procedures that are the same across all relationships, without favoring or discriminating against any clients.[17]

In general, professionals, in their interaction with clients, are supposed to be governed by these five norms. In this regard, they fit in a large category of roles that sociologists call secondary roles. Secondary role relationships make up that vast array of limited and utilitarian social connections that people engage in as a means toward particular ends—such as employer–employee, customer–clerk, and pilot–passenger. The purpose of a secondary role relationship is to accomplish ends that extend outside the relationship itself: the client gets a problem solved, the professional gets paid. The relationship is not its own reward but is a means toward other ends for each of the parties involved. Primary roles, in contrast, are small in number, intensely emotional, and highly particularistic. The relationship—close friend, spouse, parent, gang member—is defined as an end in itself and not a means to ulterior ends.

In real life, of course, these distinctions between roles tend to blur. Boss and employee sometimes become friends, professional and client sometimes fall in love. But the difference between primary and secondary roles still carries meaning. Thus, much of the distinctive nature of professional relationships is usefully captured by the ideals of emotional neutrality, narrowness of focus, achievement orientation, convergence of self-interest, and due process.

In comparison to the relative clarity of the role defined for the typical professional, teachers find themselves in a much more complicated role environment. For example, adopting a posture of social distance from students is likely to undermine their ability to teach these students effectively. Teachers need a broad understanding of the whole student—emotional life, family situation, social condition, cultural capital, cognitive capacities— which precludes the narrowly defined approach of most professional associations. By narrowing the focus to the particular task at hand—a math problem, spelling list, or science project—the teacher is likely to miss the information about the student that may help determine the most effective approach to make in promoting learning for that student.[18]

But the issue is more than a matter of developing a broad relationship with students for the purpose of understanding their learning needs and learning problems. The teacher also needs to establish an emotional link in order to be able to motivate the student to participate actively in the learning process. As we have already established, motivating students to learn is not easy. Students are conscripts in the classroom, and as a result the teacher's efforts to maintain control are often better at containing students' external behavior than at promoting learning within. John Dewey, among others, noted that "Children acquire great dexterity in exhibiting in conventional and expected ways the form of attention to school work, while reserving the inner play of their own thought, images, and emotions for subjects that are more important to them, but quite irrelevant."[19] What this means is that teachers are never sure whether what they are observing in the classroom is active engagement in an inner-directed pursuit of learning or merely formal compliance with teacher authority. And the most powerful tool teachers have to encourage engaged learning is their emotional connection with their students.

Teachers spend a lot of care and energy in constructing a social and emotional atmosphere in the classroom that is conducive to learning. This means creating a setting that is inviting and comfortable, so that attending class is a pleasurable rather than dreadful experience. In particular, it quite often means establishing a relationship with students that is warm and affectionate and using this relationship as a lever for learning. A basic rule of teaching is, "Like me, like my subject." The ultimate aim of a teacher is to get students so engaged in the intrinsic pleasure of learning that they forget she is there and pursue it for its own rewards, but the teacher's most powerful mechanism for launching them into the learning process initially is their affection for her and their eagerness to please her by learning what she asks them to learn. So the conscious or unconscious strategy for most teachers is to establish a close emotional bond with students and then seek to convert emotional engagement with the teacher into cognitive engagement with the curriculum.

I'm not arguing here that all effective teachers are teddy bears to their students, nor that students cannot learn from teachers they dislike. One of the daunting mysteries of teaching is bound up in the dazzling variety of approaches by which teachers establish an emotional relationship with students, approaches that range widely according to the gender and personality of the teacher, the nature of the subject, and the age of the students. Women and men, extroverts and introverts, science teachers and literature teachers, at the elementary level and the university level—all establish different ways of connecting with their students, but the most effective of them do indeed make this connection in some form or another.

Establishing a Teacher Persona

At the start of their careers, teachers fumble around for a way to establish an emotional link with students that is effective and sustainable, for the teaching persona that works best for them. This persona is both natural, in that it draws on characteristics and strengths of the teacher as a person, and constructed, in that it is put together in order to serve the ends of promoting learning in the classroom. Samuel Freedman provides a nice window into the process of persona construction through his portrait of a remarkably effective New York high school English teacher named Jessica Siegel.

> She wants to draw in the students, to thrill them a little. The bulletin board is part of the strategy, and so is her penchant for bright, funky attire. Today she wears four earrings and five rings, two silver on her left hand and three gold on her right, and a dress from Pakistan, bone-white cotton printed with blue designs that are as cryptic and angular as cuneiform. . . . A student once asked, "Miss Siegel, do you water that dress?"
>
> Even as Jessica tries to captivate her students, she wants to control them—not to dictate or deaden, but not to abdicate authority either. . . . It took her years to develop a classroom presence that felt organic, for she was naturally a listener, a backbencher, a person who began countless sentences, "I don't know a lot about this, but. . . ."
>
> Gradually, she created from pieces of herself a persona that might best be called The Tough Cookie. She stands this morning with right hand on the hip, head cocked slightly, eyebrows arched in mock disbelief; every so often, she shoots a phrase Jersey City style out of a gully at the corner of her mouth. "Gimme a break," she says to a lying latecomer. Her students will hear her say the same thing a hundred times before the term is over, hear her bite down hard on "Gimme" and stretch "break" into an aria of annoyance.[20]

There are several characteristics of this need to establish an affectionate relationship with students that add profoundly to the difficulty involved in being a good teacher. First, there is no guidebook for how to accomplish this for any particular teacher in a particular classroom. Like other practitioners in the professions of human improvement, teachers have to work things out on their own, without being able to fall back on standards of acceptable professional practice such as those that guide lawyers and doctors and accountants.

Second, the practice of teaching—with its requirement for a broadly diffuse relationship with students grounded in part in emotion—throws the teacher into an extraordinarily complex role that in awkward fashion puts together characteristics of both primary and secondary relationships. The teacher role combines a mandate for emotional closeness and diffuse interaction, both characteristic of primary roles, with mandates for achievement (giving students rewards based on performance, not ascribed traits); independence (encouraging students to develop and rely on their own skills and knowledge); and universalistic application of rules (treating all students the same, rewarding everyone according to the same criteria), all of which are characteristic of secondary roles. Teachers are asked to use the leverage obtained from their primary relations with students to support the teaching of a curriculum that is quite external to these primary ties. In short, this means creating affectionate ties and then using them to promote student learning. To be really good at teaching you must have a remarkable capacity for preserving a creative tension between these opposites, never losing sight of either teaching's relational means or its curricular goal.

Balancing these two kinds of roles in the same position is difficult at best. It is not surprising that teachers often resolve the tension between the primary and secondary elements in one direction or the other: by leading a forced march through a curriculum in which no one is motivated to learn, or by settling for a feel-good classroom in which no one is pushed to learn. In the latter case, teachers get so caught up in the need to be liked by their students that they lose track of the pedagogical purpose of establishing an emotional link with their classes, and they convert the teacher–student relationship into a simple primary connection, where the positive feeling in the group becomes its purpose. In these cases, the pedagogical logic reverses itself, as teachers seek to win the affection of their students by reducing the pressure on students

to learn: "If I get you to like my subject, then you'll like me."
One of the most difficult parts about teaching is that good teachers have to be willing to risk their relationship with their students in the pursuit of student learning, to use the leverage of
being liked to push for a level of student performance that may
result in being disliked.[21]

Third, teachers face the strain of trying to manage the emotional relationship with students by maintaining the teaching persona that makes this relationship work. Maintaining the teaching
persona is an exhausting task of what Arlie Hochschild calls "emotion management." In her book *The Managed Heart,* she explores
a variety of "jobs that call for emotional labor." What they have in
common is that "they require face-to-face . . . contact with the
public," "they require the worker to produce an emotional
state in another person," and "they allow the employer . . . to
exercise a degree of control over the emotional activities of
employees."[22]

She never refers directly to teachers in this study, focusing instead on the cases of flight attendants and bill collectors, but her
analysis fits teachers all too well. These kinds of jobs, she argues,
are particularly difficult and stressful because the only way you
can produce the desired emotional state in the other person is by
effectively managing your own emotions. The role of the teacher,
like the role of other emotion workers, cannot be taken on super-
ficially if you are going to be effective in this role. The aim is to
have an impact on the emotions of the student, and in emotional
matters students, like all of us, have well-developed antennas for
detecting a fake. Teachers are playing a role, but they need to play
it in a thoroughly convincing manner, to come across to their students as fully authentic. Hochschild says this calls for a kind of
"deep acting. Here, display is a natural result of working on
feeling; the actor does not try to seem happy or sad but rather
expresses spontaneously, as the Russian director Constantin
Stanislavski urged, a real feeling that has been self-induced."[23]

Good teaching, then, is deep acting. Effective teachers feel the role deeply and express it naturally, without affectation or artifice. Like the best method actors, they plunge into the role, drawing on their own emotional life for inspiration and example, and then construct a persona that is an authentic expression of real feeling, even though this feeling is brought to bear on a role that is consciously constructed to serve a particular purpose—to promote learning in the classroom. Jessica Siegel's persona is a useful artifact that she developed in order to be more effective as a teacher, but it only works because she has found an authentic emotional ground for it in her own personality. The result is a role that is not worn lightly or discarded with a flick of the wrist, but a role that arises from within a person who teaches and that takes over that person while teaching.

This is why Waller is quite right in asserting that "Teaching does something to those who teach."[24] In explaining this phenomenon, he places the greatest weight on the problem of control and the way the role of teacher as taskmaster affects the teacher more than the student: "Subordination is possible only because the subordinated one is a subordinate with a mere fragment of his personality, while the dominant one participates completely. The subject is a subject only part of the time and with a part of himself, but the king is all king."[25] With this emphasis on the inhuman consequences of control for schooling, Waller (as David Cohen has pointed out)[26] is adopting a thoroughly romantic vision of education as a contest between natural and forced learning. The implication is that a more child-centered and interest-based mode of instruction would resolve the control problem and relieve teachers from having to suffer the dire consequences of playing the teacher role.

But Hochschild suggests a more complicated interpretation. By taking on the child-centered version of the teacher role—which involves knowing the student in depth and working to draw that student into the learning process through affection and interest—a teacher is adopting a persona that requires a sizeable degree of emotion management. In short, the child-centered instructor, no less than the traditional taskmaster, is deeply shaped by the role she plays. To paraphrase Waller, the student is a student only part of the time and with part of the self, but the teacher is all teacher.

Dealing with Professional Isolation

Exacerbating the teacher's problem in trying to motivate the captive learner is the condition of structural isolation within which the teacher has to operate. American teachers normally teach behind closed doors under conditions where they are the only professional in the room. They are left to their own devices to figure out a way to manage a group of twenty-five or thirty students and move them through the required curriculum. They traditionally get little help from other teachers, who are trying to work out an accommodation with the students in their own classroom down the hall, or from administrators, who have their own problems to contend with, who are architecturally barred from knowing exactly what is going on inside the classroom, and who are therefore largely unable to help teachers do their job. Except for lunchtime conversation or the occasional visit from the principal, teachers are usually left alone to work out a way to teach effectively.

One consequence of this is to reinforce the teacher's focus on control issues. Vastly outnumbered by students and cut off from professional support, teachers are left to confront what Deborah Britzman sees as the "two rules governing the hidden tension of classroom life: unless the teacher establishes control there will be no learning, and, if the teacher does not control the students, the students will control the teacher."[27] In order to rise to the challenge of establishing and maintaining control, the teacher must turn the classroom into a personal fiefdom, a little duchy, complete with its own laws and customs.

Another consequence of isolation is to create a vision of learning to teach as a private ordeal[28] and a vision of the emergent teacher as self-made.[29] This leaves little room for the construction of a shared professional culture for teachers across classroom domains, and it certainly undercuts the value of teacher preparation programs. Teaching comes to be seen as an individual accomplishment, a natural expression of a teacher's personality. The idea that teachers are self-made "is a highly individualistic explanation which reinforces the image of the 'natural teacher,' " according to Britzman. "More than any other cultural myth, the dominant belief that teachers 'make' themselves functions to devalue teacher education, educational theory, and the social process of making value systems explicit."[30]

Chronic Uncertainties in Teaching

In 1986, U.S. Secretary of Education William J. Bennett published a booklet that was widely distributed across the United States, with the title *What Works: Research on Teaching and Learning*.[31] As Bennett put it in his foreword, the booklet was "intended to provide accurate and reliable information about *what works* in the education of our children."[32] The unintended consequence of publishing this booklet, however, was to show how little clarity and certainty there is in what we know about effective teaching. Findings reported in this document turn out not to be very helpful in defining what it takes to teach well. Some findings are mere tautologies: "How much time students are actively engaged in learning contributes strongly to their achievement"[33]—that is, students learn more if they spend more time learning. Some are misleading: "Parental involvement helps children learn more effectively";[34] but, in fact, involvement by parents with high cultural capital provides a big educational advantage for their children over the children of involved parents without this cultural capital. And most are simply too vague to be implemented: "Successful principals establish policies that create an orderly environment and support effective instruction,"[35] which begs the question about what constitutes an orderly environment and instructional support.

A troubling fact about teaching is that there is no established set of professional practices that have been proven to work independent of the particular actors involved and the particular time and place of the action. The technology of teaching is anything but certain, and teachers must learn to live with chronic uncertainty as an essential component of their professional practice.[36] One reason for this is that teachers have to operate under the kinds of daunting conditions I have been outlining in this chapter, conditions that introduce unpredictable elements of will and emotion into the heart of the teaching and learning process. Teachers can only succeed if students agree to cooperate; cooperation is problematic because students are thrust into the learning situation involuntarily; a key factor in enlisting cooperation is the teacher's ability to establish an emotional relationship with students and harness it for curricular ends; and all of this has to be worked out under conditions of immersion with students and isolation from professional peers.

Even if we focus on the more predictable factors shaping teaching and learning, however, teaching remains an uncertain enterprise for a second reason: its irreducible complexity. What we know about teaching is always contingent on a vast array of intervening variables that mediate between a teacher's action and a student's response. As a result, there is always a contingent clause hovering over any instructional prescription: This works better than that, if everything else is equal. In other words, it all depends. It depends on the subject, the grade level, and the community; on the class, race, gender, and culture of the students; on the skills, knowledge, personality, and mood of the teacher; on the time of day, day of week, season, and barometric pressure; on the content of the students' last meal and the state of their parents' marriage; on the culture and structure of the school; on the available curriculum materials, the teacher they had last year, and their prospects for getting a job when they graduate; and so on. There are simply too many people and too many factors involved in shaping the learning process for us to be able to point to a particular teaching technique and claim that it produces successful learning after controlling for other factors.

A third source of uncertainty in the work of teaching is that we are unable to measure adequately the effects that teachers have on students. The things that we can measure most precisely about teacher effects are the most trivial. A teacher can measure how many of the spelling words introduced this week a child can spell on a Friday quiz, how well a student can solve word problems of the type just covered in class, or how many facts a student can remember from a recent textbook chapter about the French Revolution. But what does this show about the larger and more meaningful aims the teacher had in mind in teaching these subjects? What does it show about how well the teacher enhanced the students' literacy and love of literature, empowered students with the capacity to use logic and numerical skills to figure out real-life problems, and provided students with the resources to understand alternative ways of bringing about social change? How can we measure these outcomes, and how can we trace specific outcomes in the lives of former students to specific teachers and particular lessons? The most important outcomes that we want education to make possible—the preparation of competent, productive, and socially responsible adults—are removed from any particular classroom interaction between teacher and student by many years and many other intervening factors. There is simply no way to attribute a causal link between a person's capacities in adulthood and the instructional technique of an individual teacher early in that person's career, because of the cumulative impact on that person of so many other teachers and choices and contingencies over time.

A fourth source of uncertainty in teaching is the complex and often contradictory purposes that societies impose on the whole educational enterprise. In some ways we want education to promote democratic equality, providing all students with the skills and values they need in order to function competently as citizens. At the same time, we also want education to promote social efficiency, providing students with the highly differentiated skills and knowledge they will need in order to function productively as workers in different occupational roles. And we also want education to promote social mobility, giving individuals the kinds of cultural and credential advantages they need in order to get ahead socially in competition with others. Yet the kind of teaching and learning that will be effective varies radically, depending on whether the primary aim is to prepare citizens or workers or social climbers, since teaching that is good for accomplishing one of these goals may be bad for accomplishing another. For example, placing students in ability groups may serve the ends of social mobility by creating distinctions between students, but it is likely to work against democratic equality for the same reason, and it may or may not serve the ends of social efficiency, depending on how well students learn useful job skills in the different groups.[37]

A fifth source of uncertainty is that teachers are not even in a position to establish clearly the identities of their clients. At one level, the client is the student. After all, the student is the one facing teachers in the classroom, the one toward whom teachers direct all of their people-improvement efforts. But keep in mind that the student has not contracted with the teacher to deliver instructional services. In this sense, the involuntary student is more an object of teaching than a client requesting professional help. At another level, the client is the parents of the student. They often see themselves as collaborating with the teacher in the larger project of socializing their children and preparing them for adult life. In private schools—and in a variety of school voucher models—the parents more or less openly contract with schools and teachers to provide professional educational services to their children in line with the parents' educational wishes.[38]

But at a third level, the teacher's client is the community at large. In public schools, it is the citizens as a whole who pay for and govern education, not just the parents of schoolchildren. And in the case of private as well as public education, the community as a whole—in addition to the student and the parents of the student—is a major consumer of the teacher's educational services. The quality of life for all members of the community depends on an educational system that is able to produce competent citizens and productive workers, and therefore everyone suffers from bad teaching and benefits from good teaching, even if they and their children are not the ones directly being taught. Keeping the client happy is not an easy matter in any profession, but consider how much more difficult it is to satisfy the demands of three entirely different clienteles, especially when they are likely to have conflicting ideas about what makes good teaching and good learning.

Why the Difficulties of Teaching Make Teachers Resistant to Reform

Teachers in general face common problems of practice. Their professional success depends on their ability to motivate an involuntary group of students to learn what the teacher is teaching. In an effort to accomplish this, teachers invest heavily in developing a teaching persona that enables them to establish a relationship with students and lure them to learn. Once they have worked out a personal approach for managing the instruction of students within the walls of their classroom, they are likely to resist vigorously any effort by reformers or administrators or any other intruders to transform their approach to teaching. Teacher resistance to fundamental instructional reform is grounded in a deep personal investment in the way they teach and a sense that tinkering with this approach could threaten their very ability to manage a class (much less teach a particular curriculum) effectively.

The teacher persona—an engaging combination of the likeable and the tough—is not something that a teacher puts on lightly or sheds with ease. Developing this persona is hard work, as it was for Jessica Siegel, carried out in isolation from professional colleagues behind the walls of the self-contained classroom, where the teacher is thrown on her own resources to deal with an unruly crowd of unwilling students. It is a form of method acting that lasts not merely for the duration of a play but for the course of an entire career. And it is not just a way of practicing a profession but a way of being. As a result, we should not be surprised to find that teachers in general tend to resist efforts by reformers to change the way they teach. To do so is to change who they are.

Once a teacher has succeeded in developing a teacher persona and has begun using it effectively to motivate learning among the reluctant students in the classroom, she is unlikely to give it up just because a new wave of reform rhetoric says she should and because school administrators issue a revised curriculum.[39] This helps explain why such transformations as the result of reform efforts are not very common, and why the changes that teachers do make in their pedagogy in the wake of reform movements are often formalistic and incremental. Recall what Larry Cuban shows in his analysis of the marginal impact of pedagogical progressivism on American teaching in the twentieth century— that teachers were more likely to adopt a few of the movement's forms (like gathering students in groups or letting them move around the classroom) than to adopt the substance of child-centered instruction; more likely to add a few elements to their core of continuing practice than to transform the way they teach. Instead of embracing reform, they are more likely to be found "hugging the middle."[40]

So when it comes to matters of practice, teaching is an extraordinarily conservative profession.[41] Pedagogical change offers the teacher little apparent benefit and great apparent risk. But this aversion to change is not simply a matter of self-preservation or personal preference; it is also potentially a matter of teacher effectiveness. If they are going to succeed in promoting learning among their students, teachers may well need the discretion they so zealously protect. As the street-level bureaucrats of the educational system, they may need the space to work out their own arrangements for handling the complex learning environment of the classroom, where general rules simply don't apply, even if they come from reformers with the highest educational aims.

THE CONFLICTING WORLDVIEWS OF REFORMERS AND TEACHERS

At heart the teacher's understanding of education is strikingly different from the reformer's understanding of education, and this difference poses a critical limitation on the ability of reformers to have a constructive impact on the way teachers teach.[42] As we have seen in this chapter, effective teachers develop a practical knowledge about how to foster learning that is heavily grounded in a particular context. For them, teaching is not an abstract system that can be applied anywhere; it's a set of specialized professional practices that they adapt to the needs of the situation at hand. To become good at the job, teachers need to develop a rich understanding of the students in their class. This means learning about their culture, social situation, past educational experiences, academic skill, subject matter knowledge, and motivation. For teachers there is no standard technology to employ in their instructional practice, not if they want to succeed. Efforts to spell out general pedagogical principles of "what works" produce either useless truisms (more study leads to more learning) or abstractions that only become workable when translated into the needs of a particular context (promote critical understanding). Instead, teachers need to build up a store of practical professional knowledge out of their own clinical experience in the classroom. And doing this requires an approach that is not only highly particular but also highly personal, since the web of effective teaching is woven from the strands of personal relationships between teacher and students.

In this sense, then, we can think of the classroom as a local ecology, like a forest, a coral reef, or a village. As with any such ecology, the individual organisms within it have a lot in common with organisms in other settings. But what makes the ecology distinctive is the evolving pattern of interaction between the organisms and their environment. An effective teacher is the expert ecologist of her classroom. This ecology is too complex and her goals for it are too broad to allow her to carry out her instructional role simply following the rules from the handbook of teaching. As astute students of the classroom have noted, teaching is not a matter of doing the right thing but of adeptly managing chronic educational dilemmas.[43] Do I respond to that question, even though it takes us off topic? Do I correct the student's error or give him time to work through the logic on his own? Do I laugh at the student's joke or use my teacher face to restore order in the room? It's a matter of balancing a wide array of equally important goals for my teaching—take advantage of a teachable moment or keep intellectual focus; promote accurate understandings or promote student inquiry; maintain a congenial learning environment or maintain an orderly learning environment— where the aim is to figure out what is my top educational priority at this point. So as a teacher I'm not applying laws, I'm choosing from an array of overlapping rules of thumb; and my primary skill as a teacher is my judgment, which shows me how to use my knowledge of the classroom ecology to decide which rule best fits the present case.

Like other social reformers, school reformers have difficulty working with local ecologies. They are located at the upper levels of the school system, far from the classroom: the education department in Washington, DC, or Sacramento; the office of the superintendent of schools or the education professor; a national task force or a professional association. Reformers see themselves operating at the hub of the school policy world while 3 million classrooms are arrayed around the periphery. From this great distance, reformers are unable to see classrooms the way teachers do, taking into account the distinctive character of each of these educational ecologies.

If teachers see education through a microscope, reformers see it through a telescope. In his book about the problem of government-initiated social reform, James Scott calls this kind of reformist vision *Seeing Like a State*.[44] In order to make education visible for their purposes, school reformers at the district, state, or national level need to construct a map; and like any map, it necessarily represents its subject in a radically simplified form. It draws on data that are easily gathered, suitable for the task at hand, and amenable to a statistical summary. This means data like student social characteristics and test scores, teacher experience and qualifications, and state and local funding. Only one thing is certain about the map that reformers create in their effort to see schooling: it leaves out almost everything. The complex ecology of the classroom disappears into the simplified columns of summary statistics.

So teachers and reformers view schooling in starkly different ways. Teachers focus on what is particular within their own classrooms; reformers focus on what is universal across many classrooms. Teachers operate in a setting dominated by personal relations; reformers operate in a setting dominated by abstract political and social aims. Teachers draw on clinical experience; reformers draw on social scientific theory. Teachers embrace the ambiguity of classroom process and practice; reformers pursue the clarity of tables and graphs. Teachers put a premium on professional adaptability; reformers put a premium on uniformity of practices and outcomes.

These differences in perception lead to a head-on conflict over what a successful school reform looks like. For teachers, a school reform works if it can be adapted to their own practice in a way that enhances the teaching and learning process in their classroom; for reformers, a reform works if it can be implemented uniformly across a large number of classrooms in a way that brings about convergent educational and social outcomes. When teachers adapt pieces of a reform effort to their own needs, reformers consider this a failure of implementation and accuse teachers of defending traditional practice and blocking educational progress. The result is a standoff of perspectives between reformers, who are seen as pursuing abstract theories that ignore classroom realities, and teachers, who are seen as protecting dysfunctional educational practices from constructive change.

In *Seeing Like a State*, James Scott provides a series of cautionary tales about state-initiated social reforms that went awry when reformers tried to impose a national theoretical vision on complex local settings. There's the story of European governments in the eighteenth and nineteenth centuries trying to mass-produce lumber by planting a single variety of fast-growing tree in neat rows, only to find that the trees gradually became stunted because of the absence of the complex ecology that had nurtured them in the wild. There's the story of the Soviet effort to accomplish a grand socialist vision by collectivizing agriculture, which destroyed village farming practices and thus led to widespread famine. And there's the story of Brasilia, the government effort to realize an urban designer's dream by the construction of a new capital city from a single comprehensive plan, which failed to leave space for the web of informal economic processes and social relationships that actually make an urban community work.

Each of these reforms was an effort to take a theoretical grid constructed at the center of power and impose it on a far-away local ecology. Grids are attractive to reformers of all stripes. They carry a seductive esthetic, since the reform setting looks neater and cleaner than the messy tableau of nature. They represent rationality, a vision of how reality could be if it followed from an orderly mind. They bring utility, by making it easy to measure, locate, and subdivide the world, as in the case of a grid structure for city streets or rural land development. And they express power. Since grids don't arise in the natural world, their presence demonstrates that someone deliberately put them in place. The problem with imposing a grid on nature or on society, however, is that the process may destroy the messy informal practices that make the ecology function.

Consider what happened when the United States used a grid to manage the surveying and development of public lands in the nineteenth century. Land was divided into sections of one square mile that were oriented along the points of the compass. A group of thirty-six sections (six miles square) made up a township and sixteen townships made a county. Roads were built along section lines, which provide a familiar pattern for travelers in rural America, driving through a grid of roads with intersections at one-mile intervals. But drivers are also familiar with a phenomenon that occurs every few miles while driving on a north–south road—when the road comes to a T intersection with another, jogs left or right for 100 feet or so, and then continues in the original direction. Scott puts an aerial photograph of such a zigzag pattern on the cover of his book, because it serves as an apt metaphor for the dilemma of reform. This recurring pattern is a fix for a geographic problem: that lines of longitude converge as you move north from the equator. A grid therefore doesn't fit the natural terrain, since roads that are heading true north cannot be parallel, and north–south section roads laid out by the compass cannot produce sections that are square. So every few miles you need to introduce a correction to keep the roads a mile apart. In spite of all the attractions of the grid for esthetics, rationality, utility, and power, therefore, it's not a model that can be implemented in the natural world without major adjustments.

IMPOSING A RECTANGULAR GRID
ON A SPHERICAL WORLD

This geographical metaphor also applies to the world of schools. Reformers run into serious problems when they try to impose the rectangular grid of school reform on the spherical world of classrooms. One side or the other has to give way. One option is that reformers allow teachers to adapt the reform plan to fit the local classroom setting, even though this hybrid mode of education is not what the reformers intended. This is the preferred choice put forward by David Tyack and Larry Cuban, who argue that a hybridized reform outcome is the best one can expect in school reform. But for most reformers and policymakers, this kind of outcome looks like a failure for school reform and a triumph for the status quo. The other option is that reformers push to implement the reform according to plan, which forces changes in the classroom that may undercut the delicate ecology of learning there. This is the preferred choice of the American standards movement in the late twentieth and early twenty-first centuries, which has used high-stakes testing and state curriculum mandates to bring teaching and learning in line with the grid of reform. But for most teachers, their defenders in schools of education, and supporters of child-centered progressivism, this approach disrupts the balance of the classroom and destroys student engagement in learning.

As I noted at the end of the last chapter, school reformers are by nature optimists. They don't doubt the virtue of their model of reform, so they have little tolerance for teacher resistance, even if it comes in the name of protecting the ecology of learning. The reform grid seems to carry the best ideas and highest values of our time, so practitioners of the old ways of doing things just need to get out of the way of progress. Social problems are too compelling; the school system doesn't work; we need to change the system to solve the problems; and concerns about a delicate learning community seem minor in the face of the need for action.

But for reform skeptics like me, teachers' hesitation to abandon the hard-won social order they have created in the classroom seems not only justified by their problems of practice but also potentially beneficial for school and society. Like the loose coupling of the system's organizational structure, the resistance of teachers to intrusions on the learning process may provide a useful buffer for the system. It deflects beneficial reforms but it also heads off harmful changes to the classroom. And the system's reluctance to embrace dramatic change at its educational core seems particularly beneficial if, like me, you are skeptical about the ability of the school system to resolve the social problems that reform forces on it. That is the topic of the next chapter.

FAILING TO SOLVE
SOCIAL PROBLEMS

6

American school reform is better at changing the form of the school system than at transforming the substance of classroom learning. And it's better at changing the form of American social life than at fixing the substance of the country's social problems. This is not to say that reform is ineffective, only that it's ineffective at carrying out the tasks we assign to it. In fact, school reform has had a major impact on many aspects of American society, by bringing the way we do things in line with the way schools do things. But at the same time it has contributed remarkably little toward accomplishing its primary goals, such as reducing social inequality, promoting economic productivity, spurring civic engagement, and improving public health.

In this chapter, I explore the failure of school reform to solve social problems, considering first its limited success in realizing the central goals it has pursued over the years and then looking at the modest accomplishments of individual school reform movements. At the end I explore the roots of education's failure as agent of social reform.

THE IMPACT OF SCHOOL REFORM ON SOCIAL EQUALITY, EFFICIENCY, AND MOBILITY

A good place to start is to consider the impact that reform has had on the three social goals I have identified as central to the educational system in the United States: democratic equality, social efficiency, and social mobility.

Democratic Equality

School systems around the world have been more effective at accomplishing their political mission than at either their efficiency or opportunity missions. At the formative stage in the construction of a nation-state, virtually anywhere in the world, education seems to have an important role to play. A wide range of historical studies in the United States and other countries support this conclusion.[1] The key contribution in this regard seems to be that schooling helps form a national citizenry out of a collection of local identities. One country after another has developed a system of universal education at the point when it was trying to transform itself into a modern state, populated by citizens rather than subjects, with a common culture and a shared national identity. As we saw in the case of the United States in the early nineteenth century, the key problem during this transitional period is how to establish a modern social order based on exchange relations and legal authority out of the remnants of a traditional social order based on patriarchal relations and feudal authority. A system of public education helps to make this transition possible primarily by bringing a disparate group of youths in the community together under one roof and exposing them to a common curriculum and a common set of social experiences. These are among the few things that schools can consistently do well.

So the evidence shows that, at the formative stage, school systems in the United States and elsewhere have been remarkably effective in promoting citizenship and forming a new social order. This is quite an accomplishment, which more than justifies the huge investment in the initial construction of these systems. And building on this capacity for forming community, schools have continued to play an important role as the agent for incorporating newcomers. This has been particularly important in an immigrant society like the United States, where—from the Irish and Ger-

mans in the mid-nineteenth century to the Mexicans and South
Asians in the early twenty-first century—schools have been the
central mechanism for integrating foreigners into the American
experience.

But the ability of schooling to promote democratic equality in
the United States has had little to do with learning, has faded
over time, and has been increasingly undermined by counterten-
dencies toward inequality. Let's consider each of these issues in
turn. First, note that when schools have been effective at community building, this had little to with the content of the curriculum or the nature of classroom teaching. What was important was
that schools provided a common socialization for all students.
What they actually learned from school subjects was irrelevant as
long as they all were exposed to the same material. The core of
learning was cultural rather than academic. The sheer irrele-
vance of the school curriculum is an important factor that helps
explain why this curriculum has changed so slowly over the last
two hundred years, while the society was changing dramatically.
Even after fifty years of an all-out assault on the traditional curriculum by both branches of the progressive movement, students
were still spending the majority of their time on the core academic subjects of math, science, English, and history. It was the
form of schooling more than its content that helped establish
and preserve the American republic.

Second, the importance of schooling in forming community
has declined over time. The common school system was critically
important in the formative days of the American republic; but
once the country's continued existence was no longer in doubt,
the political role of the system grew less critical. Reinforcing
community is a routine matter compared to the crisis-intervention
mode that characterized the early common school. As a result,
the more recent ways in which schools have come to promote
citizenship have been more formalistic than substantive. The
residue of this political goal is now found mostly in classes on
American history, speeches at school assemblies, pilgrim pageants

around Thanksgiving, presidential portraits on classroom walls, and the pause for the national anthem before football games. What had been the system's foreground rationale for existence has now retreated into the background of a system more concerned with other issues.

Third, and most important, however, the role of schools in promoting democratic equality has declined because schools have simultaneously been aggressively promoting social inequality. One of the recurring themes of this book is that every move by American schools in the direction of equality has been countered by a strong move in the opposite direction. When we created a common school system in the early nineteenth century, we also created a high school system to distinguish middle-class students from the rest. When we expanded access to the high school at the start of the twentieth century, we also created a system for tracking students within the school and opened the gates for middle-class enrollment in college. When we expanded access to college in the mid-twentieth century, we funneled new students into the lower tiers of the system and encouraged middle-class students to pursue graduate study. The American school system is at least as much about social difference as about social equality. In fact, as the system has developed, the idea of equality has become more formalistic, focused primarily on the notion of broad access to education at a certain level, while the idea of inequality has become more substantive, embodied in starkly different educational and social outcomes.

Social Efficiency

In the language of educational policy, the goal of social efficiency is alive and well. It is one of the fundamental beliefs of contemporary economics, international development, and educational policy that education plays a central role in economic development as a valuable investment in human capital.[2] As we saw in Chapter 1, this has become an increasingly central theme in the language of school reform in the United States, starting with the administrative progressives and all the way through the rest of the reform efforts in the twentieth century. Today it's hard to find a political speech, reform document, or op-ed article about education that does not include a paean to the critical role that education plays in developing human capital and spurring economic growth—and the need to improve schools in order to fix what's wrong with the economy.

Since this argument is so important in the politics of education— some refer to it as "the education gospel"[3]—I will provide an extended discussion of it in the following chapter so we can consider the implications and limitations of this argument in depth. Suffice it to say for now that I am highly skeptical about the claims that American schooling is a major factor in promoting economic growth and economic opportunity. Schooling may well have a significant economic effect at particular points of development (like the start of industrialization) and for particular kinds of education (elementary schooling); the evidence is less convincing for this proposition at a general level. A variety of studies suggest a more complex story.[4] Maybe educational investment spurs economic growth, but maybe societies start investing more heavily in education as a result of economic growth—because they can afford to and because to do so is a sign of their emergence as modern nation-states. So it is unclear if schooling and school reform have been having anything more than a sporadic impact on human capital development.

Social Mobility

In liberal democracies in general, and in the United States in particular, hope springs eternal that expanding educational opportunity will increase social mobility and reduce social inequality. This has been a prime factor in the rhetoric of the American educational reform movements for desegregation, standards, and choice. But the evidence to support this hope simply doesn't exist. The problem is this: as they relate to schooling, both social mobility and social equality are purely relative measures of social position. Both are cases of what social scientists call a zero sum game: $A + B = 0$. If A goes up then B must go down in order to keep the sum at zero. If one person gets ahead of someone else on the social ladder, then that other person has fallen behind. And if the social differences between two people become more equal, then the increase in social advantage for one person means the decrease in social advantage for the other. Symmetry is built into both measures.

Although social equality is inherently relative, it is possible to think of social mobility in terms of absolute rather than relative position. During the twentieth century in the United States, the proportion of agricultural, manufacturing, construction, and other blue-collar workers declined while the proportion of clerical, managerial, professional, service, and other white-collar workers rose. At the same time the proportion of people with a grade-school education declined while the proportion with high school, college, and graduate education rose. So large numbers of families had an experience in which parents were blue collar and their children white collar; parents had modest education and their children had substantially more education. In absolute terms, therefore, social mobility from blue-collar to white-collar work during this period was substantial, as children not only moved up in job classification compared to their parents but also attained higher pay and a higher standard of living. And this social mobility was closely related to a substantial rise in education levels. This was a great success story, and it is understandable that those involved would attribute these social gains to education. For large numbers of Americans, it seemed to confirm the adage: To get a good job, get a good education. Schooling helped people move up the ladder.

At the individual level, this perception was quite correct. In the twentieth century, it became the norm for employers to set minimum educational qualifications for jobs, and in general the amount of education required rose as you moved up the occupational ladder. This was generally more true for initial hires than for later promotions, and it didn't include the less bureaucratic and more entrepreneurial sectors (Silicon Valley startups are often populated with college dropouts); but youths overall had a strong incentive to pursue more education in order to reap social and economic rewards. Economic studies regularly demonstrate a varying but substantial return on a family's investment in education for their children. For example, one estimate shows that males between 1914 and 2005 earned a premium in lifetime earnings for every year of college that ranged from 8 to 14 percent.[5] That makes education a great investment for families—better than the stock market, which had an average annual return of about 8 percent during the same period.

What is true for some individuals, however, is not necessarily true for society as a whole. First, although gaining more education gives an individual an advantage in competing for a particular job, it is not clear that producing a large increase in the number of college graduates creates a large increase in the number of higher-level jobs for these graduates to fill. In the next chapter I will explore the relation between education and economy—the human capital question—in detail, but for now let me just say that I'm not convinced that greater education causes greater productivity and economic growth. The two are certainly correlated, but I would argue that the causation can also go the other way: economic growth leads to educational growth since such societies can afford to invest more in education, which is what consumers want and what advanced societies are expected to do.[6]

To me it seems more plausible to look at the connection between education and jobs this way: the economy creates jobs, and education is the way we allocate people to those jobs. Candidates with more education qualify for better jobs. What this means is that social mobility becomes a relative thing, which depends on the number of individuals with a particular level of education at a given time and the number of positions requiring this level of education that are available at that time. If there are more positions than candidates at that level, all of the qualified candidates get the jobs along with some who have lower qualifications;

but if there are more candidates than positions, then some qualified applicants will end up in lower-level positions. So the economic value of education varies according to the job market. An
increase in education without a corresponding increase in higher-
level jobs in the economy will reduce the value of a degree in the
market for educational credentials.

This poses a problem for the chances of social mobility between parents and children. After all, children are not competing
with their parents for jobs; they're competing with peers. And
like themselves, their peers have a higher level of education than
their parents do. In relative terms, they only have an advantage
in the competition for jobs if they have gained even more education than their peers have. Educational gains relative to peers are
what matter, not gains relative to parents. As a result, rates of
social mobility have not increased over time as educational opportunity has increased, and societies with more expansive educational systems do not have higher mobility rates.[7]

Raymond Boudon and others have shown that the problem is
that increases in access to education affect everyone, both those
who are trying to get ahead and those who are already ahead.[8]
Early in the twentieth century, working-class parents had a grade-
school education and their children poured into high schools in
order to get ahead; but at the same time, middle-class parents had
a high school education and their children were pouring into
colleges. So both groups increased education and their relative
position remained the same. The new high school graduates didn't
get ahead by getting more education; they were running just to
stay in place. The new college graduates didn't necessarily get
ahead either, but they did manage to stay ahead.

The families who are already gaining an advantage from education have more than simple greed compelling them to push
their children to ever-higher levels of educational attainment in
the face of pressure from those below them on the social scale.
They have a very realistic fear that if they don't do this their chil-

dren will face downward social mobility. Since relative position is necessarily symmetrical, what goes up must be balanced by what goes down. When you're near the top of the system, there's not much farther to go up but a long way to go down. A recent study examined the mobility between American parents and their children, comparing the relative position by income of parents in the late 1960s and their children thirty years later in the late 1990s. Families in the lowest 20 percent (lowest quintile) by income had a 58 percent chance of having their children move up by at least one quintile, while families in the top 20 percent had a 58 percent chance of having their children move down by at least one quintile and a 34 percent chance of falling two or more quintiles (below the 60th percentile).[9] With a trap door opening up beneath them, families who benefit from an educational edge feel they need to scramble for more education in order to keep their children from falling through.

So school reform in the United States has failed to increase social mobility or reduce social inequality. In fact, without abandoning our identity as a liberal democracy, there was simply no way that educational growth could have brought about these changes. School reform can only have a chance to equalize social differences if it can reduce the educational gap between middle-class students and working-class students. This is politically impossible in a liberal democracy, since it would mean restricting the ability of the middle class to pursue more and better education for their children. If we aren't willing to cap the educational opportunities for the advantaged, then increasing those opportunities for the disadvantaged will make no difference. As long as both groups gain more education in parallel, then the advantages of the one over the other will not decline. And that is exactly the situation in the American school system. It's the compromise that has emerged from the interaction between reform and market, between social planning and consumer action: we expand opportunity and preserve advantage, both at the same time. We want it both ways. From this perspective, the defining moment in the history of American education was the construction of the tracked comprehensive high school, which was a joint creation of consumers and reformers in the progressive era. That set the pattern for everything that followed. It's a system that is remarkably effective at allowing both access and advantage, but it's not one that reformers tried to create. In fact, it works against the realization of central aims of reform, since it undermines social efficiency, blocks social mobility, and limits democratic equality.

These three goals, however, have gained expression in the American educational system in at least two significant ways. First, they have maintained a highly visible presence in the educational *rhetoric,* as the politics of education continuously pushes these goals onto the schools and the schools themselves actively express their allegiance to these same goals. Second, schools have adopted the *form* of these goals into their structure and process. Democratic equality has persisted in the formalism of social studies classes, school assemblies, and the display of political symbols. Social efficiency has persisted in the formalism of vocational classes, career days, and standards-based testing. Social mobility has persisted in the formalism of the grades, credits, and degrees that students accumulate as they move through the school system.

THE SOCIAL IMPACT OF MAJOR SCHOOL REFORM MOVEMENTS

We have been considering the failure of school reform in general to accomplish its overarching goals in the last two hundred years. But another way to examine the limits of reform is to look at the social outcomes of individual reform movements in the United States. I will now consider the impact of the major reform efforts in the history of American education: the movements for the common school, progressivism, desegregation, standards, and choice.

Common School Movement

As we saw in Chapter 2, the common school movement is the exception that proves the rule about American school reform, the one reform that really worked. It established itself as the model institution for shaping the new social order in the American liberal republic, neatly balancing the responsibilities of citizenship with the liberties of the free market. Conceiving the problem as the need to create order through internal rather than external control, the common school reformers developed a school system designed to provide a shared socialization for the entire white community, one that instilled in every student a commitment to civic virtue and to a new set of social norms. As a result, they helped create a new kind of self-regulating citizen and entrepreneur, who was able to function effectively in the emerging economic and political life of the nation.

A number of factors converged to make this movement so successful. First, the crisis was frightening in its implications, overshadowing any of the social problems that prompted later school reforms. This helped to concentrate the minds of reformers and created a convergence between educational and other reform efforts unlike any seen since. So the movement for common schools emerged in a parallel and mutually reinforcing manner with movements for penitentiaries, insane asylums, juvenile reformatories, hospitals, and poorhouses. Second, the educational strand of this larger reform movement was not an extension of the larger movement, as was true with educational progressivism, but the other way around, since the common school served as the model for the others and supplied the core principle that made them operative—to socialize the new, self-regulating individual.

Third, common school reform asked education to provide something that was within its institutional capacity. Socialization was what the new social order needed, and that was exactly what the new common school was able to deliver. Schools can indeed assemble people under one roof, give them a common experience, and instill habits and norms and values into them as part of the process. Note that this success did not depend on students learning the specific academic content of the curriculum, since the content (aside for civics, perhaps) was beside the point of their central mission. One key problem with later reform movements was that they asked schools to take on social problems (such as health, poverty, race, economic growth) that could not be dealt with effectively using the primary tool that schools could supply, socializing individuals. Also, they started thinking of the schools as a system for delivering curriculum content to students, which is not what its founders had in mind.

Fourth, the common school movement enjoyed the great advantage of being able to create the American school system instead of trying to adapt an existing system that had been created for other purposes. They left all of their school reform successors to deal with the latter problem. Progressives had to wrestle with a system designed to support a liberal republic and make it the right vehicle for adapting to a corporate industrial society. And the late-twentieth-century reformers had to try to reconstruct the system again to serve the needs of a postindustrial society.

Progressive Movement

In chapters 3 and 4 we saw how the progressive movement struggled to have an impact on schools. Its biggest effect was on the rhetoric of reform. It managed to transform the way we thought about education, turning attention away from the common school's political vision of education to a more utilitarian economic vision. The idea of education for social efficiency is still in the forefront of the politics of American education, a strong legacy of the administrative progressives. We can't discuss schooling today without portraying it as a prudent investment in human capital that will serve as a major engine of the economy. In addition to this rhetorical effect, the administrative progressives had some impact on the structure of the system, in particular by creating a tracked and differentiated formal curriculum. But the movement had remarkably little impact on teaching and learning in classrooms. The educational core of the school system emerged from fifty years of continuing reform with changes that were at best superficial.

So progressives didn't transform learning, but did they succeed in addressing the larger social problems that set the reform in motion in the first place? The answer is more no than yes. The problem that prompted the progressive movement was to establish a new social order in the age of corporate industrialism, one that was appropriate for an increasingly urban and immigrant society in which the old forms of social opportunity were fading. For the working class, apprenticeship was long dead, work was increasingly deskilled, and the opportunities for moving up were blocked by a factory system that put the conception of the manufacturing process in the hands of management and left workers with the job of executing someone else's plan. For the middle class, the small shop and independent tradesman were dying, which meant that parents could no longer pass along social position to their children by giving them the store; and in the administrative realm the promotion ladder from clerk to manager was broken. The result on both sides was rampant insecurity about how to negotiate the new order and provide opportunity for one's children, as the working class saw faint hope for upward mobility and the middle class saw a real prospect for downward mobility.

As we have seen, the progressive era provided a remarkably ingenious institutional response to the problems faced by both groups, the creation of the tracked comprehensive high school. For working-class families, access to high school offered the chance for their children to acquire scarce and valuable educational credentials and pick up clerical skills, which in combination might gain them entry into white-collar work. For middle-class families, the new high school promised to buffer their children from the new hordes of high school students by placing them in the academically oriented upper track, which then would funnel them into college, the new zone of educational exclusivity. Each group of educational consumers got what it needed from the new high school, access for one and advantage for the other, and the terms of this compromise have served as the model for the American school system ever since. It was an extraordinary act of institutional innovation, which was perfectly suited to the troubles of the times.

The credit or blame for this invention, however, cannot be laid at the feet of the educational progressives. Some of the men who led the charge for administrative progressivism, such as David Snedden, were fervently opposed to the comprehensive high school. Snedden argued for a series of radically specialized, vocational high schools that would have taken American education in a very different direction. His "schools for the rank and file" would have clearly telegraphed to working-class families that their children were being channeled back into working-class jobs.[10] And this kind of class-based educational segregation would have also denied middle-class families the legitimacy that came from having their children rise to the top on their apparent merits in open competition at a comprehensive high school. The compromise version of progressivism that emerged in the *Cardinal Principles* report in 1918 embraced the comprehensive high school model, but only after it had already become an accomplished fact in the preceding decade.

As I explained in Chapter 3, the most fundamental educational change that occurred in the progressive era, the comprehensive high school, emerged through an interaction between the progressive reform movement and the educational credentials market. Working-class consumers demanded access, middle-class consumers demanded advantage, and progressive reformers adapted their doctrinaire scheme for the vocational high school to accommodate these market pressures. Therefore, this transformational change in the educational system, which constituted an effective response to the social crisis at the turn of the twentieth century, is not one we can place in the win column for progressive reformers. Instead, consumers thrust it upon them and the reformers had to go along.

If the administrative progressives were more reactive than transformative in responding to the status anxieties of their times, they were flat-out failures in trying to bring about the brave new world of social efficiency that they saw as their central mission. As we saw, they weren't able to do much more than embed the idea of school for work within the institution of schooling. Vocational courses never constituted more than a small portion of the curriculum, which continued to be dominated by the traditional school subjects against which both kinds of progressives had railed for so long. And even these vocational courses never managed to play a significant role in the preparation of students for their future occupational roles. The problem was the one that stumped Snedden, namely, that it's simply impossible for schools to provide students with the specific skills and knowledge they will need in order to be productive in particular job roles later in life.

One thing that killed vocational education was the sheer diversity of job roles. There was no way that schools could possibly provide special training programs for each of the thousands of jobs that were waiting beyond the schoolhouse door. The resulting curriculum complexity was completely unrealistic for a school system to provide, as the more pragmatic progressives like Charles Kingsley were ultimately willing to concede. A second thing that killed vocational education was the fact that preparing students with specific skills for future work in a dynamic economy is essentially futile. Graduates need to be able to function effectively in job roles that may not even exist when they're in school and to use technologies that have not yet been invented. The one thing that vocational education has always been good at is providing students with obsolete equipment on which they can learn the outmoded skills required for dying occupations. So the progressives ultimately settled for a formalistic version of vocationalism, which waved in the direction of occupational relevance without seriously trying to attain it. Boys learned to make tie racks and ash trays in shop class while girls learned about place settings and sewing in home economics.

So was there anything that the progressive education movement did on its own accord that could be seen as a successful response to the social crisis that originally got them in motion? One thing they did succeed at was Americanizing immigrants in the public schools. The flow of immigrants at the start of the twentieth century was the highest in American history, and unlike their Anglo and Saxon predecessors during the common school era, the newcomers tended to hail from southern and eastern Europe, bringing with them foreign languages and foreign (that is, non-Protestant) faiths. Fear was rampant that American culture and society couldn't handle this influx of the Other without losing its identity.

But schools came to the rescue. By expanding access to secondary education and by using the lure that some form of schooling might be useful in getting a good job, the progressives were able to draw large numbers of the new immigrants into an extended educational experience, which in turn was effective at imbuing in the newcomers a facility in the English language and a familiarity with American culture. This, of course, was hardly an innovation of the progressives. That kind of assimilation process had been at the heart of the common school movement as well, part of its effort to construct the new citizen of the republic. And—unlike so many other things they have been asked to do—assimilation is something that schools have always been able to accomplish if given the chance. They're good at building community.

Desegregation Movement

Bringing people together was also the central mission of the desegregation movement in the 1950s, 1960s, and 1970s. In this sense, the movement drew on the long history of the American school system as a medium for realizing the slogan on the dollar bill, *e pluribus unum,* turning a diversity of social classes, nationalities, cultures, languages, religions—and now races—into a single community. To do this has always been within the realm of possibility for schools, and it was the primary contribution that both the common school and progressive movements had made to the social problems that provoked them. The social problem that provoked the desegregation movement was the long-standing tradition of racial inequality in the United States, which had restricted black attendance to separate schools that were usually deficient in terms of resources and educational opportunities. So for civil rights leaders, the public school system seemed a natural place to concentrate their efforts for racial equality. Schools were both a key problem for racial equality that required a fix and also a natural medium for carrying the ideal of racial equality into other areas of American life. The South was the main target initially, since that was where racially segregated schools were mandated by law, but the movement later spread to the North, where segregation was more often a result of custom and residency.

So the desegregation movement took the one-hundred-year-old idea that schools can create community through social inclusion and extended it to race. Two additional branches of the movement for inclusion spun out of the desegregation effort. One was the effort to enhance the educational experience of girls in American schools, which meant seeking to incorporate the female experience and perspective more fully into the curriculum, encouraging girls to pursue studies in areas like math and science that had long been seen as the preserve of boys, and developing course units to challenge gender stereotypes. The other was the effort to include students with disabilities within the regular school and the regular classroom, which came to a head with the passage of the federal Education of All Handicapped Children Act in 1975.[11] This law mandated that students with handicaps should receive the special educational supports they need and should be allowed access to education in the least restrictive environment.

The Supreme Court's *Brown* decision in 1954 was a watershed moment in American history, sweeping away the long-standing legal principle that had declared racial segregation constitutional as long as the separate schools were equal. At one level, the consequences of this decision were profound, since it put the full force of law and the full weight of constitutional values behind the ideal of racial equality. In this sense, the desegregation movement was enormously successful. Within thirty years or so, Americans became surprisingly comfortable with the idea that their children would be attending schools with students from a mixture of races. Integration had become normal. For example, Gerald Grant's study of an upstate New York high school from 1950 to 1980 shows that, after a great deal of tension arose when this white school turned into a mixed-race school in the 1960s, the atmosphere became calm by the mid-seventies, as students and faculty both settled into the new institutional norm.[12]

But while whites gradually came to accept the principle of integrated schools, they were not nearly as comfortable with the possibility of sending their children to a school where minority students were anything close to a majority of the student body. In practice, American schools today are only slightly less segregated than they were before the *Brown* decision. About 70 percent of black students are currently enrolled in schools where blacks are in the majority, and more than a third are in schools where the minority proportion is more than 90 percent.[13] As a result, the impact of the desegregation movement has been more formal than substantive. It helped establish the principle of racial equality in schools, but the practice of separate and unequal schooling for whites and blacks is still standard.

The desegregation movement ran into difficulties that undercut its effectiveness, and at the heart was a problem of politics and markets. In the 1970s reformers discovered that ending legal segregation by itself was unable to create integrated schools. Since blacks and whites tended to live in different neighborhoods, their children for the most part were still attending schools with students of the same color. The effort to attack de facto segregation led reformers, and for a time the federal courts, to push for busing students to schools in other neighborhoods for the purpose of more fully integrating education. But this approach did not last very long. It ran into huge opposition from middle-class whites, who voted overwhelmingly against school busing with both their ballots and their feet. Politicians who supported busing found themselves in increasingly hot water with white voters, and districts that promoted it found that large numbers of white families were sending their children to private schools or moving to the suburbs.

This was another case of markets interacting with politics to reshape school practice. In the zero-sum struggle for social mobility, any effort to increase opportunity for one group is experienced as a loss of opportunity for another. Whites felt they were losing what had been an advantaged form of education for their children, and the prospect of sending their children to a school with a large minority population signaled a frightening prospect of social decline. At the same time, the busing movement ran into a problem with black leaders, who began to think of it as the wrong direction for both cultural and educational reasons. The idea that black children could only do well in a school with a large number of white students seemed culturally insulting, as though being around whites in itself would constitute social improvement. In addition, given the reality that busing was going nowhere fast, it seemed more sensible to focus attention on seeking improvement in the quality of education at the nearly all-black schools in many urban districts.

The desegregation movement had two limitations that were built into its DNA. As we saw in Chapter 1, the *Brown* decision took an approach to reform that depicted desegregation as an issue of consumer rights. The problem was that education had become a valuable commodity for Americans, which meant that denying a group equal access to this commodity posed a severe restriction to that group's ability to get ahead socially. So the movement in its legal form depicted education as a private good, whose benefits accrue to the owner. This made it hard to sell desegregation to whites, especially when the issue moved from attacking legal segregation to attacking the neighborhood school, since it suggested that the gain for blacks would be at the expense of whites. The broader civil rights movement pitched equality as a matter of constitutional principle, a way to realize one of the truths that Americans have long held self- evident. Portraying education as a public good like this, whose benefits accrue to society as a whole and not just to the individual educational consumer, could have broadened the appeal of the effort to achieve substantive integration of schools. But this was not the road taken by *Brown*.

Another inherent limitation to the desegregation movement was the way it characterized race as an individual phenomenon, a matter of racial prejudice, instead of a structural phenomenon, built into the larger patterns of economy, society, and social class. One advantage to this approach for school reform was that the individual view of race provided a prominent role for education in the larger quest for racial equality. If individual prejudice was the problem, then schools must be the most promising answer. Schools are a plausible institution for bringing different groups together under one roof and accommodating them to each other. And schools as an institution have a long history of being able to instill common values into students; in attacking racism this would mean teaching lessons that undermine prejudiced beliefs and replace them with more generous assessments of minorities. Of course, this would only work if indeed race prejudice was the root of the race problem, but the course of the desegregation movement seems not to have borne out this view. The issue that shut down busing and the broader effort to end de facto segregation was the competition between status groups for social advantage, which is driven not only or even necessarily by prejudiced belief but by rational calculation of relative interest.

Standards and Choice Movements

It is premature to talk about the outcomes of the standards movement and choice movement in the United States, because at this
stage (I'm writing in the year 2010) both are still works in progress. We don't know where they will end up. But it is possible to
say something about the approaches they have taken and the difficulties they have encountered up until now.

Both movements have clearly learned something about the
process of school reform from a study of its recent history, and
they have organized themselves in a way that demonstrates a de-
termination to avoid repeating the errors of their predecessors.
In particular, both have been quite strategic in organizing their
reform efforts in ways that they hope will allow them to get
around organizational and educational factors that stymied progressive reform, the factors I detailed in chapters 4 and 5. Both
have been deliberately working to make the school system more
tightly coupled, increase administrative control over instruction,
and reduce the autonomy of the teacher.

For the standards movement, this has meant using a combination of high-stakes testing, curriculum standards, and accountability measures. The standards set state-learning goals for each
grade and each subject; tests seek to determine the extent to which
students have learned this material at a sufficiently advanced level;
and in combination these factors hold both students and teachers
accountable for accomplishing learning goals. Testing is the key
link here. The point is to make the test results loom large in the
lives of both teachers and students in order to motivate the one
to teach more effectively and the other to learn more effectively.
The motivating factor for students is that test scores at certain
critical junctures will determine whether they are promoted to
the next grade, whether they will graduate from high school, and
what kind of diploma they will receive. The motivations for
teachers are more complex. One factor is professionalism. No
teacher wants to be the cause of the failure of his or her students,

so teachers can be counted on to work hard to teach to the test and thus raise their students' test scores. Another factor is pride. Teachers want to hold their heads high about their accomplishments and those of their school, but this is hard to do if the annual report cards for their school show scores that are below average or declining or both.

For the choice movement, the key to the goal of breaking down the classroom door and reshaping the teaching and learning that goes on there is not to advocate adding new layers of bureaucracy for the existing school system the way the standards movement proposes (by adding curriculum guidelines, testing machinery, promotion and graduation standards, and school report cards). Instead, choice reformers want to blow up the entire structure and start over. Unlike their counterparts in the standards movement, they have embraced the consumerism at the heart of the *Brown* decision and raised it to the central principle of schools. Instead of fighting the way consumers voted with their feet against the enforcement of the common school ideal, they have adopted the consumer approach as their own.

Choice reformers argue that the current structure of the system, still bearing the heavy stamp of the common school movement, is fundamentally flawed and needs to be replaced. Democratic control through elected school boards, they say, is inherently inefficient, nonresponsive to educational consumers, and prone to a particularly stultifying form of bureaucracy. So they seek to create schools outside of the framework of the traditional school district and freed from its political intrusions and administrative constraints. This can be done by developing charter schools— public schools with an independent charter—or in a purer form by giving every student a voucher, set at the value of the per capita public school appropriation in the area, and allowing the student to spend this money at any public or private school of the family's choice. The argument is that these measures empower the educational consumer by creating an educational market in which schools compete to attract and retain students.

Such schools, the choice reformers say, will need to be lean and entrepreneurial organizations, highly sensitive to the demands of their students. The result will be a tightly coupled school and close teacher alignment with school goals.

So the standards and choice movements learned from the organizational failures of the progressives that they needed to find a way to reduce teacher autonomy; they also learned from the political successes of the desegregation movement that they needed to reframe reform around a political argument for equality. Both movements had made only limited progress until the late 1990s, when they both added a political appeal to their arguments for reform (as we saw in Chapter 1). Since then both movements have gained momentum—the standards movement through the adoption of the No Child Left Behind law in 2002, and the choice movement through a rapid expansion of charter schools across the country and the launching of major public experiments with school vouchers in places like Milwaukee and Washington, DC.

Although the two movements have drawn similar insights from their predecessors about the process of school reform, they have drawn sharply different lessons from the history of reform about the content of schooling. The choice movement has been agnostic on the subject of what the content of learning should be, since that decision has been left up to the forces of student demand in the education market. What they have held against the administrative progressives is the top-down way in which that movement sought to establish its educational goals, and they have had the same objections to the approach taken by the standards movement.

The standards movement, in contrast, is strongly focused on content. Its whole aim has been to establish what subject matter students should learn and then set up mechanisms to ensure that they really learn this material. And its content aims have been a direct reaction to the administrative progressives. On the one hand, the standards movement has adopted the central theme of

Snedden, Kingsley, and Cubberley: the need for a school system devoted to social efficiency. Human capital theory is at the very heart of the standards movement, and its arguments continually come back to the economic value of schools. On the other hand, standards reformers are diametrically opposed to the way the progressives organized school content. In many ways, their movement is an effort to remedy the problems that progressives brought to American schooling by inflicting on it a radical form of fragmentation and differentiation. If the progressives were all about tailoring a multiplicity of curricula to the abilities and social trajectories of individual students, the standards reformers have been all about creating a single, coherent curriculum that will be shared by all students. In many ways, the standards movement has harkened back to the Committee of Ten Report from the 1890s and the common school movement from before the Civil War, both of which emphasized curriculum commonality.

What are the prospects for success in the reform efforts to promote educational standards and school choice? It's hard to say at this stage, about thirty years into these two ongoing reform efforts whose end is not yet in sight. But one thing is evident: both reforms represent radical departures from the past, from which both have been trying to learn.

In some ways, the choice movement is the more radical of the two, since it rejects the entire framework of the American school system that was created by the common schoolmen and tinkered with by progressives, inclusionists, and standards promoters. It wants to start over with an entirely different model, drawn from markets rather than politics. This is both a strength and a weakness. The strength is that it attacks directly the organizational and educational elements in the system that have been so effective over the years at deflecting, diluting, and defeating the efforts of school reformers to shape teaching and learning in classrooms. Starting over with a brand-new system modeled after a more individualistic and consumer-oriented ideal gives them the possibility of attaining their goal in the way that the common school reformers were able to do when they too started a system from scratch.

The weakness is that choice threatens a system that has a large number of stakeholders who are heavily invested in it. Teachers and their unions seem quite resistant to any move that undercuts the structures of labor negotiation and professional practice that they have developed over the years within the current system. Political leaders are reluctant to dismantle a structure that is as large and deep-rooted as this one. And citizens have a strong investment in the system through their own experience with it as students and through the central role that schooling as an institution has long played in social, political, and economic life. Throwing out the system and starting over with something radically different may just seem too risky. And there's one more factor. Polls over the years have consistently shown the same pattern in public attitudes toward schools: people feel that schools in general are in trouble and need to be fixed, but in contrast they rate their own children's schools much more positively.[14] So there is perpetually a stronger interest in reforming other people's schools than in meddling with our own.

The standards movement is content to keep the school system in much its current form, as long as it can tighten up administrative control and break down the traditional barrier to the classroom. So in this way its approach to school reform is less draconian. It proposes more than a little tinkering with the system but less than a total tear-down. But in a different sense it is more radical than the choice movement, since it is the first educational reform movement in American history that is seeking to make students learn the content of the academic curriculum. This may seem like a strange statement, since one would think that any school system is trying to teach content. True, schools in general expect teachers to teach the curriculum. But as we have seen, the connection between this expectation and the practice of teaching in individual classrooms has been weak indeed. And reform movements have either not tried or not succeeded in promoting a particular kind of learning. Common school reformers were not interested in promoting particular forms of knowledge; they just wanted students to learn something in common, the content of which was more or less arbitrary. The administrative progressives made a case for the economic value of having students learn particular job-related skills and knowledge in school, but they did not manage to change the system in a way that would allow schools to realize this goal. They were not able to change teaching and learning in the classroom, so their reform of the curriculum was more formalistic than substantive. The inclusion movement involved some curriculum changes, but its main focus was on creating a different mix of bodies in the classroom rather than a different kind of learning.

In contrast, standards reformers have pitched all their hopes on the effort to increase student mastery of the academic curriculum. They argue that by learning math, science, English, and social studies, in greater depth and in alignment with curriculum standards, students will become more productive workers and America will become a stronger nation. This is brand new in the history of American school reform. Schools have long tried to attain social goals such as equality, efficiency, and mobility. They have sought to instill attitudes like civic virtue and racial tolerance. They have worked to incorporate immigrants and minorities into the community. And they have tried to mediate the conflicting tensions in the social class system. But they have never before tried hard to get students to learn academic subjects. Given their strategic effort to work around factors that have impeded reformers in the past—such as loose coupling and teacher autonomy—they may have a chance of making some progress toward this goal. But, as I explain in the following chapter, it is not at all clear that increasing the achievement level of American students in the core academic subjects will in fact succeed in raising productivity and spurring the economy. The connection between academic learning and economic growth is uncertain at best, and it may be that learning the curriculum is less useful for American students than learning to do school.

ROOTS OF THE FAILURE OF SCHOOL REFORM
TO RESOLVE SOCIAL PROBLEMS

In closing, let me summarize the reasons for the continuing failure of school reform in the United States.

The Tensions among School Goals. One reason for the failure of reform to realize the social goals expressed in it is that these goals reflect the core tensions within a liberal democracy, which push both school and society in conflicting directions. One of those tensions is between the demands of democratic politics and the demands of capitalist markets. A related issue is the requirement that society be able to meet its collective needs while simultaneously guaranteeing the liberty of individuals to pursue their own interests. As we have seen, these tensions cannot be resolved one way or the other if we are going to remain a liberal democracy, so schools will inevitably fail at maximizing any of these goals. The result is going to be a muddled compromise rather than a clear-cut victory in meeting particular expectations. The apparently dysfunctional outcomes of the educational system, therefore, are not necessarily the result of bad planning, deception, or political cynicism; they are an institutional expression of the contradictions in the liberal democratic mind.

The Tendency toward Organizational Conservatism. There is another layer of impediment that lies between social goals and their fulfillment via education, and that is the tension between education's social goals and its organizational practices. Schools gain their origins from social goals, which they dutifully express in an institutional form, as happened with the construction of the common school system. This results in the development of school organization, curriculums, pedagogies, professional roles, and a complex set of occupational and organizational interests. At this more advanced stage, schools and educators are no longer simply the media for realizing social aspirations; they become major actors in the story. As such, they shape what happens in education in light of their own needs, interests, organizational patterns, professional norms, and teaching practices. And this then becomes a major issue in educational reform. Such reforms are what happens after schooling is already in motion organizationally, when society seeks to assign new ideals to education or revive old ones that seem to be in disuse, thus initiating an effort to transform the institution toward the pursuit of different ends. But at that point society is no longer able simply to project its values onto the institution it created to express these values; instead it must negotiate an interaction with an ongoing enterprise. As a result, reform has to change both the values embedded in education and the formal structure itself, which may well resist. As we saw in chapters 4 and 5, a combination of loose coupling, weak instructional control, and teacher autonomy have made the organization of American schooling remarkably effective at blocking reforms from reaching the classroom.

Sociologist Arthur Stinchcombe wrote a classic essay in 1965 about the problem of why organizational forms tend to resist change.[15] He noted that a particular type of organization tends to reflect the values and concerns and technologies and needs of the period in which it first arose, and then it continues on in much the original form, even when the social conditions around it change substantially. He saw three factors in particular that help explain why an organizational form may persist over time. It turns out that all three apply to the case of education in the United States.

One factor is that at their formation organizations acquire a rationale for their existence, which becomes the way for them to explain themselves to the public and which anchors the ideology of the people who work within them. For the school system in the United States, the common school movement provided the system's rationale as "the school of the republic." It was the place that would instill citizenship and help create the moral order of a republican market society. The school system transmitted this belief in the value of the system to its students and institutionalized the belief in the process of socializing its teachers and administrators. This original political goal of American schooling has remained fundamental to its identity and its social legitimacy. Both the standards and choice movements found out quickly that they would not be able to make headway unless they tapped into that political rationale to justify their own reform efforts. And this has continued as a source of resistance by the public to any attempts to do more than tinker with the system, since a frontal assault on it would constitute an assault on its political values. This has put reformers in the delicate position of having to push for a change in the system without directly challenging its legitimacy.

A second reason that a form of organization may resist change is that it may not have any serious competitors. As the publicly governed and supported system of education in the United States, the public school system has never had to face this kind of challenge. From the beginning, religious and independent schools have existed alongside the public system, but enrollments in the nonpublic sector of education have never exceeded 10 percent of the total number of students. The choice movement in particular has attacked on this point, declaring that schools are a public monopoly and aiming to liberate education from this stranglehold in order to allow multiple types of new schools to arise. But with its ability to control schooling for 90 percent of the families in the country, the public school system has not felt threatened by the competition from the nonpublic sector and has not felt compelled to adapt to the alternative forms of schooling around it.[16]

A third reason for organizational conservatism is that an organization type may persist in the face of competition with other types because it is effective in what it sets out to do. Why turn to another model if the existing system is working? Reformers, of course, need to prepare the way for their proposed changes in

education by showing in detail that the present system of schooling is failing to meet its goals. This is a standard claim in any
reform tract: first show what's wrong and then show how to fix
it. But the argument I developed in chapters 4 and 5 suggested
that the loose coupling of the system and the considerable autonomy of the classroom teacher may have persisted for so long,
frustrating the aims of one set of reformers after another, because
these forms of organization are in fact effective at promoting
learning. It may be that schools and teachers need to be buffered
against intrusions from the outside in order to work out the best
way to adapt instruction to the needs of particular groups of
students.

The Curse of the Doctrinaire. Another problem that leads to the failure of school reform is the issue that James Scott raises about modern efforts at social engineering in general: arrogance abounds.
School reformers spin out an abstract vision of what schools, and
by extension society, should be, and then they try to bring reality
in line with the vision. But as we saw at the end of Chapter 5, this
abstract reformist grid doesn't map comfortably onto the lumpy,
parochial, and idiosyncratic ecology of the individual classroom.
Trying to push too hard to make the classroom fit the grid may
destroy the ecology of learning there; and adapting the grid
enough to make it workable in the classroom may change the
reform to the point that its original aims are lost. Reformers are
loath to give up their aims in the service of making the reform
acceptable to teachers, so they tend to plow ahead in search of
ways to get around the obstacles. If they can't make change in
cooperation with teachers, then they will have to so in spite of
them. In a sense, then, school reformers tend to have more than a
touch of the doctrinaire in them. They see a crying need to fix a
problem through school reform, and they have developed a theory for how to do this, which looks just great on paper. Standing
in the state capital or the university, they are far from the practical realities of the classroom, and they tend to be impatient with

demands that they should respect the complexity of the settings in which they are trying to intervene.

The Marginality of School Reform to School Change. Finally, we need to remind ourselves that school reform has always been only a small part of the broader process of school change. A study of reform such as this one focuses on reform movements—the deliberate efforts by groups of people to change schools in a direction they value and to resolve a social problem that concerns them. And we measure the success of these movements by the degree to which the outcomes match the intentions of the reformers. But there's another player in the school change game, and that's what I've been calling the educational market. By this I mean the combined actions of educational consumers who are pursuing their own interests through the schooling of their children. From the colonial days, when the expressed purpose of schooling was to support the one true faith, consumers were pursuing literacy and numeracy for reasons that had nothing to do with religion and a lot to do with enhancing their ability to function in a market society.

That very personal and practical dimension of education was there from the beginning, even though no one wanted to talk about it, much less launch a reform movement in its name. And this individual dimension of schooling has only expanded its scope over the years, becoming larger in the late nineteenth century and then dominant in the twentieth century, as increasingly educational credentials became the ticket of admission for the better jobs. The fact that public schools have long been creatures of politics—established, funded, and governed through the medium of a democratic process—means that they have been under unrelenting pressure to meet consumer demand for the kind of schooling that will help them move up, stay up, or at least not fall down in their position in the social order. This pressure comes from individual consumer actions (attending school or not, going to this school not that one, enrolling in this program not some other program) and political actions (supporting expansion of educational opportunity, preserving advantage in the midst of broad access).

These actions by consumers and voters have brought about significant changes in the school system, even though these changes have not been the aim of any of the consumers themselves. They have not been acting as reformers with a social cause but as individuals pursuing their own interests through schooling, so the changes they have produced in schooling by and large have been inadvertent. Yet these unintended effects of consumer action have often derailed or redirected the intended effects of school reformers. They created the comprehensive high school, pushed vocational education to the margins, and blocked the advance of de facto desegregation. Educational consumers may well keep the standards movement from meeting its goals if they feel that standards, testing, and accountability are threatening educational access and educational advantage. They may also pose an impediment to the choice movement, even though it is being carried out explicitly in their name, since consumers may feel more comfortable tinkering with the system they know than in taking the chance that blowing up this system might produce something that is less suited to serving their needs. In the American system of education, it seems, the consumer—not the reformer—is king.

THE LIMITS OF
SCHOOL LEARNING

7

As we have seen in the previous chapters, America has had a long-standing compulsion to fix its most pressing social problems by reforming schools. For the common school men, the school's mission was to establish a new social order that would integrate a market economy with a republican government. For the progressives, the mission was to restructure the social order in order to meet the political and social needs of the new corporate industrial economy. For the last one hundred years, however, reformers have put forward a more mundane and utilitarian goal for American schools, to promote social efficiency. In practice, this has meant trying to focus the efforts of educators on the task of preparing students to be productive workers—or, in the language of modern economists, to enrich the nation's supply of human capital. Schools are being asked to provide the kinds of skill and knowledge that are called for in an economy that has been steadily shifting its emphasis from manual to mental work.

As we have also seen, however, educational consumers—the families who have been sending their children to school—have been pushing for a different educational goal: social mobility. They have been demanding a school system that would support their efforts to get ahead or stay ahead in a competitive society, where school has become the primary mechanism for deciding

which individuals get what jobs. In contrast with school reformers, consumers have been less interested in the vocational skills
that school could provide than in the occupational doors it could
open. Access to a good job and a secure social position were their
main concerns, and school was the way to gain these ends.

These reformer and consumer visions of education are starkly
different. One difference revolves around the definition of who
benefits from education. The social efficiency vision of the reformers portrays education as a public good. As an investment in the
country's stock of human capital, it makes the workforce more
productive, which in turn promotes economic development. This
investment pays dividends for everyone in the society, including
those without children in school, by increasing the standard of living, enhancing economic opportunity, and expanding the tax
base. In contrast, the social mobility vision of the consumers portrays education as a private good. Its benefits flow exclusively to
the student who receives a particular level of education, and its
value is that it offers this student an advantage in the competition
for jobs that is not enjoyed by students who failed to receive the
same level and quality of education.

Another difference between the two visions is in the value that
each places on the form versus the content of schooling. The social
efficiency vision locates the source of education's value in the
skills and knowledge that students pick up in school. From this
perspective, the learning that students acquire in the classroom
enables them to be more productive, by supplying the abilities
needed in a technologically developing economy. The social mobility vision, however, focuses on access to jobs rather than acquisition of job skills, emphasizing the way in which educational
credentials allow prospective employees to meet the minimum
requirements for better positions. From this perspective, what
students learn in the classroom is irrelevant; what matters is that
they have acquired a form of educational currency—a diploma—
which they can cash in on a good job.

So, for our understanding of the American school system, it matters a lot which of these views has in fact prevailed. If the reformers succeeded in their mission, making human capital production the driving force in American education in the twentieth century, then the most salient outcome of education during this period was learning the curriculum. But if instead the consumers succeeded, making social mobility the driving force in education, then the primary outcome of education was not classroom learning but educational credentialing.

In my view, school consumers won out over school reformers in the twentieth century. As a result, we have a school system that is focused on credentialing more than learning and whose benefits flow to the degree holder more than to economy or society. If I am right about this, then the human capital argument for schooling—which is so dominant in the language of school reform and the politics of education in the United States today—is at best overstated or at worst simply wrong. In this chapter, therefore, I explore the evidence for education as an investment in human capital, which boils down to an examination of the limits of school learning.

SCHOOLING AS A SOCIAL INVESTMENT IN HUMAN CAPITAL

The strongest argument I have seen in support of the human capital vision of education comes from a book published in 2008 with the title *The Race between Education and Technology*, which was written by economists Claudia Goldin and Lawrence Katz.[1] In this book the authors have put together an impressive array of data on American education and economy in the twentieth century, which they connect to a sophisticated historical analysis of the rapid expansion of education during the century and its links to a rapidly developing economy. They argue that the extraordinary expansion of the American economy in the twentieth century was to a large degree the result of an equally extraordinary expansion in educational enrollments during this period. It is no coincidence, they say, that what turned out to be the American Century economically for the United States was also the Human Capital Century.

The numbers are indeed staggering. In the United States, education levels rose dramatically for most of the twentieth century. If you compare those who were age 24 in 1900 and 1975, the average number of years of schooling rose a total of 6.2 years, which is an increase of 0.82 years per decade.[2] This means that the average education level of the entire U.S. population rose from less than 8 years of grade school to 2 years of college in only 75 years. For the first half of the century, the growth was primarily in high school enrollments, which started in 1900 at about the same rate of attendance as Great Britain (10 percent), but by the late 1930s it reached 68 percent while Britain lagged behind at 42 percent.[3] By midcentury, when high schools were filling up, the growth of U.S. enrollment shifted to higher education. For those born in 1900, about 10 percent attended college and 4 percent graduated with a bachelor's degree, but for those born in 1950, 50 percent attended college and 24 percent graduated.[4]

As the book's title suggests, the authors see the social and economic history of America in the twentieth century as a race between education and technology. For the first two-thirds of the century, they say, education was resoundingly winning the race, as the supply of educated workers regularly exceeded the demand, and this excess provided an enormous boost to economy. It meant that employers were able to hire large numbers of workers with a high school and later college education, who brought the kinds of higher-level skills that were needed in a technologically advancing workplace. Since supply exceeded demand, employers were able to get these advanced skills without having to pay a high premium; and by stockpiling human capital in the workforce, they were able to introduce new technologies quickly without having to wait until they could find workers with the required abilities. The result was a virtuous circle of high education levels and high technology, which reinforced each other and stoked economic development. The dramatic expansion of schooling, they argue, drove the dramatic expansion of the economy. The authors estimate that the growth in education in the United States accounted for between 12 and 17 percent of the growth in economic productivity across the twentieth century, with the average educational contribution at 13.5 percent. Put another way, they say that increased education alone accounted for economic growth of about one-third of 1 percent per year from 1915 to 2005.[5]

But exactly how did the growth in education produce this economic effect? In particular, how did the academic learning that students acquired in high school increase their productivity in the workforce? The authors acknowledge that technological advance by itself does not necessarily create a demand for greater skill, much less the kinds of skills that are picked up in school. During the nineteenth century, they note, industrial technology had the opposite effect, when a combination of two factors—an increase in the division of labor and the use of machinery driven by steam and electricity—turned skilled workers into unskilled workers, whose job was to carry out simple manual tasks. They calculate that in 1870 three-quarters of the workforce consisted of agricultural laborers, unskilled manufacturing workers, and domestic servants.[6] Education beyond the basics was of little practical use in these occupations.

At the start of the twentieth century, an increase in corporate administration—at the same time that it created new opportunities for office workers with greater education—also brought about a degree of deskilling in white-collar work. But after 1900, the authors say that new production technologies—particularly the development of continuous processing and batch processing, both of which require fewer hands and more machinery—increased the need for skilled workers to maintain the equipment and reduced the demand for unskilled operatives. Increasingly the better blue-collar jobs called for workers who could read blueprints, make calculations, and understand the basic chemistry and physics of the production process. These were the kinds of capabilities that students were picking up in high school, and as a result high school graduates were becoming more and more useful to have on the payroll.

The authors make clear that the kinds of skills that were most useful in the twentieth century workforce were general skills. They argue that this represented a shift from the kinds of specific skills that could be picked up on the job through apprenticeship (they give the example of learning to operate a telegraph key) to the kinds of general skills—reading, writing, math, and science—that were best acquired through formal education. So they are not talking about the narrow vocational training advocated by social efficiency extremists such as David Snedden. Instead, they are focusing on the economic usefulness of a liberal education. As a result, whereas in 1870 only 10 percent of jobs required more than an elementary education, by 1920 more than 25 percent required high school or college.[7] Between 1950 and 2000, the proportion of the workforce who were high school dropouts declined from 59 percent to 8 percent, while the proportion who were college graduates rose from 8 percent to 32 percent.[8]

The payoff for students who invested in further education was substantial throughout the twentieth century. The authors estimate that from 1914 to 2005, the average male worker earned a wage premium of between 5 and 11 percent per year for every additional year of high school and between 8 and 14 percent for every additional year of college.[9] The authors point out, however, that the pattern until the 1950s was quite different from the pattern after then. In the first part of the century, the returns on education actually declined substantially, with the return on a year of high school falling from 11 percent in 1914 to 5 percent in 1949 and then slowly climbing to 8 percent in 2005, while the return on a year of college slowly fell from 10 percent to 8 percent in 1949 and then quickly climbed to 14 percent in 2005.

During the first part of the century the earnings advantage en-joyed by those with more education declined compared to those with less education, and at the same time the advantage of white-collar workers declined compared to blue-collar workers. By 1940, the returns on a year of high school and a year of col-lege were surprisingly close, 8 versus 9 percent.[10] The reason for this decline in the return on education and the reduction of the gap between blue- and white-collar work, they argue, was that the supply of educated workers was expanding so quickly, well in advance of the demand from the economy. Workers still re-ceived a nice return on their investment in education, but the ad-vantage dropped as the number of graduates grew, which paid great dividends to the economy.

In the last part of the century, however, this pattern changed. The return on education—particularly college education—grew sharply, and the gap between white- and blue-collar work grew as well. The reason, say the authors, was not a sudden increase in demand from a high-technology economy but a sharp decline in the rate of growth in the education of the workforce. After growing for fifty years at the rate of 0.82 years per decade, the growth in the education level of workers born between 1951 and 1975 slowed down, increasing by a total of only one-half year. For the first time in the twentieth century, maybe the first time since the days of the common school movement, the dream that American children would have substantially more educa-tion than their parents was beginning to fade.[11] This declining American investment in education, say the authors, threatens both to increase America's social inequality and to reduce its economic vitality.

SCHOOLING AS A PERSONAL INVESTMENT
IN EDUCATIONAL CREDENTIALS

I take issue with some parts of the argument that Goldin and Katz make about education as the source of American economic growth, and I also give a different interpretation to much of their evidence. Let's consider a series of issues that emerge from the authors' extraordinarily rich presentation of data and analysis about education and economy in twentieth-century America.[12]

The Problem of Benefit and Cost

One problem is that the size of the human capital effect that Goldin and Katz identify is relatively small. On average they estimate that the growth in educational attainment accounted for less than 14 percent of the growth in economic productivity over the course of the twentieth century. That's not negligible but it's also not overwhelming. The authors claim that this is a minimum estimate, since they figure that an educated workforce also contributes indirectly to economic growth by making it easier for employers to introduce new technologies. Since the extent to which this intuition is true is unknown, we are left with their original estimate, which allows a lot of room for other, more substantial factors than schooling to have shaped the size and direction of economic growth.

This wouldn't be a concern if education were a modest investment drawing a modest return, because every little bit helps when it comes to economic growth. But that's clearly not the case. Education has long been the largest single expenditure of American state and local governments, which over the course of the twentieth century devoured about 30 percent of their total budgets. In 1995 this came to $378 billion in direct payments for elementary, secondary, and higher education.[13] If this huge expenditure of public funds is seen as an investment in economic growth, then it should have an equally huge impact on that growth. After all, these funds could be spent on other public goods that might be more productive socially, like health care or the environment; or the funds could be left in the private economy, where they could be invested in business or in consumption. Add to this the enormous and essentially incalculable cost of the investment that families and individuals make in education—both direct costs, like college tuition, and indirect costs, like the money that students would have made if they were in the workforce instead of in school. In short, as costly as education is, it would seem that its economic benefits would need to be more substantial than they are in order to justify these expenses as a prudent investment in the nation's wealth instead of a large drain on this wealth.

The Problem of Cause and Effect

Another problem is that it is hard to establish that in fact education was the cause and economy the effect in this story. The authors make clear that the growth in high school and college enrollments both exceeded and preceded demand for such workers from the economy. Employers were not begging high schools to produce more graduates in order to meet the needs for greater skill in the workplace; instead they were taking advantage of a situation in which large numbers of educated workers were available, and could be hired without a large wage premium, for positions that in the past had not required this level of education. So why not hire them? And once these high school graduates were on the job, the employers may have found them useful to have around (perhaps they required less training), so employers began to express a preference for high school graduates in future hiring. But the fact that the workforce was becoming more educated didn't mean that the presence of educated workers was the source of increases in economic productivity. It could just as easily have been the other way around.

Producing a large increase in high school graduates was enormously expensive, especially considering that the supply of these graduates greatly exceeded the economic demand for them. But strong economic growth provided enough of a fiscal surplus that state and local governments were able to afford to do so. In short, it makes sense to think, counter to the Goldin and Katz interpretation, that it was economic growth that made educational growth possible. We expanded high school because we could afford to;

and we wanted to do so not because we thought it would provide social benefits by improving the economy but instead because we hoped it would provide us with personal benefits.

The authors point out that the growth of high school enrollments was not the result of a reform movement. There was no reform organization that set out to expand high schools in order to produce human capital. Instead, the demand for high school came from educational consumers. Middle-class families saw high school and college as a way to gain an edge—or keep their already existing edge—in the competition for good jobs. And working-class families saw high school as a way to provide their children with the possibility of a better life than their own. The demand came from the bottom up, not the top down. Administrative progressives later capitalized on the growth of the high school by trying to harness it for their own social efficiency agenda, as we saw in the 1918 *Cardinal Principles* report. But by then the process of high school expansion was already well under way, with little help from them.

In short, we can reasonably think of economy as the cause and education as the effect. Even though this interpretation reverses the causal direction of the story that Goldin and Katz tell about the Human Capital Century, it nonetheless fits their data. They deploy a sophisticated statistical analysis in trying to identify the contribution that education made to economic growth, but all their regression equations really do is establish that these two phenomena were correlated. Which was cause and which was effect is something inferred by the analysts and not imposed by the data. I think it's at least equally plausible to infer that causation went the other way.

Consider one fact about the growth of educational opportunity that is a particular point of pride for the authors: unlike the European model in the late nineteenth and early twentieth centuries, the American high school system educated girls at a high rate. In fact, girls graduated from high school at a substantially higher rate than boys through the twentieth century, and this was especially true in the early part of the century, when girls had a graduation rate that was 39 percent higher than boys.[14] But during the same period, most women were not entering the workforce. In 1910 the female proportion of the U.S. labor force was 18 percent and by 1940 it had only risen to 25 percent, when female graduation rates reached 60 percent.[15] So a large portion of the investment in high school education was going to students who were not part of the formal economy and thus could not be considered as a contribution to gains in economic productivity. The early education of girls at a high level was a great thing and a reason for pride in the American educational system, but it seems to have been a remarkably inefficient way to promote economic growth.

An Emphasis on Access over Learning

The case of girls is an interesting one because it points to one of the central insights of the Goldin and Katz book: the major accomplishment of the American school system was not necessarily that it provided education but that it provided access to schooling. The system may or may not have been effective at teaching students the kinds of skills and knowledge that would economically useful, but it was quite effective at inviting students into the schools and keeping them there for an extended period of time. Early in the book, the authors identify what they consider to be the primary "virtues" of the American educational system as it developed before the Civil War and continued into the twentieth century. In effect, these virtues of the system all revolve around its broad accessibility. They include: "public provision by small, fiscally independent districts; public funding; secular control; gender neutrality; open access; and a forgiving system."[16]

Most of these we discussed in Chapter 2 as part of the analysis of the common school movement and the kind of school system that it produced. Providing schools through local districts made the system quite responsive to the demand of local voters and educational consumers, which is how high school expansion could take place so quickly without a national reform movement to guide it. Public funding, secular control, gender neutrality, and open access made the school system a big tent that incorporated the entire community, without major barriers of class, faith, or gender (racial barriers fell much later). And the forgiving quality of the system meant that it was highly tolerant of students who did not show great academic promise. It was willing to keep students in school even if they failed in their studies, to promote them even if they trailed behind their classmates in achievement, to invite them back even after they had dropped out, and to provide alternative routes to schooling even if the first few didn't work out.

Note that none of these virtues of the American school system speaks to *learning* the curriculum. Instead, all have to do with the *form* of the system, in particular its accessibility and flexibility. I thoroughly agree; indeed this has been my argument throughout this book. But for the human capital argument that Goldin and Katz are trying to make, these virtues of the system pose a problem. How was the system able to provide graduates with the skills needed to spur sustained economic growth when the system's primary claim to fame was that it invited everyone in and then was reluctant to penalize anyone for failing to learn? In effect, the system's greatest strength was its *low academic standards*. If it had screened students more carefully on the way in and graded them more scrupulously on their academic achievement, high school and college enrollments and graduation rates never would have expanded so rapidly and we would all be worse off. But of course, this doesn't fit the narrative of the Human Capital Century, does it? Goldin and Katz are arguing that high school provided a rich store of general knowledge and skill that proved highly useful in the technologically advancing workplace of the twentieth century. Yet their depiction of the system's virtues seems to tell a different story altogether. Let's explore some of the characteristics of this counternarrative.

Schooling, Signals, and the Labor Queue

In his classic analysis of the connection between education and economic equality, economist Lester Thurow poses a contrast between two opposing visions of how education relates to the economy.[17] The human capital argument sees the job market as a competition for wages among potential workers who have varying degrees of economically useful skill. The idea is that individuals bring with them a set of skills, mainly acquired through education, and then the market assigns differential wages to those skills based on their potential contribution to productivity. Higher skills get higher wages because they generate more productivity.

An alternative is to think of the job market as a competition for jobs rather than wages. The idea here is that prospective workers do not bring specific job-relevant skills to the workplace but instead bring general capacities for learning those skills on the job. From this perspective, education provides a signal to the employer about an applicant's trainability.[18] Hiring someone with more education can be reasonable since it may reduce training costs and therefore may mean that the employee will become productive more quickly than someone less trainable. Prospective employees compete for jobs according to their level of education, with the highest education feeding into the best-paying positions. In practice this creates what Thurow calls a labor queue, in which candidates are lined up according to education from high to low and this queue is matched up against the parallel hierarchy of jobs. Education levels, however, tend to be lumpy rather than continuous, since the most salient characteristic is not so much years of schooling but degrees earned: high school diploma, associate's degree, bachelor's degree, and postgraduate degree. So workers tend to be grouped by degree level and the labor queue is a hierarchy of these groupings. The queue is further complicated by additional ranking factors, including the quality of the institution that offered the degree, the program the student pursued, grades, and work experience.

This job competition model better fits the Goldin and Katz analysis, since it portrays education as providing a broad set of capacities that allow workers to learn how to carry out a wide range of jobs once they enter employment. This is exactly the kind of liberal education that high school and college provided in the United States in the twentieth century and that paid off so handsomely for workers. Whereas the wage competition model suggests that formal education provides an unrealistically narrow kind of vocational training, the job competition model merely assumes that more education makes workers more trainable.

As a measure of trainability, education is useful for employers. To array workers in a labor queue and then allocate jobs according to position in the queue is much easier for employers than trying to test worker job skills in advance or operating by trial and error. And it has a certain logic: more educational attainment suggests higher-level cognitive skills and greater ability to learn on the job. Without knowing what a student actually learned in school or whether this knowledge is relevant to the job, employers can still reasonably assume that a student who completed a degree program is more likely to succeed in learning the new job than someone who didn't. It's a crude measure but a plausible one.

But the labor queue poses problems in establishing a strong causal link between education and actual, as opposed to predicted, productivity. First, it's not clear how employers are able to gain systematic evidence that their education-based hiring strategy is really paying off economically. Once employers come to accept education as a signal of productivity and rearrange their hiring practices accordingly, which happened early in the twentieth century in the United States, then how are they going to encounter any negative feedback on these practices?[19] They hire educated workers; things work out okay; so they keep picking candidates from the queue based on education level. It seems unlikely that many employers were willing to go to the trouble and expense to set up experimental conditions, in which they hired one group with more education and another with less for the same job and then compared work performance. In fact, studies suggest that businesses in general have not sought out disconfirming evidence about the effectiveness of hiring by level of education.[20] Like the rest of us, they have come to assume without warrant that more education makes an employee more useful.

Even if hiring the more educated employee does in general help productivity, it's not clear that a further increase in education levels will produce further gains in productivity. This is critically important because of the steady pattern of increasing education in the workforce across most of the twentieth century, when in the United States average education levels grew at the rate of close to one year of additional schooling per decade. Keep in mind that the labor queue establishes a relative rather than absolute measure of education. If employers consistently hire workers with the highest level of education that is available at a given time, after higher-paying positions have already scooped up workers farther ahead in the queue, then the average level of education of each employer's workforce is going to keep growing over time in conjunction with the rise in the average education level in the country.

The extra education level of the more recent employees may provide no benefit at all for the employer. For national human capital policy, this poses a serious problem, which Goldin and Katz wrestle with at the end of their book. Even if increased education has been productive for the economy at certain points in our history, there's no necessary reason to think that increasing education levels now—such as by ramping up the growth in college graduate rates, as the authors propose—will provide any benefits to future economic growth. Instead, all that this policy may do is increase the costs of education for both governments and consumers without showing any positive return on this investment.

As a signal of trainability, education in the job competition model is also useful for individual consumers. The labor queue provides them with a clear strategy for how to get ahead: get more education. The point is to position yourself as high in the labor queue as you can manage so you will be able to pick off the most attractive jobs. And this is indeed the strategy that consumers followed in the twentieth century in the United States. As Goldin and Katz point out, consumers pursuing social opportunity were the main driving force behind the expansion of high school and college enrollments during this period.

But the problem for consumers has been and continues to be that everyone else is pursuing the same strategy that they are. As I noted in the last chapter, students are not competing with their parents for jobs but with their peers. As peers in parallel acquire more education than their parents have, then the individual consumer's relative position in the queue is unchanged and his or her relative income gain is zero. On the other hand, consumers can't afford to drop out of the race for higher educational credentials for fear of falling back in the queue and undergoing downward mobility. As a result, pursuing more education becomes a defensive measure for individuals, a case of having to run in order to stay in place. And at the same time, pursuing a strategy of increasing educational enrollments becomes a counterproductive policy for American society, a very expensive and radically inefficient mechanism for promoting economic growth.

This helps put in perspective the problem at the heart of the Goldin and Katz book. They deplore the relative decline in the growth of educational attainment in the United States in the late twentieth century, since they feel that this change is both reducing social equality and stifling economic growth. But, if we think about this from the perspective of relative position in the labor queue rather than from the perspective of absolute investment in human capital, the reduction in growth of education seems inevitable. Now that high schools are nearly full, educational growth must take place at the college and graduate levels, which are radically more expensive for the state to support and also radically more expensive for consumers to acquire.

For governments, this realization led to a series of taxpayer revolts and recurring fiscal crises starting in the 1970s, just at the point when enrollments started leveling off. Since then, free tuition at public colleges and universities has disappeared and the proportion of higher education funding that comes from the state has been steadily declining. Some flagship state universities now are public institutions in name only, since the state is contributing less than 10 percent of their budget. This in turn has meant that educational consumers must pick up a larger share of the direct cost of higher education through increased tuition and fees, which has led to a rapid accumulation of student debt among college students. At the same time, the opportunity costs of higher education are much greater than for high school, since college students must forego earning adult salaries in the workforce in order to attend classes. While having to pay high direct and indirect student costs for higher education, consumers must also confront the frustrating realization that all this effort and all this debt may not accomplish anything more than to allow them to remain at the same social level as their less-educated parents. It's no wonder that both governments and consumers may have grown weary of running in this seemingly endless race for more education.

DOING STUDIES OR DOING SCHOOL

So where does this leave us? In using educational criteria for screening workers, employers are in effect hiring a credential, which is visible, rather than hiring job skills, which are not. By doing so employers may be acquiring workers whose general education makes them more trainable than those who don't have the credential, but increasing education requirements for jobs don't necessarily provide any dividend in the form of increased productivity. For the educational consumer, getting more creden-tials than the competition does indeed pay off in the job market. But keeping ahead of the pack is not easy, when everyone else is jockeying for position in the same job queue. And the value of a diploma in getting a job is independent of what is learned in school, since employers and consumers alike tend to assume that the degree represents learning without ever trying to verify this. Under such circumstances, following the logic of human capital theory (that what is learned in school is critical for economic pro-ductivity) leads to a counterproductive educational policy: ramp-ing up standards for academic learning and raising the penalty for those who fail to learn the curriculum fully. This policy, which has been the aim of the standards movement in the late twentieth and early twenty-first centuries and became national policy with the adoption of the No Child Left Behind law, ignores the lesson that the form of American education is more consequential than its content and that school access is more important than school learning.

Let's consider the implications of following the lead of the standards movement by examining a prototypical piece of pub-lic rhetoric about the urgent need to invest in human capital by raising academic standards. The case in point is a recent film that vividly makes this argument. School learning matters, it says; and if American students don't get serious about learning the curriculum, our economy will suffer irreparable harm, as countries with higher educational standards leave us in the dust. This film has received a lot of visibility, but its greatest value for us is that it crystallizes the policy ramifications of the human capital vision of education. In effect it is a video version of the *Nation at Risk* report, updated for the twenty-first century.

Two Million Minutes: A Case in Point

In 2008, an American venture capitalist named Bob Compton pro-duced an hour-long documentary film comparing the experience of

American and foreign high school students. His mission: to show the need for Americans to catch up with the rest of the world in academic learning or suffer the grievous consequences. He called the film *Two Million Minutes*, which is the amount of time American students spend in high school. The description on the jacket of the DVD explains the film's argument about school learning and economic development.[21]

> The battle for America's economic future isn't being fought by our government. It's being fought by our kids.
>
> Regardless of nationality, as soon as a student completes the 8th grade, they have just Two Million Minutes to prepare for college and ultimately a career.
>
> For some, high school is little more than a necessary rite of passage—the standard American backdrop for prom nights, tailgate parties and teenage rebellion. But for other students around the world, these Two Million Minutes are spent with tutors and textbooks as they sharpen their minds for the "New Knowledge Economy." One in which America's best and brightest may find themselves irreversibly outdated. And the clock is already ticking.[22]

The film follows the high school experiences of a pair of students (male and female) in three different settings—the United States, China, and India—while supplementing these stories with commentary by economists, businessmen, and educational leaders. Let me summarize the approach that each of these pairs of students takes to their high school studies.

Brittany and Neil are seniors at Carmel High School in Carmel, Indiana, a suburb of Indianapolis. We see them doing a lot of things during the course of the week—socializing, engaging in extracurricular activities, working—but we don't see a lot of studying. They seem to focus on doing school rather than doing studies. Brittany tells us that kicking back and having fun is as important as getting good grades; Neil admits he doesn't have to put much effort into his studies in high school, though he figures he'll have to work harder in college. Neil's mother is amazed that his grades are as good as they are (he was a National Merit finalist) given all the other things he does. The film focuses more on Neil than on Brittany, showing us that he simultaneously plays the following roles: class president; former captain of the football team (who used to spend twenty hours a week in practice during the season); president of the school environment club; graphic designer for the school newspaper; and worker in an Italian restaurant (where he goes on the job every day at 5). By the end of the year, Brittany was accepted as a premed student at Indiana University, and Neil received free tuition at Purdue in a computer graphics program.

Xiaoyuan and Ruizhang are students at a special high school in Shanghai that has the reputation of sending graduates to the top universities in China. Studying is clearly their top priority, which we learn from their own mouths and from observing their study-intensive weekly routines. Both are intent on gaining admission to the very best universities. The film focuses primarily on Xiaoyuan, whose dream is to go to Yale but who has a backup plan as well. If she doesn't get into a top university, she intends to go instead to a music conservatory, so she supplements her demanding academic studies with hours of instruction and practice on the violin. We learn that Chinese students have a longer school year and school day than American students and that they spend considerably more time on homework. By the end of high school, the narrator tells us, they spend twice as much time in school and study as their American counterparts. By the end of the school year, both students experience a degree of disappointment. Ruizhang is admitted into prestigious Peking University, but he fails to get into the advanced math program that he had hoped for. Xiaoyuan does not get into Yale, but she is admitted to Tsinghua University, where she was going to study finance.

Apoorva and Rohit attend a university preparatory institution in Bangalore called St. Paul's English School. We follow them as they get up very early to study before school and stay up late studying at night; they also go to study support sessions at school on Saturdays. We hear from both the students and their parents about how their studies are the key for them to gain access to the right universities, which in turn is central to their hopes for the future. Apoorva wants to be an engineer, and Rohit wants to be a physicist. Anxiety pervades the high school experience for both generations. The narrator tells us that American students have a lot more fun, while Indian students spend a lot of time hunched over their studies. Rohit and his friends talk wistfully about playing soccer and other forms of play, but they assert that their top priority is always pursuing their academic program at the highest level. By the end of the year, both students fall a bit short of the target they were aiming for: Rohit gets into a top university in Bangalore but not the India Institute of Technology, which he has been talking about all year long; and Apoorva is also not accepted into the university of her choice, so she decides to study computer engineering at a college near home.

Creating Scholars or Creating Hustlers

It is tempting to raise questions about the validity of the comparison the film presents between the high school experience of American students and their counterparts elsewhere in the world. For example, the film looks at students in two selective schools in urban centers of high technology (Shanghai and Bangalore) compared with students in a rather ordinary upper-middle-class high school in the Indianapolis suburbs, of the sort that could be found in almost any prosperous American community. Why not use as a comparison Bronx Science or Palo Alto High, where you would find a lot of American students who are also studying too hard and stressed out by the competition? (My colleague, Denise Pope, runs a popular program called Stressed Out Students [SOS], which is designed to help alleviate the overwhelming achievement pressures facing Silicon Valley students.) Or consider the overweighting of economists as talking heads in the film (Robert Reich and Richard Freeman), which raises the question: Why is human capital production the most important goal for education? Or consider the focus on education for technology, which raises the question: Why does everyone have to become an engineer?

This sort of mismatched comparison is the norm in the human capital genre of school reform rhetoric, but it's more fruitful to direct attention to the film's central argument about what constitutes a socially beneficial form of education. Essentially, the film says that students in China and India are putting their time in high school to good use by concentrating on their studies (particularly science and math), which will help them get good jobs and help their countries out-produce the United States economically. Meanwhile, American high school students are spending their time on everything but their studies, and those studies in turn give short shrift to science and math. This is how a once-dominant country can slide into decline and be overtaken by leaner, hungrier, and more ambitious competitors. Time is running out.

As presented in the film, both the Asian and American models of education are effective at providing individuals with an opportunity to get ahead. All six students seem on track to get a good university education and qualify for a good job. The issue is the social consequences of the two models, which are quite divergent. The Asian model is a classic example of what Ralph Turner called a sponsored mobility system. Students are required to specialize early in a particular field of study dictated by their intended occupational destination, and they study this field intensively. The American model is a classic case of a contest mobility system, which encourages students to delay specializing their studies until the last possible moment, with the aim of keeping their occupational options open. The result is an educational system that stresses general education at all levels and deters deep learning in a particular field.[23]

The sponsored mobility system produces specialists, with a strong knowledge of one area but little flexibility in switching fields or adapting to change. The contest mobility system produces generalists, with thin knowledge about everything but good prospects for changing careers and adapting to a future unanticipated by their schooling. The sponsored system promotes intensive learning of the curriculum, and schools award diplomas based on a student's demonstrated mastery of this curriculum. The contest system tends to discount learning in favor of tokens of learning (grades, credits, and degrees), and it measures educational attainment in hours of attendance rather than tested performance, as embodied in the American system of accumulating credit hours toward a degree. The sponsored system gives students the incentive to study hard now and reap the reward later. The contest system encourages students to lag in their studies early but take them more seriously as they rise in the system and get closer to the point of specialization and employment. For most Americans, high school is not a time to study hard—and neither Neil nor Brittany did—but college is understood to be harder (as Neil anticipated). Even more demanding is graduate school, where an increasing number of Americans receive their terminal educational experience.

Given the dramatic differences in the core structure of the Asian and American models of education, it is not surprising to see how much harder Xiaoyuan, Ruizhang, Apoorva, and Rohit worked at their high school studies than did Brittany and Neil. As Neil's mother and one of the commentators pointed out, however, this does not mean that the Americans were not working hard in high school. In fact they were amazingly busy doing things other than homework. Neil was a poster child for a busy student: football, student government, environment club, school newspaper, job, and socializing with friends. The film makes a strong argument that the Asians are using their time on things that matter while the Americans are wasting their two million minutes on marginalia. I make the opposite argument.

How does society benefit from having students master the formal curriculum in high school with the zeal that the four Asian students demonstrate (to the great approval of the film's commentators)? The educational machinery in which they are caught is very good at creating good students, but how does it contribute to making good citizens and good parents? Despite the testimonials of the economists, how does it even make good workers? There is a connection between science and math knowledge and the work of engineers. But how many engineers do we need? For everyone else, the classic school subjects (language, math, science, and social studies) have little direct connection to any work people do in the real world. Contest mobility systems may promote educational formalism, by focusing on the tokens rather than the substance of learning (degree accumulation), but sponsored mobility is equally formalistic, by focusing on the mastery of school subjects (curriculum accumulation).

The difference is that all of the noncurricular things that the American students in the film were doing had the potential to enhance their ability to contribute to society. They were picking up skills about how to function in a work environment, network, compete, lead, improve the environment, and juggle priorities. They were also learning how to work the system to their advantage, how to do the minimum needed to satisfy school so they could do what they really wanted elsewhere. Isn't it more productive for economy and society to produce a smaller number of zealous students and a larger number of accomplished hustlers? Doesn't the contest mobility system do a pretty good job of preparing actors for life in a market economy, which values entrepreneurship over scholarship?

Both students and society may be better off if schools focused less on producing scholars and more on producing hustlers. As we have seen, American schools are not terribly effective at turning out graduates with a deep command of the academic subjects in the elementary and secondary curriculum. Our test scores internationally are at best in the middle of the distribution, which shows that other school systems are consistently more effective at teaching this material. But it is not clear that accumulating this kind of academic knowledge is particularly useful. For during the same period in the latter twentieth century that U.S. test scores were mediocre, U.S. economic development was stellar.

Maybe the lesson from this is that it is dangerous for both individuals and societies to take school too seriously. The result of an intensive focus on academic learning may be, at the individual level, a generation of stressed-out students as well as, at the societal level, an accumulation of academic skills and knowledge that is not especially functional for modern political, social, and economic life. It may turn out to be advantageous for a society to have an American-style approach to education, which discounts academic learning and encourages students to game the system.

Of all the students depicted in the film, Neil was the most adept at managing his two million minutes of high school in a way that allowed him to contain academic demands and thus focus attention on the array of extracurricular activities most in line with his personal goals. And pursuing these personal goals—through his participation in football, student government, school newspaper, environment club, restaurant work, and peer group—may well prove to be more beneficial to his future prospects and his country's political, social, and economic prosperity than if he had concentrated instead on attaining the top grades in the most demanding classes. In the course of his tenure in high school he was learning how to bend school to his own ends instead of training himself to be a good student. The American educational system, therefore, may not be very good at producing graduates with a strong command of the school curriculum, but it may be reasonably effective at producing graduates who are self-directed, entrepreneurial, and creative.

Implications

All this suggests that efforts by American school reformers to spur economic growth by increasing the rigor of academic studies may be misguided and even counterproductive. Why would we want our students to ramp up their mastery of the school curriculum if this might undermine the kind of education that has historically proven useful both for individual consumers and for society as a whole? Reformers seem to be drawing the wrong lessons from the history of American education. The standards movement in particular assumes that the characteristic of American education that has made it successful has been its ability to teach students the formal curriculum. But the historical evidence suggests strongly that American schools have never been very effective at promoting academic learning and that this was a surprisingly good thing for both students and society. We never did need to produce a large number of graduates who have mastered the academic curriculum and we still don't. Instead, as Claudia Goldin and Lawrence Katz have shown, the primary value of American schooling has been its accessibility to all and its low academic standards. We let everyone in, at ever higher levels of the system, and we don't punish people for failing but instead give them multiple possibilities to reenter the system and try again.

Interestingly, educational consumers seem more aware of this than educational reformers. Consumers have consistently acted, both as students and as voters, to keep the system wide open and academically forgiving. They show a strong preference for a school system that makes both admission and graduation easy. At one level, this is because they recognize that the key goal for pursuing education is to get a good job, and that the primary way that schools make it possible to achieve this goal is not by providing a deep understanding of the curriculum but by providing degrees. At another level, consumers seem to recognize instinctively that what useful skills students do learn in school have less to do with mastering academic subjects than with mastering the school's social environment. School teaches them how to juggle priorities, how to interact effectively with both peers and superiors, and how to manipulate an institutional context in a way that serves their own individual ends. The best preparation for life, in short, may not come from getting an education but from doing school.

LIVING WITH THE
SCHOOL SYNDROME

8

Americans may not be well educated but we are well schooled. We don't score high on international comparisons of student achievement, but historically we have spent more time and money on our system of elementary, secondary, and higher schooling than any other nation on earth. One reason for this persistent pattern of educational largesse is that we are chronic social reformers, who are on a mission to solve a series of seemingly intractable social problems and who routinely turn to school as the most accessible if not the most effective way to accomplish that mission. From this angle, we see schools as the primary way to accomplish our highest social ideals, or at least to represent these ideals in institutional form. Another reason for our heavy investment in schooling is that we are chronic social climbers, who are engaged in a relentless race with our peers to get ahead in the social order or at least to avoid falling behind. From this angle, we see schools as the primary way to accomplish our greatest individual ambitions and to stave off our worst personal fears.

In combination, these impulses—one idealistic and collective, the other pragmatic and individual—have led to the school syndrome that I have been describing in this book. What makes school a syndrome instead of a strategy for Americans is the sheer compulsiveness of the way we keep turning to school for the answer to every social and individual problem. We never let our repeated failure to accomplish our ends through schooling get in the way of our continuing faith that schooling will come through for us this time around. If we can just change the curriculum, revamp the structure of the system, increase access, and differentiate outcomes, then school reform will lead to better social problem solving and greater individual opportunity.

As we have seen, the school reform effort that created the American school system, the common school movement, was the most successful reform movement in the history of American education; indeed, we can say that it was the only such movement that had a substantial impact on both school and society. It laid out an educational structure of local control, open access, loose coupling, and low academic standards that has persisted to the present day. And in the process of establishing this system, it successfully accomplished its primary social goal, which was to create a way to form the citizens and entrepreneurs who were needed for the market-oriented American republic of the mid-nineteenth century. Once in motion, however, this school system came to have a mind of its own. As a thriving educational enterprise, it presented a tempting opportunity for reformers to put it to their own social uses, but it acquired an organizational momentum that made it hard to control and particularly difficult to turn around. Radically decentralized into a series of autonomous organizational units (systems, schools, and classrooms) and harnessed to a compelling common school rationale, the school system (to paraphrase Larry Cuban) had "plans for reformers."

Although reformers often were able to change the rhetoric of education and sometimes were able to tinker with its organizational form, they were remarkably ineffective in transforming how teachers taught and what students learned. This inability to get into the classroom became increasingly frustrating for reformers in the twentieth century, leading to two current movements that have been deliberately engineered to create a more tightly coupled school system that will do what it's told. The standards and choice movements have developed approaches, each in its own way, to bring schools in line and shape classroom learning. It turns out, however, that this concentrated effort to control academic learning may be unnecessary and even counterproductive to the achievement of reform goals. Because something else we have seen about the American school system over time is that its main social impact has come through its form rather than its content. The system has never been so much about education as about schooling. Its primary accomplishments, such as they are, have come largely through its ability to bring together all the members of a community in a single institutional space and subject them to a common social experience.

Another thing we have found about the American school system is that reformers have had a more modest impact on it than consumers. Reformers tried hard to change the system in order to change society, but ever since the common school men, their impact has been quite limited. Educational consumers, on the other hand, have had a significant impact on both, and they weren't even trying. Their aim wasn't to change school or society but simply to use education as a way to get ahead or stay ahead.

So let's see where we are in our effort to understand the roots and ramifications of the American school syndrome. First, I review the major school reform movements in the last two hundred years and their weak effects, following this up with an analysis of why we continue to pursue school reform in spite of its severe limitations. Then I recount why consumers have had a more substantial effect than reformers during the same period, and I close with a summary of the unusable lessons for school reformers that we can draw from this study.

THE MODEST IMPACT OF SCHOOL REFORMERS

The common school movement was able to set up a school system that would blend oil and water to form a new social order in antebellum America. It did so by instilling in students a civic commitment to the public good as members of a cooperative republican community, combined with a personal inclination to preserve individual liberty and pursue self-interest as actors in a competitive market economy. The school system accomplished this goal through the commonality of the educational experience that students underwent within it, combined with the competition for school attainment that determined which students passed or failed, dropped out or graduated. Both outcomes derived from the form and process of schooling rather than from any particular curriculum content that students might have learned along the way. The central aim of the common school movement was to promote democratic equality, since the reform arose from the effort to protect the republic from the threat posed by the burgeoning market economy. But the other two central goals of American education were also present within the system they created. The system sought to promote social mobility by allocating its rewards based on individual achievement; and it sought to promote social efficiency by providing the kind of balance between individual and collective interests that were needed to keep a market-based society functioning effectively.

Progressive reformers shifted the emphasis strongly in the direction of social efficiency, as they tried to reorient the school system toward providing graduates with the right job skills and placing them into the positions where they were needed in the corporate industrial economy of the early twentieth century. But they were much less effective than their predecessors in harnessing the system to that goal. The narrow form of vocational education was a bust, since the preparation it provided was too narrow and backward-looking to be economically efficient and too complex to be implemented in schools. And as I argued in Chapter 7, the contribution of education to economic growth in the twentieth century was at best modest and sporadic. To the extent that education did help out economically, it was partly the result of providing general skills (reading, writing, and figuring) and general knowledge (about the physical and social world) rather than mastery of academic skills and school subjects. And it was also partly the result of teaching students how to maneuver their way through the school system, by mastering the game of "how to succeed in school without really learning."[1] The benefits came less from having students learn the curriculum than from having them learn how to pursue their own interests in an organizational setting, meeting external expectations while also doing what they wanted.

In one area progressives were more effective, but that was because they were building on the earlier success of the common school movement—by using the commonality of the school system to assimilate immigrants into American political, social, and economic life. The civil rights movement also picked up on this characteristic of the system and put it to good use initially in trying to reduce the social differences between blacks and whites by ending legal segregation of American schools. The movement succeeded at first and then ran into the wall of de facto segregation, which was much harder to crack through the political and legal systems and which still left most blacks confined to schools where they were the overwhelming majority. The limitation that this movement confronted was in part a result of the strategy it adopted, defining the right to education as a private good rather than as a public good. The argument was that schooling provided a credential that was critically important for anyone seeking to get ahead in American society, so denial of equal access to this credential was a violation of consumer rights. The movement therefore took the political issue of democratic equality and changed it into the consumer issue of social mobility. Under the same logic of consumer rights, many white families saw busing as a threat to the value of their own children's right to an advantageous educational credential and so chose to oppose it. On both sides of this issue, however, the concern was about what students would attend which school and not about what subjects they would learn there.

In the 1980s, the standards movement brought the focus back to education as a public good, in particular as an investment in human capital. After experiencing only limited success with this approach, which didn't have particularly strong resonance with the public, the leaders imported the consumer rights issue from the civil rights movement and created an amalgam of social efficiency and equality of access in the form of the No Child Left Behind law. During the same period, the choice movement focused initially on social mobility as an issue of individual liberty (parents should be able to choose the school for their children and schools should adapt to parental demands), and then, after equally modest success, adopted the same equality of access appeal, which called for poor families to have the same choices that rich families have always had.

We don't know yet how the standards and choice movements will turn out, since both are still in play at the time I am writing (2010). But we have seen that the ability of the progressive movement and the civil rights movement to achieve their reform goals has been modest at best. And, in both cases, whatever impact the school system has had on reform goals has come from the system's form and process, not its academic content. Consistently, the central factors have been the accessibility of the system and the shared experience of doing school.

WHY WE PERSIST IN SCHOOL REFORM, DESPITE ITS REPEATED FAILURES

School reform has not proven to be a particularly effective way to solve social problems. In fact, it has not even been able to do much about reforming schools. Yet we continue to come back to schools time after time in an effort to make things right. We still have a preference for educationalizing social problems instead of seeking to address these problems in ways that might be more effective.[2] Why is that? This tendency, it seems, arises in response to several central characteristics of American culture and society. It comes in part from some of our most cherished social ideals and in part from some of our most deeply embedded social interests.

Social Ideals

Utility. At core, the urge to educationalize social problems arises from a deep American commitment to the idea that education both is and should be socially useful. Education may well have strong intrinsic value for many of us personally. We may see it as a source of individual enlightenment, intellectual stimulation, spiritual development, playful exploration, esthetic enhancement, and personal enjoyment. But these are not the reasons that we pour such enormous amounts of time, effort, and money into it. It is not why states spend a third of their budget on public education, why we require students to attend, or why employers set minimum levels of education for jobseekers. We do all this mostly because we see education as a critically necessary investment in the improvement of personal, political, economic, and social life. Its primary value for us is extrinsic, measured by the return this investment is expected to yield to ourselves and our society.

Individualism. Liberal democracies in general are prone to understand social life as the sum of the traits and actions of its individual members, and this tendency is particularly prominent in the United States, which is a critical factor in explaining why Americans tend to see education as the central institution for solving social problems.[3] The American worldview tends to reduce social problems to individual problems, locating the root cause of everything from poverty and illness to criminality and racism in the capacities and motives of individuals. If these are indeed the primary roots of social problems, then education is the natural solution, because its central focus is on changing the capacities and motives of individual students.

For example, consider the problem of racism. Leah Gordon's finely textured study of the link between individualism and educationalization in the United States shows how, in the years after World War II, American social science shifted from a sociological view of racism (seen as the result of social inequality and social conflict) to a psychological view (seen as the result of personal prejudice).[4] This change provided strong intellectual reinforcement for two educational efforts to attack racism—the racial desegregation of schools and the development of instructional programs to undermine race prejudice—which sought to accomplish this end by equalizing individual capacities and changing individual beliefs. Of course, if race is seen as a problem arising not from individual prejudice but from basic inequalities in the social structure, then the educational solution makes less sense. But since Americans tend to individualize this and other social problems, education naturally appears to be the obvious mechanism to use in solving these problems.

Optimism. Another major ground for educationalizing social problems that is also characteristically American is a faith in progress. We are a perennially optimistic people, believing that social improvement is not just possible but likely. In part, this is an extension of individualism, which portrays personal will as able to overcome nearly any social constraint, but it also connects with a faith in utility. If we want education to be useful in solving social problems, and if we believe it is effective in this pursuit because it is able to attack the roots of these problems in individual capacities and motives, then we have reason to be optimistic about the possibility that educational reform will be able to produce social progress. James G. March discusses this mind-set in an essay titled "Education and the Pursuit of Optimism," which opens by noting: "The modern history of American education is a history of optimism. We have believed in the successes of our past and the good prospects for our future."[5] Education, he notes, has become our all-purpose tool for realizing our hopes to improve society by fixing its problems; but once we invest all our hopes in the vehicle of educationalization, we can no longer afford to find failure in the enterprise of educational reform.

Social Interests

Professional Interest. Building on the social ideals of utility, individualism, and optimism, we have constructed an educational profession with a strong interest in extending the reach of the school system to deal with social problems. The profession attracts people who have a vision of saving the world by fixing the child. This means educators do not have to be drafted into the ranks of the educationalizers; they volunteer for duty, eager to take on new missions and work their magic on new problems. In his account of educationalization in contemporary Great Britain, David Bridges shows how this tendency is fed by the idealism of the educators, who share "an honest conviction that they can thereby contribute in some general or more specific way social benefit, perhaps even to the building of a better world."[6] But he also notes a strong element of self-interest in the willingness of educators to take on new social problems, since this brings in new resources to support the educational enterprise. "The elementary point is that if educational institutions can convince government that they are the ones who can deliver on social and economic change then they can call in the additional financial support which is attached to the advance of such policies."[7] In this way, educationalizing social problems offers educators the opportunity to do good and do well at the same time.

Political Interest. Like educators, politicians also have an interest that is both idealistic and pragmatic in promoting education as the answer to social problems. One of the primary motives for anyone seeking political leadership is the urge to fix what's wrong in the community, and education offers a plausible mechanism for doing this. Operating within the cultural frame of utility, individualism, and optimism, it seems only natural for an American mayor, governor, or president to ask schools to take on the responsibility for carrying out a particular social reform, which educators are then only too eager to accept. If the problem exists at the individual level and school is the primary tool for tinkering with the skills and beliefs of individuals, then there would appear to be no better place to turn for help.

Of course, schools also offer some pragmatic political advantages over other, more direct approaches to social engineering. Particularly in the American context, where schooling is radically decentralized and loose coupling is the organizational norm, promoting social reform through educational reform is notoriously slow and indirect. The push for change needs to move from the state government to the state educational bureaucracy, local school districts, individual schools, and individual classrooms, where teachers need to carry out the reform in the instruction of individual students. As Richard Elmore and Milbrey McLaughlin pointed out, in their essay on the problem of school reform in the United States, *Steady Work*, school change and political policy operate on radically different timelines, noting that "there is abundant evidence that the time it takes reforms to mature into changes in resource allocation, organization, and practice is substantially longer than the electoral cycles that determine changes in policy."[8]

By the time the mayor or governor or president is leaving office after four or at most eight years, the school reform process may just be getting in gear. This time lag allows the politician to enjoy all the benefits of initiating a major effort to solve a social problem without ever having to take responsibility for the outcomes of this reform effort, which are likely to occur on someone else's watch. The next leader can easily blame the failure of the problem-solving effort on the flaws in the predecessor's policy. Or—and this is a particular political advantage that comes from educationalizing social problems—both new leader and old can always blame the educational system for failing to carry out the reform effectively. So the politician can have it both ways—taking credit for initiating reform and blaming the failure of reform on the schools—which, of course, then means initiating a new educational reform to make schools more effective in solving the problem the next time around. This is one reason why Elmore and McLaughlin call school reform "steady work." Both as savior and whipping boy, education as the answer to social problems is an indispensable political tool.

Political Opportunity. Another factor that makes educationalization attractive to politicians is that schools are readily accessible to their influence. They may not be effective in solving the social problem, but they are an institutional arena that politics can affect. As David Bridges points out, schools are government property; they are already established in every community (no need to hire staff, set up an organizational structure, or rent offices); they already have the children of the community under their control and subjected to programs designed to shape their skills and beliefs; and the system is quite used to receiving new mandates from above and undergoing continual retraining for the latest reform effort.[9]

As we saw, the common school movement had established the American school system as a means for solving a critically threatening social crisis in the early years of the republic. Once the machinery was in place, it was only natural that future reformers would turn to it as the solution to future problems facing American society. So the progressives enlisted it in the quest for establishing a new socially efficient public order, civil rights leaders asked it to promote racial equality, the standards movement sought to turn it toward economic productivity, and the choice movement sought to put it under market control to promote greater liberty. The school system may not be an effective tool, but it has continually served as the tool at hand.

Structural Limits. The urge to educationalize social problems also arises from a pragmatic consideration of what kinds of social reforms are feasible within the limits of the social and political structure of a liberal democracy. This is particularly true in the United States, where the liberal component of liberal democracy has been emphasized more heavily than in most Western

European countries. A system such as ours—which values individual liberty at least as much as the public good and which values the freedom to accumulate and dispose of property at least as much as the benefits that derive from greater equality—removes from the table many of the most direct mechanisms for resolving social problems.

Americans have been unwilling to deal with medical problems by adopting universal health care, so instead we have leaned on the weak reed of schooling to solve the problem through mechanisms like school nurses and health education programs. We have been unwilling to redistribute wealth and subsidize income in order to equalize social opportunity, so instead we have offered the opportunity for more education in the hope that this would allow individuals to get ahead in society. We have been unwilling to attack the structural roots of racial inequality, such as by desegregating the racially homogeneous neighborhoods that most Americans live in, so we have opted instead for desegregating schools and increasing the number of black and brown faces in school textbooks. Under these kinds of restrictive limits on what is socially and politically possible, schools often look like the best option for attacking our most pressing problems.

Formalism. Ultimately, all of these elements, which provide the foundation for the American tendency to use schools to solve social problems, make us willing to accept a response to social problems that is more formal than substantive. Schools may not be able to do much to resolve these problems, but schools do align nicely with our cultural values and our sociopolitical structure, and they do stand as a formally credible if not substantively effective way to respond to demands for reform. In this way, our fixation on school reform rests on a kind of confidence game. We believe that schools are a good way to deal with social problems, in part because they express our values (utility, individualism, and optimism), in part because they have the troops, and in part because they are accessible to the reformist impulse in a way that other institutional arenas are not. So we assign them the responsibility for resolving these problems, but we are unable to accept the possibility that they are not up to the task.

At best, we are willing to accept what schools can do as sufficient. So we accept educational opportunity as a proxy for social opportunity and multicultural textbooks as a proxy for a multicultural society. At worst, we can always blame schools for getting it wrong and then demand that they redouble their efforts to reform themselves in order to reform society. Either way, we need to keep the faith that educationalizing problems really works. This is not a con game in the criminal sense, in which con artists deliberately dupe the suckers. Instead it's a form of good salesmanship, where the first principle is to sell yourself first. We sell ourselves on the value of education in solving social problems, and then we buy what we're selling. The whole thing rests on the uncertain foundation of our collective willingness to continue in believing the con. Whatever the problem, we continue to keep the faith in schools as the answer.

I have been arguing that when we educationalize social problems we are expressing a willingness to accept the kinds of formal and symbolic outcomes that education can actually provide— things like instructional programs and educational credentials —in place of a concrete resolution to the problem itself. This is because, when we get right down to it, a liberal democracy is primarily interested in having the educational system embrace and institutionalize the central values of the culture, in its language and in the system's formal structure. I am arguing that we hold the school system responsible for expressing our values rather than for actually realizing them in practice; that the rapid expansion of the system is less a result of its effectiveness in carrying out those goals in practice than in its ability to represent those goals in formal terms.[10]

Therefore, the history of schooling is the history of formalism.[11] Schooling transforms social goals into institutionalized expressions of those goals. Even though it does not realize these goals, schooling does create a set of academic forms—structures, processes, currencies, and languages—that play useful roles for society. The grammar of schooling is not only an expression of the organizational inertia of the educational system but also a mechanism by which it shapes society. So in educationalizing social problems, we may not be doing much to resolve these problems, but we are doing a great deal to school ourselves.

THE IMMODEST IMPACT OF SCHOOL CONSUMERS

Educational reform has been only one part of the story of school change, and, as we have seen, this part has been less consequential than the other part—the education market—which was more effective both in shaping the school system and in shaping the impact of school on society. The education market is the sum of the actions of all educational consumers as they pursue their individual interests through schooling. From early in the history of American education, American families and individuals have looked on education as an important way to get ahead and stay ahead in a market society. Even before formal schooling was commonplace, families sought to provide their children with the kinds of literacy and numeracy skills that were essential for anyone who wanted to function effectively in the commercial life of the colonies.

The introduction of universal public education in the common school era made such basic skills available to everyone in the white population at public expense. This meant that a common school education became established as the baseline level of formal skill for the American populace in the nineteenth century. For the small number of students who gained a more advanced education at an academy, high school, or college, this educational advantage gave them an edge in the competition for the equally small number of clerical, managerial, and professional roles. Late in the nineteenth century, the number of office jobs increased, which raised the value of a high school education, and by the start of the twentieth century, employers increasingly came to use educational qualifications to decide who was qualified for particular jobs, including both white-collar and blue-collar positions. At this point the economic returns on the consumer's investment in education became quite substantial all across the occupational spectrum.

For our purposes, in trying to understand the factors affecting school change in the United States, the consumer effect on the school system is quite different in both form and function from the reformer effect. One distinction is that reformers treat education as a public good. They see their reform efforts as the solution of a social problem, and the benefits of this reform will be shared by everyone, whether or not they or their children are in school. In contrast, consumers approach education as a private good, which is the personal property of the individual who acquires it.

Another distinction is that reformers are intentionally trying to change the school system and improve society through their reform efforts. In contrast, consumers are simply pursuing their own interests through the medium of education. They're not trying to change schools or reform society; they're just trying to get ahead or at least not fall behind. But in combination their individual decisions about pursuing education do exert a significant impact on the school system. These choices shift enrollments from some programs to others and from one level of the system to another. They pressure political leaders to shift public resources into the educational system and to move resources within the system to the locations that are in greatest demand. At the same time these educational actions by consumers end up exerting a powerful impact not only on schools but also on society. When consumers used education to address their own social problems, the social consequences were no less substantial for being unintended.

A third distinction between the approach that reformers and consumers take to schools is that reformers assert the importance of school learning but consumers don't. As we have seen, the connection between reform and learning in practice has been rather weak. School reformers have not been terribly effective in bringing school and society in line with its goals, but what modest impact they have had tended to come more from the form of schooling than its content. In contrast, consumers take a less ideological and more pragmatic approach to schooling. What is most salient about schooling for them is not its use value (what usable knowledge it provides) but its exchange value (what doors it will open). Front and center in the consumer agenda for gaining the greatest benefit from schooling is to acquire its marketable tokens of accomplishment. These include gold stars, test scores, grades, track placements, academic credits, and—most of all—diplomas. From the consumer perspective, the form of schooling is everything. School provides the educational currency that students can cash in for a good job and a comfortable life.

The American school system was a deliberate creation of the common school movement; but once the system was set in motion, consumers rather than reformers became its driving force. Consumers drove the extraordinary expansion of American school enrollments to a level higher than anywhere else in the world, starting with the surge from primary school into grammar school in the late nineteenth century, into high school in the first half of the twentieth century, and into college in the second half. Reformers didn't make school expansion happen; they just tried to put this consumer-generated school capacity to use in service of their own social goals, particularly the goal of social efficiency. Not only did consumers flood the system with students, but they also transformed the system's structure. They turned the common school, where everyone underwent the same educational experience, into the uncommon school, where everyone entered the same institution but then pursued different programs. Their most consequential creation in this regard was the tracked comprehensive high school, which established the model for the reconstructed (not reformed) educational system that emerged at the start of the twentieth century and is still very much with us.

At the heart of this reconstructed system is the peculiarly American balance between access and advantage. This balance was not the brainchild of school reformers proposing it as the educational solution to a social problem. Instead, it was the unintended outcome of the actions of individual consumers competing for valuable credentials in the education market. Like any other market, the education market consists of a diverse array of actors competing for advantage by acquiring and exchanging commodities; the difference is that the commodities here are educational credentials. As a result, the education market does not speak with a single voice but with competing voices, and it exerts its impact not by pushing in a single direction but by pushing in multiple directions. When the common school system was introduced into a society with an unequal distribution of social advantages, families naturally started to use it in their efforts to improve or preserve their social situation. As we saw, the common schoolmen inadvertently set off the competition for educational advantage when they created the public high school as a way to lure middle-class families into the public school system. So from the very start, the American school system simultaneously provided broad access to schooling at one level and exclusive access to schooling at a higher level. The race was on.

For most of the nineteenth century, the high school remained largely a middle-class preserve within the school system. During the same period, working-class enrollments gradually expanded from the lower grades into the grammar school grades. By the 1870s and 1880s, grammar school enrollments were nearing universality in the United States, which led naturally to growing consumer demand for access to the high school. Before the end of the century, the system yielded to this demand and began opening a series of new high schools, which led to a rapid expansion of high school enrollments. Increased access for working-class families, however, undercut the advantage that high school attendance had long brought to middle-class families. How was education supposed to meet both of these consumer demands within the same school system?

It turns out that the education market was much more adept at constructing such educational solutions to complex social problems than was the school reform process. With a little help from the progressives, consumer demand created the tracked comprehensive high school. It provided broad access to high school for the entire population while at the same time preserving educational advantage for middle-class students in the upper academic tracks, which started feeding graduates into college. This reconstructed school system really could have it both ways. But how did the education market bring about this remarkable institutional response to a pressing set of social problems?

In a functioning liberal democracy, consumer demand quickly translates into political demand. Working-class families did not have the social position or wealth of their middle-class counterparts, but they did have the numbers. It was then and is now very difficult for a democratic government to resist strong demand from a majority of voters for broad access to an attractive, publicly provided commodity such as schooling. At the same time, middle-class citizens retained substantial influence in spite of their smaller numbers, so government also had difficulty ignoring their demands to preserve a special place for them within the public school system. If democracy is the art of compromise, the comprehensive high school is the ultimate example of such a compromise frozen in institutional form.

One additional factor makes the education market so effective at shaping the school system. Markets are dynamic; they operate interactively. Individual educational consumers are playing in a game where everyone knows the rules and all actors are able to adjust their behavior in reaction to the behavior of other actors. By the start of the twentieth century, a new rule was emerging in American society: the educational level of prospective employees sets their qualifications for a particular occupational level. To get more pay, get more schooling.

The problem was that some people already had an educational edge, and they had the means to maintain that edge. Their children were in high school and yours weren't. So you demanded and gained access to high school, only to find that the ground had shifted. First, it was no longer the same high school but a new one with its own internal hierarchy that placed your children at the bottom. Second, high school was no longer the top of the educational line; college was. The middle-class students in the upper tracks were now heading to college, leaving your children in the same relative position they occupied before—one step behind in the race for educational advantage. The only real difference was that now everyone had more education than before. In the nineteenth century, the credential of advantage was the high school diploma. In the early twentieth century, it was the college degree. By the late twentieth century, it was the graduate degree. The race continues.

Over the years, therefore, educational consumers have been more effective than school reformers in shaping the American school system. Consumers were the ones who developed the institutional core of the system: its delicate balance between access and advantage, and the corresponding organizational structure of the system, combining equality and hierarchy. Consumers have also been more effective than reformers in the impact they have exerted on American society through the medium of schooling. These social effects were not the intention that was guiding consumer behavior in the education market; instead, consumers were trying to use education for their own personal ends, and the societal consequences of their actions were a side effect. For individuals, the school system often has served their purposes: some have found that gaining more education enabled them to get ahead, and others have found that it helped them hold onto their competitive edge. But collectively the social impact of market pressure on schools has cost consumers dearly.

As we saw in Chapter 6, the system of schooling that consumers created has not been able to increase social equality, nor has it been able to increase upward mobility. The population as a whole has seen its standard of living and quality of life rise as the economy has grown, but schooling has had no effect on the relative position of social groups in the social hierarchy. The rise in the education level of Americans in the last 150 years has been extraordinarily rapid, but this change has not succeeded in shuffling the social deck. People who had an educational edge on the competition were by and large able to maintain this edge by increasing their schooling at the same rate as those below them in the status order. The effect of this process over time was to increase the average education level of everyone in the labor queue, which artificially inflated educational requirements for jobs. As a result, people were spending more time and money on schooling just to keep from falling behind. They were forced to run to stay in place. The education market, therefore, had the cumulative effect of undercutting the educational goal that most twentieth-century school reformers tried to attain: it sharply reduced America's social efficiency.

Schools have been ineffective in realizing the social goals of reformers, and their impact on educational consumers collectively has been counterproductive, but schools have been remarkably effective at reshaping American society in their own image. By educationalizing social problems, we have educationalized society itself.

One source of education's social impact is funding. Governments spend an extraordinary portion of their annual budgets on the educational systems, from preschool through the most advanced graduate programs at universities. Families and individuals invest an enormous amount of money in direct costs for school supplies, tutoring, test preparation, uniforms, college counseling, and especially for college tuition, fees, and loans. And then there is the opportunity cost of what students could have been earning if they were not in school.

A second source of education's impact is time. Education devours somewhere between twelve and twenty-five years of a person's life just in attending classes in a modern developed society. In addition, the institution absorbs the efforts of the largest profession in modern societies—educators—plus a large number of collateral personnel who support the educational enterprise.

A third source of education's impact is process. Education forces families and governments and businesses to organize themselves around academic schedules, academic priorities, academic activities, academic procedures, and academic credentials. All three of these social effects of schooling continue to grow as the education market continues to pressure students to pursue ever higher levels of schooling.

This process of educationalizing society is in part an unintended consequence of the process of building the school system, kicked off by our need to find institutional expression of our ideals and our faith in the efficacy of individual solutions to social problems. But this process does have its social uses, which help reinforce and preserve the expansion of schooling once it is in motion. Educationalizing society integrates social life around a set of common experiences, processes, and curricular languages. It gives stability and legitimacy to a social structure of inequality that otherwise might lead to open conflict. It gives stability and legitimacy to government by providing an institution that can be assigned hard social problems and that can be blamed when it fails to solve them. It provides orderly and credible processes by which people can live their lives, giving employers grounds for selecting a workforce, workers a way to pursue jobs, and families a way to pass on privilege and seek social opportunity, even if the rationales for these processes (human capital, individual merit) are not very credible. Most of all, it gives us a way to express serious concern about social problems without actually doing anything effective to solve those problems. In this sense, then, the ability of schools to formalize substance—to turn anything important into a school subject or a school program or a school credential—is at the heart of their success in educationalizing society.

IS THE SCHOOL SYNDROME CURABLE?

As I bring this book to a close, I imagine that the story I have been telling may leave many readers feeling depressed about the promise and prospects for American schools. I have shown that the school system has been remarkably unsuccessful at carrying out the more recent social missions we have assigned to it. After its early successes, it has done very little to foster its core goals of democratic equality, social efficiency, and social mobility. It has not been able to promote equality of race, class, and gender; or to enhance public health, economic productivity, and good citizenship; or to reduce teenage sex, traffic deaths, obesity, and environmental destruction. In fact, in many ways it has had a negative effect on these problems by draining money and energy away from social reforms that might have had a more direct impact. Educationalizing social problems has consistently pushed education to expand its scope well beyond both what it should do and what it can do, and the result is a record of one failure after another. Yet, as I noted in the book's introduction, at the same time the American school system has been an enormous institutional success. It started small and at the fringes of American society, and then grew into a mammoth institution that devours our resources and shapes the way we live.

So how are we to understand the success of this institution in light of its failure to do what we asked of it? One way of thinking about this is that education may not be doing what we ask, but it is doing what we want. We want an institution that will pursue our social goals in a way that is in line with the individualism at the heart of the liberal ideal, aiming to solve social problems by seeking to change the hearts, minds, and capacities of individual students. Another way of putting this is that we want an institution where we can express our social goals without violating the principle of individual choice that lies at the center of the social structure, even if this comes at the cost of failing to achieve these goals. So education can serve as a point of civic pride, a showplace for our ideals, and a medium for engaging in uplifting but ultimately inconsequential dispute about alternative visions of the good life. At the same time, it can also serve as a convenient whipping boy, which we can blame for its failure to achieve our highest aspirations for ourselves as a society.

In this sense, then, we can understand the whole grand educational enterprise as an exercise in formalism. We assign formal responsibility to education for solving our most pressing social problems in light of our highest social ideals, with the tacit understanding that by educationalizing these problem-solving efforts we are seeking a solution that is more formal than substantive. We are saying that we are willing to accept what education can produce—new programs, new curricula, new institutions, new degrees, new educational opportunities—in place of solutions that might make real changes in the ways in which we distribute social power, wealth, and honor.

So is the American school syndrome curable? I think not. It's too deeply embedded in our values and traditions and too integral to our identity as a liberal democracy, which is always trying to establish an uneasy balance between equality and inequality and thus necessarily constructs a school system that fosters both access and advantage. A change in the school system in any fundamental way—the essence of the reform ideal—can only really happen if we are willing to change American culture and society in an equally fundamental way. This would mean backing away from our commitment to liberal democracy, individualism, utilitarianism, and social optimism. Since these kinds of changes are unlikely, we are also unlikely to change the way we do school and the way we keep trying to reform society through school.

Sure, the system is messy, grossly inefficient, and deeply unfair. It keeps hope of advancement alive while continuing to preserve advantage. But there is something intriguingly elegant about the American school system. It's not doing what we ask of it, but it's remarkably effective at doing what it does. It deftly reconciles opposites and obligingly accommodates all of our higher and lower impulses. It offers a medium for expressing our public ideals and for acting out our private ambitions. It allows schools to change continuously and to remain very much the same. It organizes large parts of American life around its own routines and interests while presenting itself convincingly as a humble servant of the public will. It fails us regularly, but it retains our confidence, and we keep investing large sums of public and private money into it. I find it hard not to admire a system that is able to keep all of these balls in the air at the same time.

UNUSABLE LESSONS FOR SCHOOL REFORMERS

At the end of books on education there is a mandatory chapter that offers suggestions for how to fix the system. Never mind that the preceding chapters have presented a complex and realistic analysis of why the system continues to be dysfunctional. The genre still mandates an upbeat conclusion that offers a neat set of bullet points for setting things straight: five ways to end the string of failures and do reform right the next time around. As an education skeptic—who admires the system for its elegance and resilience and who is pessimistic about the process of social engineering—I am reluctant to follow in this tradition, which would require me to deny the evidence of the previous seven chapters in a final burst of reckless enthusiasm.

But the fact is that there are some lessons that can be drawn from the analysis in this book, which—if followed, a big if— might head off some of the problems that school reformers have encountered in the past. I feel reasonably comfortable about offering these lessons primarily because, unlike many reform agendas, I don't think they are likely to do any harm. Why? Because I am quite confident that no one will follow them. The school system is too well entrenched, too closely connected to who we are as a people to be upset by a few feeble bullet points. Consider the list of suggestions that follows as an academic exercise in the most pejorative sense of the word. Don't worry; none of this will really happen. It's just a thought experiment.

Scale Down Your Ambitions. The biggest problem with school reform efforts is their overreaching ambition. David Snedden wanted
schools to serve as the mechanism for creating the socially efficient society. John Dewey wanted schools to be the embryo for
democracy. George W. Bush wanted schools to promote personal
liberty and social equality. These things are not going to happen.
It is best to think about educational goals at a more modest level.
Overreaching produces either abject failure or serious damage.
For the former, think Dewey; for the latter, think Snedden.

Build on What Schools Can Do. Schools are able to do some things
well, so it pays to focus on these kinds of efforts. They can provide students with a broad set of basic skills (reading, writing,
calculating, analyzing, reasoning) and a broad understanding of
major aspects of the natural and social world, the kinds of broad
capacities we tend to consider part of a liberal education. Schools
can be very effective at assimilating immigrants, transients, and
other social newcomers into a local community and into the
broader political, cultural, and social fabric of American society.
They can have a modest effect in increasing the comfort level
between people across social barriers of race, class, and gender
by getting them accustomed to interacting with each other in the
hothouse environment of the school. They can provide students
with a variety of social skills and strategies for pursuing self-
interest in an institutional setting by teaching them how to game
the process of doing school without having to do much academic learning. Most of all, schools are good at credentialing.
Their most important social function is to certify that students
have completed a particular level of schooling by conferring degrees. This in turn helps assign graduates to particular positions
in the queue of prospective workers, providing both employers
and employees with a predictable and apparently legitimate
method of deciding who gets which jobs. Schools do this not only
by certifying the quantity of schooling that students have acquired but also by labeling the quality of this schooling, as iden-

tified by the rank, reputation, and relative exclusivity of the school or program that students have attended.

Don't Pursue Goals That Schools Can't Accomplish. There are lots of things that schools can't do well, so it's best to drop these from the school reform agenda. Schools may be able to make us more comfortable and less fearful of the Other, but they can't equalize differences like race, class, and gender that are deeply embedded in the social structure. More schooling raises the education level of the population but it doesn't reduce social inequality. Likewise, schooling can offer some individuals the opportunity to get ahead of others, but simple logic dictates that it can't do this for everyone, since when one person gets ahead then someone else has to fall behind. (Only in Lake Wobegon can everyone be above average.) Education may be able to help promote economic growth—but only at certain historical points, at certain educational levels, and at very high cost to both governments and individuals. So we need to be quite wary of thinking that education is the cure for any, much less every, economic woe. Schooling can try to expose students to the issues surrounding major social problems and try to teach them behaviors that might help mitigate these problems, but in combination these efforts do very little to help with issues like improving public health, promoting peace, or preserving the environment. These things—like equality, opportunity, and economy—require not educational action but political action, since only the political sphere is able, even if usually unwilling, to exert a significant impact on these issues. The question, then, is whether we want to continue to approach these issues obliquely and ineffectually through the medium of school reform or to take direct and substantive action through the mechanism of political reform.

Don't Keep Pushing for the Upward Expansion of the School System. Consumers are going to continue to push for access to ever-higher levels of education, in an endless competition between those who want to get ahead through schooling and those who want to stay ahead through schooling. This creates tremendous political pressure on public officials to keep expanding the supply of higher education, but there's no good public policy reason for officials to accelerate this process. Endless expansion does nothing to increase mobility and equality and relatively little to spur the economy, but it is quite effective in sending both families and governments to the poorhouse. Continuous expansion raises the average education level of the population, which may be a good thing in many ways. It gives more people access to higher levels of American and world culture, to more forms of esthetic appreciation, to more ways of expanding their intellectual horizons, and to more ways of pursuing personal fulfillment. As a result, I would never be one to say that we are overeducating citizens, but I would say that we are overcredentialing them. From this angle, all that this expansion does is keep inflating the credential requirements for jobs as the credential levels of people in the labor queue keep rising.

Extending education indefinitely is not only expensive financially, but it also defers the start of adult life further into the future. For people currently entering higher-level jobs, work begins after completing graduate school, which means they aren't able to become economically productive and start families until the mid- or late twenties at the earliest; and this deferred starting point keeps getting pushed upward. Does everyone need to go to college? Will everyone soon need to go to graduate school? That's where we're heading. From the individual perspective the answer is yes, because if you don't keep gaining substantially more education than your parents you are sure to fall behind your peers and drop down the social scale. From the societal perspective the answer is no, since the social costs are high and the social benefits are somewhere between modest and miniscule.

Assume That Consumers, Not Reformers, Are Driving the System. One lesson from this study of school reform in America is that the major changes in the system have come from the actions of educational consumers, not educational reformers. This suggests that reformers would be well advised to try to build their movements on top of the efforts of consumers, trying to ride the consumer wave instead of trying to roll back the consumer tide. Social efficiency was the most prominent goal of the two biggest reform movements in the twentieth century, the administrative progressivism and the standards initiative (*Cardinal Principles* and *A Nation at Risk*), but it didn't get very far in shaping either school or society. Instead, we ended up with a remarkably inefficient system that produced many more graduates than we needed.

What we see in most recent movements, however, is a tendency for school reformers to pick up the social mobility argument, which had long been the credo of consumers, and put it to their own uses. This started with the desegregation movement, which made consumer rights the primary focus of its argument for change. Then we saw both the standards and choice movements at the end of the century belatedly adopting the same argument and incorporating it into their reform agenda, as they asserted that standards and choice would enable disadvantaged families to have access to the same school learning and the same school choice that advantaged families had always had. Falling in line with the consumer may make these reform movements more effective even though it does no good for school and society.

Focus on the Form, Not the Content, of Schooling. Another lesson from this study is that the broader social consequences of schooling, such as they have been, have come primarily from the form of the system rather than the content of academic learning that occurs within it. One key factor about the form of the system is access. Perhaps the central issue and primary impact of American schooling has come from its extraordinary accessibility to all parties at all levels of the system. Another factor is advantage. The system is great at sorting students and giving them labels that certify higher or lower levels of merit. A third factor is shared experience. This effect has been attenuated by the way schools at higher levels have sorted students by ability and social background, but none-theless schools at the lower levels have played a major role in creating citizens, incorporating newcomers, and forming the core of a common American culture. A fourth factor is school process. If learning the curriculum has never been a major function of American schooling, which has long prided itself on low academic standards, then the process of schooling has played a much greater role. Americans have learned well how to do school, and in the course of this they have picked up some useful skills in interacting with peers, dealing with authority, and pursuing their own inter-ests in an institutional setting.

The fifth and most important factor, however, is credentialing. This is the most consequential social product of the school sys-tem over the years, which has created its own form of cultural currency—grades, credits, and degrees—and given itself the mo-nopoly on distributing this currency. In the process, schools have reorganized society in their own image, turning family life and economic life into adjuncts of the school system. If reformers are going to have any impact on school and society, they need to ac-knowledge that the form of the school system is the key medium for bringing about both desirable and undesirable social outcomes. Give up on tinkering with the curriculum and instead focus on tinkering with the form and process of the school system.

Don't Assume You Have the Answer. Another lesson from this study is that reformers are usually cut off from the information and exper-tise they need in order to come up with a policy that might actu-ally bring about improvement in school and society. Reformers tend to occupy the center of power, not the center of practice. This means they are far removed from the classrooms where both schooling and educating take place, so they are not in a position to see what's going on or to know how the system really works at the ground level. As a result, reformers tend to develop a highly abstract and theoretical form of knowledge about schooling, which forms the basis for the educational policies they construct.

Absent from these models of understanding schools is the concrete and practical form of knowledge about schooling that is present in the practice of classroom teachers, who serve as the street-level bureaucrats of the school system. Without taking into account this kind of local practical knowledge, reformers are likely to come up with policies that won't work, won't be adopted by teachers who find them potentially disruptive of effective practice, or, worst of all, will be implemented anyway and in the process trample all over the delicate ecology of classroom teaching and learning. Learning from this lesson would mean that reformers would need to follow the kind of strategy proposed by David Tyack and Larry Cuban in their book *Tinkering Toward Utopia*. Build into every reform effort a space for schools and teachers to adapt the reform to local conditions, which means that reformers would not try to implement the reform in its pure state but would allow it to hybridize within each local ecology.[12]

Be a Pessimist. A particularly dangerous thing about school reformers is not only that they are so sure about the accuracy of their analysis but also that they are so optimistic about the benefits of their reform for school and society. Reformers tend to assume the worst about the current state of the school system ("*anything* would be an improvement") and assume the best about the effect of their proposed changes ("this change would *have* to be a help"). Better to be a pessimist; assume that you might just be wrong and that the reform might actually make things worse. Hope for a sunny day, but carry an umbrella in case it rains.

For a reformer this means adopting the caution that comes with lack of certainty. Do good if you can, but at least try to do no harm. In practice this directs reformers to start small to see if the idea works out in a pilot setting, which would allow them to learn from the interaction with local practice and adapt the policy in ways that make it more workable and less harmful. With such concerns in mind, reformers would not try to tighten the coupling of the school system in order to make it more responsive to demands from above; instead, they would work to preserve the loose coupling of the system as a failsafe mechanism for preventing the possibility that a reform might bring about catastrophic systemic failure. Finally, as James Scott suggests to social engineers in *Seeing Like a State,* school reformers should have Plan B waiting in the wings, so they can respond to bad news by having a way to back out of the reform effort, reversing the changes they made in order to avoid permanent damage.

THE RESILIENCE OF THE SCHOOL SYSTEM

Of course, none of this is really going to happen. As we have seen, the American school system is highly resilient. Not only can it resist the best efforts of reformers to change schools, but it can also resist the efforts of people like me to change the way reformers do their work. No reformer worth his salt would take the wimpy and self-negating approach to school change that I have suggested here. There's a name for reformers who choose to scale back their ambitions, focus only on what schools can do, think they might be wrong, and worry about doing harm. It's "loser." A school reformer is a political actor whose job is to gather support behind a particular policy, and you won't be able to convince supporters to march behind a banner that says "Think Small" or "Maybe We Can't." You don't breed confidence if you speak in tentative tones, if you acknowledge that your critics may be right, and if you plan for failure.

So reformers often feel they need to speak with more confidence, certainty, and simplicity than they actually feel (in quiet moments of critical reflection). Or they may feel compelled to sell themselves first on a reform idea that seems to offer high promise of solving a big problem—letting both the promise and the problem deflect them from looking at the idea too critically—and then start marketing it with vigor to the larger public. Or maybe they harbor no doubts at all. As we have seen, often simple ideas jump to the fore in a reform movement based on ideological clarity of vision, leaving complex ideas in their dust. Whatever the case, following my advice would doom any reform effort before it even got started.

One thing that reformers need to take into consideration is how much they are committed to having an impact on school and society regardless of whether this impact turns out to be positive or negative. If their hopes for doing good are higher than their fears of doing harm, then drawing on the lessons I have culled from the study of school reform would be bad tactics, since it would simply make things easier for another reformer who is more sure of being right. And employing these lessons in a reform effort would not only be bad tactics but also bad strategy.

To embrace the idea that the form of education is more important than its content is to deny the fundamental basis for the system's legitimacy. We are willing to invest vast amounts of time, money, and social energy in the school system because it educates our young, providing them with knowledge that is useful for both students and society. To deny the centrality of academic learning in the social function of schooling, as I do here, and to say that the system's most salient social product is not learning but credentialing, is to belie the system's core rationale as an institution of education. Without this rationale, the system looks like a sham, which offers tokens of accomplishment that we all choose to accept as representing mastery of a body of useful knowledge, even though it is really only a measure of time spent in school. The credential market works for parents and students, for employers and employees, only as long as everyone agrees to maintain the fiction that the exchange value of diplomas represents the acquisition of knowledge with use value. It's a game that relies on all parties to maintain their confidence that diplomas signal substance, that schools promote education, that learning matters. If it doesn't, then our whole process of assigning jobs, pursuing opportunity, and awarding merit in the United States is a fraud. Understandably, no reformer wants to go there.

One other aspect of these lessons makes it unlikely that anyone would implement them: to take a pessimistic stance toward school reform undercuts the central means for realizing the American Dream. We all know the adage: To get a good job, get a good education. Without schooling as a means, the chances of getting ahead in American society suddenly would seem quite remote. After all, the rise in our hopes for advancement for our children are tied to the rise in their education level. However, if the rise in education signifies not skill enhancement but credential inflation, and the result is to juggle positions in the labor queue rather than to move upward in the social order, then the story of social mobility fades to black. In particular, my suggestion to slow down the expansion of educational opportunity would seem at best uncharitable and at worst immoral—especially coming from a guy with a Ph.D. It looks suspiciously like I'm trying to close the door of opportunity after passing through it myself, in an effort to preserve the scarcity and thus the value of the system's highest credentials. The resulting structure would look dangerously close to Snedden's vision of "schools of the rank and file."

Shutting down the expansion of higher education is simply unthinkable in the political culture of the United States, and to propose doing so is political suicide. So it won't happen. But—as part of this impracticable thought experiment—consider where the current pattern of expansion is taking us. As master's programs start filling up, which is already happening, there will be greater pressure to expand access to doctoral programs, which are becoming the new zone of special educational advantage. So it seems likely that we're going to need to invent new forms of doctoral degree programs to meet this demand, something that universities (always on the lookout for a new marketing opportunity) are quite willing do. When that happens, of course, there will be demand for a degree beyond the doctorate (the current terminal degree in American higher education), in order to give some people a leg up on the flood of doctoral graduates pouring into the workplace. In some ways this has already happened for science Ph.D.'s, who have to complete an extensive postdoctoral program if they want a faculty position in an American university. We may end up going the direction of many European universities, which require that candidates for professorships first complete a Ph.D. program and then prepare a second dissertation called a habilitation, which is in effect a super-doctorate. This puts people well into their thirties before they complete their educational preparation.

Political will is unlikely to halt our movement in this direction, but more practical considerations may have some effect. The reason is that the cost of education programs rises exponentially at each higher level of the system, both for governments and consumers. Resistance already became apparent in the last quarter of the twentieth century. The rate of enrollment growth in higher education declined during this period, when fiscally constrained state governments resisted increasing appropriations for this sector, and as a result the costs of college increasingly shifted to consumers in the forms of higher tuition and higher student loans. The prospect of paying ever more taxes or taking on ever more loans may put a damper on the rate of expansion of higher education among citizen-consumers. However, the American belief in the value of schooling is so strong that we seem willing to continue shouldering a growing burden in one way or the other— even though the social benefits of our huge investments are small—in order to preserve the dream of getting ahead and to allay the fear of falling behind. Most likely, costs will only slow rather than stop the expansion of schooling.

At its heart, the school syndrome arises from Americans' insistence on having things both ways through the magical medium of education. We want schools to express our highest ideals as a society and our greatest aspirations as individuals, but only as long as they remain ineffective in actually realizing them, since we don't really want to acknowledge the way these two aims are at odds with each other. We ask schools to promote equality while preserving privilege, so we perpetuate a system that is too busy balancing opposites to promote student learning. We focus on making the system inclusive at one level and exclusive at the next, in order to make sure that it meets demands for both access and advantage. As a result the system continues to lure us to pursue the dream of fixing society by reforming schools, while continually frustrating our ability to meet these goals. It locks us in a spiral of educational expansion and credential inflation that has come to deplete our resources and exhaust our vitality. And we can't find a simple cure for this syndrome because we won't accept any remedy that would mean giving up one of our aims for education in favor of another. We want it both ways.

NOTES

REFERENCES

ACKNOWLEDGMENTS

INDEX

NOTES

INTRODUCTION

1. *Steady Work* is the title of a monograph by Elmore and McLaughlin (1988); "tinkering" comes from the title of a book by Tyack and Cuban (1995).

1   FROM CITIZENS TO CONSUMERS

1. Chubb and Moe (1990); Betts and Loveless (2005).

2. In the 1990s, I developed an interpretation of the history of American education as a shifting terrain defined by the relative influence, at particular points in time, of three major goals for public education: democratic equality (preparing competent citizens), social efficiency (preparing productive workers), and social mobility (preparing individuals to get ahead socially) (Labaree, 1997). This chapter is in part an attempt to complicate that earlier story, in particular by exploring the ways in which the political goal of education has itself evolved over time.

3. Cremin (1957), p. 87.

4. Cremin (1957), p. 92.

5. Mann (1841), p. 81.

6. Mann (1841), p. 81.

7. Tyack and Cuban (1995).

8. Labaree (1988).

9. Ravitch (2000); Angus and Mirel (1999).

10. Krug (1961), pp. 86–87.

11. Tyack and Cuban (1995).

12. Tyack and Cuban (1995), p. 87.

13. The terms "administrative" and "pedagogical" progressives come from David Tyack (1974). I discuss the tension between the two and the reasons for the victory of the administrative wing in Chapter 4.

14. Committee on the Reorganization of Secondary Education (1918), p. 1.

15. Committee on the Reorganization of Secondary Education (1918), p. 3.

16. Committee on the Reorganization of Secondary Education (1918), p. 5.

17. Committee on the Reorganization of Secondary Education (1918), p. 16.

18. 347 U.S. 483.

19. National Commission on Excellence in Education (1983), p. 7.

20. National Commission on Excellence in Education (1983), p. 8.

21. National Commission on Excellence in Education (1983), p. 22.

22. National Commission on Excellence in Education (1983), p. 24.

23. National Commission on Excellence in Education (1983), p. 25.

24. Chubb and Moe (1990), p. 218.

25. Chubb and Moe (1990), p. 37–38.

26. Chubb and Moe (1990), p. 35.

27. Public Law 107–110.

28. Betts and Lovelace (2005), p. 1.

29. Betts and Lovelace (2005), pp. 1–2.

30. Fuller (2002).

31. Bowles and Gintis (1999).

2   FOUNDING THE AMERICAN SCHOOL SYSTEM

1. Lockridge (1974), p. 13.

2. Lockridge (1974), p. 77.

3. Cremin (1970), p. 181.

4. Tyack and Cuban (1995).

5. Tyack (1967), p. 102.

6. Tyack (1967), p. 105.

7. Tyack (1967), p. 109.

8. Tyack (1967), p. 109.

9. The term "market revolution" has a controversial history among American historians. Charles Sellers wrote an influential book with this title in 1991, in which he argued that the market revolution was the signal event in the United States in the first half of the nineteenth century, around which all other issues revolved. In his view, the emergence of a market economy had a devastating effect on nearly all but the wealth-

iest members of society, which was kept in check only by the rise of Jacksonian democracy. A number of historians responded critically to this interpretation, including Daniel Walker Howe, who wrote his own alternative account of this period in his 2007 book, *What Hath God Wrought?* In that work he argued that the market had always been a factor in American life, so there was no sudden market revolution in the 1820s, and the economic and social changes that did take place during this period were largely positive and generally welcomed by most members of society. The view of the market revolution that I am pursuing here lies somewhere in between these two polar histories of the period. Like Sellers, I see the changes in the 1820s as transformative rather than incremental; but like Howe, I see them as having positive qualities that led people at all levels of society to welcome the changes, even as they simultaneously feared where these changes would lead. If there is a hero in my story, it is not the capitalists or the workers or the Jacksonian Democrats; it is the Whig reformers who designed institutions that would allow republican community to coexist with the new market economy. As it happens, in pursuing this argument I draw on Howe's earlier book, *The Political Culture of the American Whigs* (1979).

10. Johnson (1978).

11. For a classic account of the social organization of work in a pre-capitalist setting, see Thompson (1967).

12. This analysis draws inspiration from an essay by Michael Katz, "The Origins of Public Education" (1987).

13. Katz (1987).

14. I am drawing here on a perceptive account of the Whig phenomenon by Howe (1979), in which he depicts it broadly as a cultural force in antebellum American life instead of limiting it to the members of the Whig party.

15. Kaestle and Vinovskis (1980).

16. Dunlop (1851); emphasis in original.

17. I'm grateful to my colleague, Mitchell Stevens, for pointing out to me the way decentralization makes it so easy to initiate school reforms, even if not to realize reform goals.

18. NPR, http://www.npr.org/templates/story/story.php?storyId= 5178603 (accessed October 30, 2008).

3   THE PROGRESSIVE EFFORT TO RESHAPE THE SYSTEM

1. Cremin (1961); Rodgers (1982); and Kliebard (1986).

2. Braverman (1974).

3. Wiebe (1967).

4. This section draws on Kliebard (1986) and on a more detailed account in Labaree (2004, chapter 7).

5. Cremin (1961), p. x.

6. Kliebard (1986).

7. Church and Sedlak (1976).

8. Tyack (1974).

9. Lagemann (1989), p. 185.

10. I will discuss the differential impact of the two kinds of progressivism on the various layers of the school system in Chapter 4.

11. Hirsch (1996).

12. In Chapter 4 I explore why the administrative progressives were also more effective in shaping the school system.

13. Fishlow (1966), cited in Rury (2005), p. 64.

14. NCES (1993), table 5.

15. NCES (1993), table 8.

16. NCES (1993), table 8.

17. Angus and Mirel (1999), tables A.2, A.5, and B.11.

18. Commission on the Reorganization of Secondary Education (1918), p. 5.

4   ORGANIZATIONAL RESISTANCE TO REFORM

1. Rossi (1987), pp. 4–5.

2. Fullan (2001), p. 69.

3. Cuban (1988).

4. Elmore and McLaughlin (1988).

5. This model is a generalization of a model for curriculum reform that I and others have used elsewhere. In that scheme, the four levels are the rhetorical curriculum, formal curriculum, curriculum in use, and received curriculum (Labaree, 2007a, chapter 7). Cuban (1992) calls the latter three levels the intended, taught, and learned curriculum.

6. Cuban (1988), p. 101.

7. Commission on the Reorganization of Secondary Education (1918), p. 1.

8. Ravitch (2000), p. 459.

9. U.S. Bureau of the Census (1975), table H 412.

10. Cremin (1961), pp. 306–308.

11. Angus and Mirel (1999), tables A.2, A.5, and B.11.

12. Dewey (1902/1990), p. 205.

13. Zilversmit (1993); Cuban (1993). Diane Ravitch agrees with this assessment: "Cuban and Zilversmit identified progressive education with the child-centered, socially conscious, intellectually stimulating environ-

ment that Dewey had advocated. They rightly concluded that this ideal version of progressivism had not been institutionalized in American public schools." Ravitch (2000), p. 527, fn. 6.

14. Cuban (1993), p. 75.
15. Zilversmit (1993), p. 34.
16. Zilversmit (1993), p. 168.
17. Semel (2006), p. 13.
18. Cremin (1961), p. 328; emphasis in original.
19. When Cremin details the concrete effects of progressivism on schools in the first half of the twentieth century, his list echoes the agenda of the administrative progressives. The only effects he sees arising from the child-centered progressives were student projects and student activity (Cremin, 1961, pp. 308–310).
20. Weick (1976); Bidwell (1965).
21. Perrow (1999).
22. NCES (2007), tables 3, 4, 5, and 83.
23. NCES (1993), *120 Years of American Education*, tables 14 and 20.
24. Lortie (1975).
25. Brill (2009).
26. Carnegie Task Force (1986); Holmes Group (1986).
27. Urban (1989).
28. Sedlak (1989), p. 272.
29. Perrow (1984).
30. Elmore and McLaughlin (1988).
31. This concern about unintended consequences is enhanced by another characteristic of the reform skeptic: a strong sense that schools are a particularly weak medium to use in trying to address the most important social problems. This is the subject of Chapter 6.

5 CLASSROOM RESISTANCE TO REFORM

1. This discussion derives primarily from Chapter 3 of my book *The Trouble with Ed Schools* (2004). That account in turn draws on seminal work by Willard Waller (1932/1965), Dan Lortie (1975), David Cohen (1988), and Richard Elmore and Milbrey McLaughlin (1988).
2. Elmore and McLaughlin (1988).
3. Lipsky (1980).
4. As Michael Fullan has noted, it is just as helpful to schooling to block a harmful reform as it is to implement a beneficial reform. Fullan (1991), p. 18.
5. Cohen (1988), p. 55.

6. Cohen (1988), p. 57.

7. Fenstermacher (1990).

8. Quoted in Jackson (1986), p. 81.

9. Waller (1932/1965), pp. 195–196.

10. Cusick (1992), p. 46.

11. Waller (1932/1965), p. 196.

12. Sedlak et al. (1986).

13. Powell, Farrar, and Cohen (1985).

14. Labaree (1997).

15. Waller (1932/1965), p. 383.

16. I am grateful to Brian Vance and other members of my fall 1998 doctoral seminar for reminding me of the potential differences in the teacher–student relationship that arise in educational systems driven by external examinations.

17. These five characteristics of professional–client relationships are drawn from the "pattern variables" developed by Talcott Parsons, which are five pairs of alternative orientations that can be used to define distinctive types of role relationships. He called them: affective neutrality versus affectivity, specificity versus diffuseness, achievement versus ascription, self versus collectivity-orientation, and universalism versus particularism. Parsons (1951).

18. Gary Fenstermacher puts it this way: "Teachers may . . . at times wish for social distance from the complex, tangled, and sometimes destructive lives of their students, but they cannot teach well and ignore the many dimensions of the lives of their students. Teaching well requires as broad and deep an understanding of the learner as possible, a concern for how what is taught relates to the life experience of the learner, and a willingness to engage the learner in the context of the learner's own intentions, interests, and desires. Social distance of the variety favored by many physicians inhibits the capacity of teachers to do their job well." Fenstermacher (1990), p. 137.

19. Dewey (1904/1964), p. 319.

20. Freedman (1990), pp. 29–30.

21. I owe thanks to two members of my Michigan State doctoral seminar—Jo Lesser and Dana Sammons—for pointing out that the emotional link between teachers and students can undermine learning as well as promote it.

22. Hochschild (1983), p. 147.

23. Hochschild (1983), p. 35.

24. Waller (1932/1965), p. 375.

25. Waller (1932/1965), pp. 383–384.

26. Cohen (1989).

27. Britzman (1986), p. 449.

28. Lortie (1975), p. 74.

29. Britzman (1986), p. 451.

30. Britzman (1986), p. 451.

31. U.S. Dept. of Education (1986).

32. U.S. Dept. of Education (1986), p. v; emphasis in original.

33. U.S. Dept. of Education (1986), p. 34.

34. U.S. Dept. of Education (1986), p. 19.

35. U.S. Dept. of Education (1986), p. 50.

36. Lortie (1975); Jackson (1986); Floden and Clark (1988); Cohen (1988).

37. For more on this line of argument, see Labaree (1997), chapter 1.

38. In this regard, a parallel case to teachers is veterinarians, who identify the pet as the patient and the owner as the client.

39. In a study of efforts to transform the way teachers teach math in the United States in the 1990s, Stephen Mattson (2003) concludes that changing pedagogy is like changing religious beliefs; it calls for a tumultuous personal transformation that is akin to a conversion experience.

40. Cuban (2007).

41. Cohen (1988); Lortie (1975); and Britzman (1986).

42. This section draws heavily from Scott (1998).

43. Lampert (1985).

44. Scott (1998).

6   FAILING TO SOLVE SOCIAL PROBLEMS

1. Tyack (1966); Meyer et al. (1979); Ramirez and Boli (1987); Cummings (1997).

2. Schultz (1961); Hanushek and Kimko (2000); Goldin and Katz (2008).

3. Grubb and Lazerson (2004).

4. Rubinson and Browne (1996); Ramirez (2006).

5. Goldin and Katz (2008), table 2.7.

6. I owe this last observation to my colleague, Francisco Ramirez (2008a).

7. Blossfeld and Shavit (2000).

8. Boudon (1974); Blossfeld and Shavit (2000).

9. Hertz (2006), table 3.

10. Snedden (1900, 1920, 1929).

11. Public Law, 94–142.

12. Grant (1988).

13. Cohen (2004).

14. *Phi Delta Kappan* and Gallup have found this a consistent pattern over the years in their annual poll of public attitudes toward education. In 2008, for example, the poll found that 48 percent of the respondents gave their community's schools a grade of A or B, while 72 percent graded their oldest child's school at the same level. PDK (2008), tables 11 and 12.

15. Stinchcombe (1965).

16. Political economist Albert Hirschman (1970) labels public education as a lazy public monopoly. As a political entity, it is most responsive to pressure from the political system, but in practice its most dissatisfied customers are less likely to voice their concerns within the public school district than to take the easier and more efficient option, to exit the system by sending children to private schools or moving to another school district. This removes pressure on the school system to make changes.

7 THE LIMITS OF SCHOOL LEARNING

1. Goldin and Katz (2008).

2. Goldin and Katz (2008), p. 19.

3. Goldin and Katz (2008), table 1.1, p. 27.

4. Goldin and Katz (2008), p. 283.

5. Goldin and Katz (2008), table 1.3, p. 39.

6. Goldin and Katz (2008), p. 167.

7. Goldin and Katz (2008), p. 167.

8. Goldin and Katz (2008), table 3.1, p. 96.

9. Goldin and Katz (2008), table 2.7, p. 84.

10. Goldin and Katz (2008), p. 113.

11. Goldin and Katz (2008), p. 19.

12. I am grateful to Michael Katz for sharing with me his essay review of the Goldin and Katz book; his arguments were helpful to me in understanding both the strengths and the weaknesses of this book. See Katz (2009).

13. Carter et al. (2006), table Ea pp. 287–347.

14. Goldin and Katz (2008), p. 229.

15. U.S. Bureau of the Census (1975), Series D, pp. 29–41.

16. Goldin and Katz (2008), p. 130.

17. Thurow (1972).

18. Spence (1973).

19. Spence (1973).

20. Berg (1971).

21. The film is available on the producer's website: http://www
.2mminutes.com/.

22. *Two Million Minutes* (2008).

23. Turner (1960).

8   LIVING WITH THE SCHOOL SYNDROME

1. This was the title of one of my earlier books (Labaree, 1997).

2. I first encountered the concept of educationalizing social problems
at a meeting of the research group "Philosophy and History of the Discipline of Education," held annually at Catholic University of Leuven,
Belgium. See Smeyers and Depaepe (2009).

3. I am grateful to my colleague Francisco Ramirez (2008b) for suggesting that individualism is at the heart of our tendency to seek solutions to social problems by means of education.

4. Gordon (2008).

5. March (1975), p. 5.

6. Bridges (2008), p. 466.

7. Bridges (2008), p. 463.

8. Elmore and McLaughlin (1988), p. 36.

9. Bridges (2008).

10. Meyer (1977); Meyer and Rowan (1977); Meyer and Rowan
(1983).

11. This is what Emile Durkheim noted a century ago, at the end of
his review of *The Evolution of Educational Thought,* across 1,000 years
of European history. "In this way we can explain a law to which I have
frequently drawn attention and which, in fact, governs the whole of our
academic evolution. This is the fact that from the eighth century onwards
we have moved from one educational formalism to another educational
formalism without ever managing to break the circle. In different periods this formalism has been successively based on grammar, on logic or
dialectic, then on literature; but in different forms it has always been formalism which has triumphed. By this I mean that throughout this whole
period the aim of education has always been not to give the child positive
knowledge, the best available conception of the way specific things really
are, but to generate in him skills which are wholly formalistic, whether
these consist in the art of debate or the art of self-expression." Durkheim
(1938/1969), p. 280.

12. Tyack and Cuban (1995).

REFERENCES

Angus, David L., and Mirel, Jeffrey E. (1999). *The failed promise of the American high school, 1890–1995.* New York: Teachers College Press.

Berg, Ivar. (1971). *Education and jobs: The great training robbery.* Boston: Beacon.

Berlin, Isaiah. (2000). The hedgehog and the fox: An essay on Tolstoy's view of history. In Thomas Hardy (ed.), *The proper study of mankind: An anthology of essays* (pp. 436–498). New York: Farrar, Straus and Giroux.

Betts, Julian, and Loveless, Tom. (2005). *Getting choice right: Ensuring Equity and efficiency in educational policy.* Washington, DC: Brookings Institution Press.

Bidwell, Charles E. (1965). The school as a formal organization. In James M. March (ed.), *Handbook of organizations* (pp. 972–1018). Chicago: Rand McNally.

Blossfeld, Hans-Peter, and Shavit, Yossi. (2000). Persisting barriers: Changes in educational opportunities. In Richard Arum and Irenee R. Beattie (eds.). *The structure of schooling.* Mountain View, CA: Mayfield.

Boudon, Raymond. (1974). *Education, opportunity, and social inequality: Changing prospects in Western society.* New York: Wiley.

Boudon, Raymond. (1986). Education, mobility, and sociological theory. In John G. Richardson (ed.), *Handbook of theory and research for the sociology of education* (pp. 261–274). New York: Greenwood.

Bowles, Samuel, and Gintis, Herbert. (1999). *Recasting egalitarianism: New rules for communities, states, and markets.* London: Verso.

Braverman, Harry. (1974). *Labor and monopoly capital: The degrada-tion of work in the twentieth century*. New York: Monthly Review Press.

Bridges, David. (2008). Educationalization: On the appropriateness of seeking or offering a response by educational institutions to social and economic programs. *Educational Theory,* 58(4) (November), 461–474.

Brill, Steven. (2009). The rubber room: The battle over New York City's worst teachers. *New Yorker*, August 31. http://www.newyorker.com/ (accessed 1/1/10).

Britzman, Deborah P. (1986). Cultural myths in the making of a teacher: Biography and social structure in teacher education. *Harvard Educational Review*, 56(4), 442–456.

Brooks, David. (2002). Notes from a hanging judge. *New York Times,* January 13. http://www.nytimes.com/ (accessed 1/13/02).

Brown v. Board of Education of Topeka, 347 U.S. 483 (1954).

Carnegie Task Force on Teaching as a Profession. (1986). *A nation prepared: Teachers for the 21st century.* New York: Carnegie Forum on Education and the Economy.

Carter, Susan B. et al. (eds.). (2006). *Historical statistics of the United States* (millennial edition online). New York: Cambridge University Press.

Chubb, John E., and Moe, Terry M. (1990). *Politics, markets, and America's schools.* Washington, DC: Brookings Institution.

Church, Robert L., and Sedlak, Michael W. (1976). *Education in the United States.* New York: Free Press.

Cohen, Adam. (2004). The supreme struggle. *New York Times,* January 18. www.nytimes.com (accessed 1/18/04).

Cohen, David K. (1988). Teaching practice: Plus ça change. In Philip W. Jackson (ed.), *Contributing to educational change: Perspectives on research and practice* (pp. 27–84). Berkeley, CA: McCutchan.

Cohen, David K. (1989). Willard Waller, on hating school and loving education. In D. J. Willower & W. L. Boyd (eds.), *Willard Waller on education and schools.* San Francisco: McCutchan.

Commission on Reorganization of Secondary Education. (1918). *Cardinal principles of secondary education.* Bulletin no. 35, U.S. Department of Interior, Bureau of Education. Washington, DC: U.S. Government Printing Office.

Cremin, Lawrence A. (ed.). (1957). *The republic and the school: Horace Mann on the education of free men.* New York: Teachers College Press.

Cremin, Lawrence A. (1961). *The transformation of the school: Progressivism in American education, 1976–1957.* New York: Vintage.

Cremin, Lawrence A. (1970). *American education: The colonial experience, 1607–1783.* New York: Harper and Row.

Cuban, Larry. (1988). Constancy and change in schools (1880s to the present). In Phillip W. Jackson (ed.), *Contributing to educational change: Perspectives on research and practice* (pp. 85–105). Berkeley, CA: McCutchan.

Cuban, Larry. (1992). Curriculum stability and change. In Philip Jackson (ed.), *Handbook of research on curriculum.* New York: Macmillan.

Cuban, Larry. (1993). *How teachers taught: Constancy and change in American classrooms, 1890–1980,* 2nd ed. New York: Teachers College Press.

Cuban, Larry. (2007). Hugging the middle: Teaching in an era of testing and accountability, 1980–2005. *Education Policy Analysis Archives,* 15(1), 1–27.

Cummings, William. (1997). Patterns of modern education. In William Cummings and Noel McGinn (eds.), *International handbook of education and development: Preparing schools, students, and nations for the twenty-first century* (pp. 63–85). New York: Pergamon.

Cusick, Philip A. (1992). *The educational system: Its nature and logic.* New York: McGraw-Hill.

Dewey, John. (1902/1990). The child and the curriculum. In *The school and society and the child and the curriculum.* Chicago: University of Chicago Press.

Dewey, John. (1904/1964). The relation of theory to practice in education. In Reginald D. Archambault (ed.), *John Dewey on education* (pp. 314–338). Chicago: University of Chicago Press.

Dunlop, Thomas. (1851). Introductory address of the commencement of the Central High School of Philadelphia, February 12, 1851. Philadelphia: Board of Controllers.

Durkheim, Emile. (1938/1969). *The evolution of educational thought: Lectures on the formation and development of secondary education in France.* Boston: Routledge and Kegan Paul.

Education of Handicapped Children Act. (1975). Public law, 94–142.

Elmore, Richard F., and McLaughlin, Milbrey W. (1988). *Steady work.* Santa Monica, CA: Rand.

Fenstermacher, Gary D. 1990. Some moral considerations on teaching as a profession. In John I. Goodlad, Roger Soder, and Kenneth A. Sirotnik (eds.), *The moral dimensions of teaching* (pp. 130–151). San Francisco: Jossey-Bass.

Finkelstein, Barbara. (1989). *Governing the young: Teacher behavior in popular primary schools in nineteenth century United States.* Philadelphia: Falmer.

Fishlow, Albert. (1966). Levels of nineteenth-century American investment in education. *The Journal of Economic History,* 26(4), 418–436.

Floden, Robert E., and Clark, Christopher M. (1988). Preparing teachers for uncertainty. *Teachers College Record,* 89, 505–524.

Franklin, Barry M. (1986). *Building the American community: The school curriculum and the search for social control.* Philadelphia: Falmer.

Freedman, Samuel G. (1990). *Small victories: The real world of a teacher, her students, and their high school.* New York: HarperCollins.

Friedman, Milton. (1962). *Capitalism and freedom.* Chicago: University of Chicago Press.

Fullan, Michael G. (1991). *The new meaning of educational change,* 2nd ed. New York: Teachers College Press.

Fuller, Howard. (2002). Education matters to me: Full court press. *Education Next,* 2(3), 88.

Goldin, Claudia, and Katz, Lawrence F. (2008). *The race between education and technology.* Cambridge, MA: Belknap Press of Harvard University Press.

Gordon, Leah. (2008). The question of prejudice: Social science, education, and the struggle to define "the race problem" in postwar America, 1940–1970. Unpublished Ph.D. dissertation, University of Pennsylvania.

Grant, Gerald. (1988). *The world we created at Hamilton High.* Cambridge, MA: Harvard University Press.

Grubb, W. Norton, and Lazerson, Marvin. (2004). *The education gospel: The economic power of schooling.* Cambridge, MA: Harvard University Press.

Hanushek, Eric, and Kimko, Dennis. (2000). Schooling, labor force quality, and the growth of nations. *American Economic Review,* 90 (December), 1184–1208.

Hertz, Tom. (2006). *Understanding mobility in America.* Washington, DC: Center for American Progress.

Hirsch, E. D., Jr. (1996). *The schools we need and why we don't have them.* New York: Doubleday.

Hirschman, Albert O. (1970). *Exit, voice, and loyalty: Responses to decline in firms, organizations, and states.* Cambridge, MA: Harvard University Press.

Hochschild, Arlie. 1983. *The managed heart: Commercialization of human feeling.* Berkeley: University of California Press.

Holmes Group. (1986). *Tomorrow's teachers.* East Lansing, MI: Author.

Howe, Daniel Walker. (1979). *The political culture of the American whigs.* Chicago: University of Chicago Press.

Howe, Daniel Walker. (2007). *What hath God wrought? The transformation of America, 1815–1848.* New York: Oxford University Press.

Jackson, Philip W. (1986). *The practice of teaching.* New York: Teachers College Press.

Johnson, Paul E. (1978). *A shopkeeper's millennium: Society and revivals in Rochester, New York, 1815–1837.* New York: Hill and Wang.

Kaestle, Carl F., and Vinovskis, Maris A. (1980). *Education and social change in nineteenth-century Massachusetts.* Cambridge, UK: Cambridge University Press.

Kantor, Harvey, and Tyack, David. (1982). Introduction: Historical perspectives on vocationalism in American education. In Kantor and Tyack (eds.), *Work, youth, and schooling: Historical perspectives on vocationalism in American education* (pp. 1–13). Stanford, CA: Stanford University Press.

Katz, Michael B. (1987). Origins of public education. In *Reconstructing American education* (pp. 5–23). Cambridge, MA: Harvard University Press.

Katz, Michael B. (2009). Can America educate itself out of inequality? Reflections on the race between education and technology. *Journal of Social History,* 43(1), 183–195.

Kingsley, Clarence D. (1919). *School and Society,* 10(236), 18–20.

Kliebard, Herbert M. (1986). *The struggle for the American curriculum, 1893–1958.* Boston: Routledge and Kegan Paul.

Kliebard, Herbert M. (1999). *Schooled to work: Vocationalism and the American curriculum, 1876–1946.* New York: Teachers College Press.

Krug, Edward (ed.). (1961). *Charles W. Eliot and popular education.* New York: Teachers College Press.

Labaree, David F. (1988). *The making of an American high school: The credentials market and the Central High School of Philadelphia, 1838–1920.* New Haven: Yale University Press.

Labaree, David F. (1997). *How to succeed in school without really learning: The credentials race in American education.* New Haven: Yale University Press.

Labaree, David F. (2004). *The trouble with ed schools.* New Haven: Yale University Press.

Labaree, David F. (2007a). *Education, markets, and the public good.* Routledge: London.

Labaree, David F. (2007b). Citizens and consumers: Changing visions of virtue and opportunity in U.S. education in the 19th and 20th centuries. Paper presented at conference on "Republican and Non-Republican Imaginations," University of Applied Sciences, Zurich.

Lagemann, Ellen Condliffe. (1989). The plural worlds of educational research. *History of Education Quarterly,* 29(2), 185–214.

Lampert, Magdalene. (1985). How do teachers manage to teach? Perspectives on problems in practice. *Harvard Educational Review,* 55, 178–194.

Lazerson, Marvin, and Grubb, W. Norton. (1974). Introduction. In Lazerson and Grubb (eds.), *American education and vocationalism: A documentary history* (pp. 1–50). New York: Teachers College Press.

Lipsky, Michael. (1980). *Street-level bureaucracy: Dilemmas of the individual in public services.* New York: Russell Sage Foundation.

Lockridge, Kenneth A. (1974). *Literacy in colonial New England: An enquiry into the social context of literacy in the early modern West.* New York: Norton.

Lortie, Dan C. (1975). *Schoolteacher: A sociological study.* Chicago: University of Chicago Press.

Mann, Horace. (1841). *Fifth annual report to the Massachusetts Board of Education.* Boston: Board of Education.

Mann, Horace. (1848). *Twelfth annual report to the Massachusetts Board of Education.* Boston: Board of Education.

March, James G. (1975). Education and the pursuit of optimism. *Texas Tech Journal of Education,* 2(1), 5–17.

Mattson, Steven Matthew. (2003). *A changing metaphor: Instructional reform as evangelism.* Unpublished Ph.D. dissertation, Michigan State University.

Meyer, John. (1977). The effects of education as an institution. *American Journal of Sociology,* 83(1), 55–77.

Meyer, John W., and Rowan, Brian. (1977). Institutionalized organizations. *American Journal of Sociology,* 83(2), 340–263.

Meyer, John W., and Rowan, Brian. (1983). The structure of educational organizations. In John W. Meyer and William R. Scott (eds.), *Organizational environments: Ritual and rationality* (pp. 71–97). Beverly Hills, CA: Sage.

Meyer, John, Tyack, David, Nagel, Joanne, and Gordon, Audri. (1979). Public education as nation-building in America: Enrollments and bureaucratization in the American states, 1870–1930. *American Journal of Sociology,* 85(3), 591–613.

National Center for Educational Statistics. (1993). *120 years of American education.* Washington, DC: Government Printing Office.

National Center for Educational Statistics. (2007). *Digest of education statistics 2006.* Washington, DC: Government Printing Office.

National Commission on Excellence in Education. (1983). *A nation at risk: The imperative for educational reform.* Washington, DC: U.S. Department of Education.

No Child Left Behind Act. (2002). Public Law, 107–110.

Parsons, Talcott. (1951). *The social system.* Glencoe: Free Press.

Perrow, Charles. (1984). *Normal accidents: Living with higher-risk technologies.* Princeton, NJ: Princeton University Press.

Phi Delta Kappa. (2008). 40th PDK/Gallup Poll. www.pdkintl.org (accessed 2/16/09).

Powell, Arthur, Farrar, Eleanor, and Cohen, David K. (1985). *The shopping mall high school: Winners and losers in the educational marketplace.* Boston: Houghton-Mifflin.

Ramirez, Francisco. (1997). The nation-state, citizenship, and educational change: Institutionalization and globalization. In William Cummings and Noel McGinn (eds.), *International handbook of education and development: Preparing schools, students, and nations for the twenty-first century* (pp. 47–62). New York: Pergamon.

Ramirez, Francisco O. (2008a). Personal communication, March 20.

Ramirez, Francisco O. (2008b). Personal communication, May 20.

Ramirez, Francisco O., and Boli, John. (1987). The political construction of mass schooling: European origins and worldwide institutionalization. *Sociology of Education,* 60(1), 2–18.

Ramirez, Francisco O. et al. (2006). Student achievement and national economic growth. *American Journal of Education,* 113(1), 1–29.

Ravitch, Diane. (2000). *Left back: A century of failed school reforms.* New York: Simon and Schuster.

Rodgers, Daniel. (1982). In search of progressivism. *Reviews in American History,* 11(4), 113–132.

Rossi, Peter H. (1987). The iron law of evaluation and other metallic rules. In Joann L. Miller and Michael Lewis (eds.), *Research in Social Problems and Public Policy,* 4 (pp. 3–20). Greenwich, CT: JAI Press.

Rubinson, Richard, and Browne, Irene. (1996). Education and the economy. In Neil Smelser and Richard Swedborg (eds.), *The handbook of economic sociology.* Princeton: Princeton University Press.

Rudy, Willis. (1968). Review of *David Snedden and Education for Social Efficiency* by Walter H. Drost. *The Journal of American History,* 55(1) (June), 170–71.

Rury, John L. (2005). *Education and social change: Themes in the history of American education,* 2nd ed. Mahwah, NJ: Lawrence Erlbaum.

Schultz, Theodore W. (1961). Investment in human capital. *American Economic Review,* 51(1), 1–17.

Scott, James. (1999). *Seeing like a state.* New Haven: Yale University Press.

Sedlak, Michael W. (1989). Let us go and buy a schoolmaster. In D. Warren (ed.), *American teachers: Histories of a profession at work* (pp. 257–290). New York: Macmillan.

Sedlak, Michael W. et al. (1986). *Selling students short: Classroom bargains and academic reform in the American high school.* New York: Teachers College Press.

Sellers, Charles. (1991). *The market revolution: Jacksonian America, 1815–1846.* New York: Oxford University Press.

Semel, Susan E. (2006). Introduction. In Susan E. Semel and Alan R. Sadovnik (eds.), *"Schools of tomorrow," schools of today: What happened to progressive education.* New York: Peter Lang.

Smeyers, Paul, and Depaepe, Marc (eds.). (2009). *Educational research: The educationalization of social problems.* New York: Springer.

Smith-Hughes Act of 1917, in U.S., *Statutes at Large,* XXXIX, Part I, 929–936.

Snedden, David. (1900). The schools of the rank and file. *The Stanford Alumnus,* I, 185–198.

Snedden, David. (1920). *Vocational education.* New York: Macmillan.

Snedden, David. (1929). The socially efficient community. *Journal of Educational Sociology,* 2(8) (April), 464–470.

Spence, Michael A. (1973). Job market signaling. *Quarterly Journal of Economics,* 87(3), 355–374.

Stinchcombe, Arthur L. (1965). Social structure and organizations. In James G. March (ed.), *Handbook of organizations* (pp. 142–193). Chicago: Rand McNally.

Thompson, E. P. (1967). Time, work-discipline, and industrial capitalism. *Past and Present,* 38 (December), 56–97.

Thurow, Lester. (1972). Education and economic equality. *Public Interest,* 28 (Summer), 66–81.

Turner, Ralph. (1960). Sponsored and contest mobility and the school system. *American Sociological Review,* 25(6), 855–867.

Two million minutes. (2008). Film produced by Robert Compton, Chad Heeter, and Adam Raney. Available at http://www.2mminutes.com/.

Tyack, David. (1966). Forming the national character. *Harvard Education Review,* 36(1), 29–41.

Tyack, David. (1974). *The one best system.* Cambridge, MA: Harvard University Press.

Tyack, David B. (ed.). (1967). *Turning points in American educational history.* Waltham, MA: Blaisdell Publishing.

Tyack, David, and Cuban, Larry. (1995). *Tinkering toward utopia: Reflections on a century of public school reform.* Cambridge, MA: Harvard University Press.

Urban, Wayne J. (1989). Teacher activism. In Donald Warren (ed.), *American teachers: Histories of a profession at work* (pp. 190–212). New York: Macmillan.

U.S. Bureau of the Census. (1975). *Historical statistics of the United States: Colonial times to 1970.* Washington, DC: Government Printing Office.

U.S. Department of Education. (1986). *What works: Research about teaching and learning.* Washington, DC.

Waller, Willard. (1932/1965). *The sociology of teaching.* New York: Wiley.

Weick, Karl. (1976). Educational organizations as loosely-coupled systems. *Administrative Science Quarterly,* 20(4), 1–19.

Wiebe, Robert. (1967). *The search for social order.* New York: Hill and Wang.

Wirth, Arthur G. (1972). Charles A. Prosser and the Smith-Hughes Act. *The Educational Forum,* 36(3) (March), 365–371.

Zilversmit, Arthur. (1993). *Changing schools: Progressive education theory and practice, 1930–1960.* Chicago: University of Chicago Press.

ACKNOWLEDGMENTS

Like most of my earlier writing, this book emerged from my work as a teacher, in particular from teaching the class on the History of School Reform in the United States at the Stanford University School of Education over the last half-dozen years. When I teach a class, I have to develop a story about the issues that surround the topic and that arise from the relevant literature. Then, after trying out the story for a while, I need to see if it has enough durability to put it on paper. Teaching allows the flexibility to develop an idea, but print is where the idea has to show its ability to survive critical scrutiny. As I tell my students, talking about ideas in the classroom is like singing in the shower; it may sound good there, but the real test comes in the recording studio. I hope this book survives that test.

I am grateful to a large number of colleagues and students for help in constructing this book. My students at Stanford have been remarkably tolerant about following along with my trial-and-error efforts to develop an argument about the nature of American schooling, the limits of school reform, and the persistence of educational consumerism. Likewise, my colleagues here and elsewhere have been very helpful in stimulating my thinking, responding to questions, reacting to ideas, and giving specific comments aimed at improving the story I tell here. These colleagues include a number of Stanford faculty members, including David

Tyack, Larry Cuban, Mitchell Stevens, Chiqui Ramirez, Leah Gordon, Denis Phillips, and Ray McDermott; a group of scholars in the history and sociology of education from across the United States, including Jeff Mirel, Cleo Cherryholmes, Bill Reese, Tom Popkewitz, Nick Burbules, Michael Katz, Norton Grubb, Glenn Adams, Lani Guineer, and Lynn Fendler; and another group of scholars in Europe, including Daniel Tröhler, Fritz Osterwalder, Marc Depaepe, Paul Smeyers, Jean-Claude Croizet, and Jón Torfi Jónasson. It takes a village to raise a book.

In the past few years I've had the good fortune to try out some of the ideas in this book at a variety of scholarly forums. These have included the annual meetings of the American Educational Research Association, the History of Education Society, and the American Sociological Association. They also included some more intimate settings, such as the annual meetings of the Research Community on the Philosophy and History of the Discipline of Education at Catholic University in Leuven, Belgium; the conference on Republican and Non-Republican Imaginations hosted by the Pestalozzian Research Institute in Zurich, Switzerland; the conference on The Century of the School at Centro Stefano Franscini, Ascona, Switzerland; the doctoral colloquium on Schools and Education in Modern Times at University of Berne; and a lecture at the Faculty of Education, Queens University, Kingston, Ontario.

David Tyack, Larry Cuban, and Norton Grubb provided detailed feedback on the proposal for this book and thus helped me figure out how to frame the argument. David Tyack gave me some trenchant comments and suggestions about the first draft of the full manuscript; and Mitchell Stevens did the yeoman service of providing insightful comments on both the first and second drafts of the manuscript. I am very grateful to these colleagues for their time, effort, and constructive commentary. My editor at Harvard, Elizabeth Knoll, has given me wise counsel and strong support for this project over the last several years. Dean Deborah Stipek granted me the sabbatical that allowed the time to complete the manuscript. And I am deeply grateful for the tolerance, love, and support that I received from my wife, Diane Churchill, throughout the turbulent course of this book's evolution.

Finally, I want to express my gratitude for the scholarly example, friendship, and support of two emeritus faculty members at the Stanford School of Education. David Tyack and Larry Cuban were the primary reason I wanted to come to Stanford seven years ago. I have admired and used their work for years, and I found myself in the wonderful position of taking over the class in the history of school reform that they had taught together for the previous decade. They drew on their experience with the course in writing their seminal book, *Tinkering Toward Utopia,* and I drew on my own experience with the course in writing *Someone Has to Fail.* My book is dedicated to these two dear colleagues and friends.

Some of the material in this book has appeared in print in an earlier form. I am grateful to the publishers for permission to reuse that material as revised here:

Labaree, David F. (2000). On the nature of teaching and teacher education: Difficult practices that look easy. *Journal of Teacher Education,* 51(3) (May), 68–73. With kind permission of Sage Publications.

Labaree, David F. (2004). Teacher ed in the present: The peculiar problems of preparing teachers. In *The trouble with ed schools* (pp. 39–61). New Haven: Yale University Press. With kind permission of Yale University Press.

Labaree, David F. (2008). Limits on the impact of educational reform: The case of progressivism and U.S. schools, 1900–1950. In Claudia Crotti and Fritz Osterwalder (eds.), *Das jahrhundert der schulreformen: Internationale und nationale perspektiven, 1900–1950* (pp. 105–133). Bern: Haupt. With kind permission of Haupt Verlag.

Labaree, David F. (2008). The winning ways of a losing strategy: Educationalizing social problems in the U.S. *Educational Theory,* 58(4) (November), 447–460. With kind permission of John Wiley and Sons.

Labaree, David F. (2009). Educational formalism and the language of goals in American education, educational reform, and educational history. In Paul Smeyers and Marc Depaepe (eds.), *Educational research: Proofs, arguments, and other reasonings* (pp. 41–60). Dordrecht: Springer. With kind permission of Springer Science and Business Media.

Labaree, David F. (2009). Participant in moderated discussion of the film *2 Million Minutes*. *Comparative Education Review*, 53(1), 113–137. With kind permission of University of Chicago Press.

Labaree, David F. (2010). What schools can't do. *Zeitschrift für Pädagogische Historiographie*, 16:1, 12–18. With kind permission of the Pädagogische Hochschule Zürich.

INDEX

Ability grouping of students, 153
Abstract reformist grid, school
  reform and, 192
Academic curriculum: hostility
  toward traditional, 5; need to
  refocus attention on, 33;
  progressive antagonism
  toward, 91–92
Academic high schools, 99
Academic learning: connection
  between economic growth and,
  188–189, 220; efforts to
  control, 224
Academies, 43–44
Access: administrative progressives and, 99; balance between
  advantage and, 3, 22, 75, 82,
  103–105, 156, 172, 176, 194,
  237–238, 240, 244, 249;
  common school movement
  and, 223; democratic demands
  for, 101; desegregation
  movement and, 226; differential, 115–116; to education
  opportunity, 10, 30, 31, 33, 40,
  51, 52, 78, 92, 94, 96, 110,
  166, 170, 175, 176, 178, 179,
  181, 194, 205, 215, 220, 222,

232, 249; emphasis on, over
  learning, 205–207, 212; to
  employment, 17, 96, 137, 196;
  formalism and, 233; to good
  life, 94; increasing, 170–171;
  No Child Left Behind and,
  227; political demands for, 22,
  30, 95; principals versus
  teachers and, 126; progressive
  movement and, 174, 176;
  tracked comprehensive high
  schools and, 172; to word of
  God, 45
Accommodation, classroom
  bargaining, 139
Accountability measures,
  standards movement and, 183
Achievement orientation in
  professional-client relationship,
  142
Administrative control, weakness
  over teaching, 125–129
Administrative progressivism,
  24–27, 82, 92–93; accomplishments of, 107; assessing impact
  of, 112–117; effectiveness of,
  94; establishment of professional administration for